# MR. CHINA'S SON

# MR. CHINA'S SON

## A Villager's Life

### HE LIYI
*with Claire Anne Chik*

WESTVIEW PRESS
*Boulder • San Francisco • Oxford*

Copyright © 1993 by He Liyi and Claire Anne Chik

Published in 1993 in the United States of America by Westview Press, Inc., 5500 Central Avenue, Boulder, Colorado 80301-2877, and in the United Kingdom by Westview Press, 36 Lonsdale Road, Summertown, Oxford OX2 7EW

Cut paper designs used on part title pages and on cover are from *Chinese Folk Designs* by W. M. Hawley (Dover Pictorial Archive Series).

Library of Congress Cataloging-in-Publication Data
He, Liyi, 1930–
    Mr. China's son : a villager's life / He Liyi ; with Claire Anne Chik.
        p.   cm.
    ISBN 0-8133-1731-2 — ISBN 0-8133-1730-4 (pbk.)
    1. He, Liyi, 1930–      . 2. Authors, Chinese—Biography.   I. Chik,
Claire Anne, 1952–      .  II. Title.
PL2861.E26Z473   1993
828—dc20
[B]                                                                                                    93-21592
                                                                                                          CIP

Printed and bound in the United States of America

(∞)  The paper used in this publication meets the requirements
        of the American National Standard for Permanence of Paper
        for Printed Library Materials Z39.48-1984.

10      9      8      7      6      5      4      3      2      1

# CONTENTS

# INTRODUCTION
# MARTHA WARD

**Y**ou are about to read a compelling and riveting autobiography. The man who wrote it, Mr. He Liyi, has told a wondrous story of cultural chaos in China and of personal lives thwarted and fulfilled. The idea of looking at history from the bottom up, and of delving into the relevance of lived experience, has never been more meaningful than in this account. That Mr. He writes with such grace and humor is only part of the magic of this book.

The author is a member of the Bai minority group of China and lives in Yunnan Province in a special region called the Dali Autonomous Prefecture. As he says, "I live in a distant mountain corner of northwestern Yunnan in the southwestern corner of China." Born in 1930, he attended college and studied English in Kunming, the capital city of the province, from 1950 to 1953. But when the Anti-Rightist Movement started, he was "disciplined." Married to a peasant woman, he became a farmer and later a "chalk-eater." He experienced what he describes as "years of unspeakable humiliation and suffering." Yet by Part 3 Mr. He has translated a collection of the folktales of China's minority populations and published the book in England.

Many of us tried to follow the extraordinary happenings in China after the Communist government took over in 1949. We knew very little of what was happening to one-fourth of the world's people. There were rumors of millions starved to death, exiled to labor camps, or executed; stories circulated of the harshness and pain of living and dying in China. As a Chinese man told me about those years of upheaval, "Every one of us has a story; most of us can never tell it." What happened to Mr. He in the decades between college and his book of folktales? What tales could he tell?

## Mr. China

This story is about the machinations of one man to survive and even explain what happens to a person caught in the turmoil of his nation building and tearing itself up simultaneously. On October 1, 1949, Mao Zedong proclaimed the People's Republic of China in Beijing. The new government assumed control of a country exhausted by two generations of war and social conflict. Inflation and the disruption of transport and communication systems had devastated the economy. Chinese Communist leaders, most of whom had made the famous "Long March," urgently needed to establish social order and national infrastructures very quickly. They modeled the new social institutions they needed after the Soviet example. But this brought anything connected to their mutual enemy, the United States, into automatic disfavor. As Mr. He writes, "The leaders of Mr. China started a love affair with Russia."

With the Communist Party in control, this period in China was characterized by vast internal conflicts. In 1957 the Anti-Rightist Movement encouraged the flowers of free expression and individuality to bloom, only to denounce and cut them down as weeds. Mr. He's accounts of "self-criticism meetings" and "struggles" give an extraordinary view of the daily confrontations among citizens, bureaucrats, party hacks, and even crazy people about what shape the new China should take.

The authority of the Chinese Communist Party began to reach into every phase of ordinary life. In 1958, for example, the "Great Leap Forward" brought new economic programs aimed at rapidly raising industrial and agricultural production above the impressive gains already made. Local leaders formed cooperatives or communes. Backyard factories dotted China's landscape. But the results were disastrous, as normal cultural and economic patterns were disrupted, even destroyed. Within a year, the Chinese leadership retreated, blaming poor planning and the weather. The resulting famine killed at least 20 million people, perhaps as many as 30 million. We will never officially know.

By 1960 the love affair with Russia had ended. Sino-Soviet relations deteriorated sharply as Russia withdrew all of its advisers; citizens like Mr. He became more isolated than ever from the rest of the world. Mr. He relates almost casually the stories of these times: Wolves steal a baby, lovers are separated abruptly, careers are assigned capriciously, and the metaphors of cooking pots and hunger sneak into ordinary consciousness. He calls 1958 the "period of big-pot rice" because everyone was supposed to eat communally and share food. Later he defines jobs as the secure but lowly "iron rice bowl" or the more prestigious "golden rice bowl."

In the spring of 1966 another movement, the Great Proletarian Cultural Revolution, set China on a course of political and social anarchy that lasted the better part of a decade. Radical young people's groups, the Red Guard, attacked party and state organizations at all levels. Complex factions developed. Watchers outside China had very little information or insight into these baffling and precarious times; those living in China had even less. The entire fabric of Chinese collective life was affected: Schools closed, monuments and market systems were destroyed, and countless individuals were sent to labor camps, exile, or death. Even the most intimate moments, such as between husband and wife or between parent and child, were subordinated to the national mania of Mao's revolutionary vision. Nourishing meals for the coming months—matters of life and death—could be tied to an event as simple as a chance meeting with a village functionary or the death of a pig. We can follow the history of China in the course of Mr. He's personal difficulties: At the depths of the Cultural Revolution he is forced to become a capitalist; and he steals shit.

Mao's demise in September 1976 set off a scramble for succession, paving the way toward the arrest of his wife and the other members of the so-called Gang of Four. The new leaders renounced the mass political movements of prior years and adopted agrarian policies aimed at expanding rural income and incentives. They endorsed experiments in rudimentary capitalism and entrepreneurship. And, turning away from the central planning that had dominated Mao's reign, they approved direct foreign investment and allowed consumer goods to be imported. In 1978 the Communist Party denounced the Cultural Revolution and slowly began finding and rehabilitating the survivors and victims of thirty years of tumult. This autobiography, as you will see, is the product of that lightening-up as it reached into Mr. He's remote mountain corner.

## A Way with Words

This book is remarkable for a number of reasons. Mr. He wrote it from scratch in English; it has not been translated. We must not take this extraordinary achievement for granted. I can only imagine the challenge it must have been for a Chinese villager, at the age of fifty, to resurrect a language studied in college and write an account with such flowing form, grammar, and idiom. This book required less editing than do many of my students' essays. Yet Mr. He had to use a different writing system for a language totally unrelated to Chinese—indeed, one he had not heard spoken for decades. He says of this period, "I abandoned all other trivial pursuits. I had only one goal and that was to lay siege to the English language and recapture my lost territory as soon as possible. I made this poor and mountainous corner my permanent home and the English language my daily bread."

His love of English put Mr. He in the path of suffering and disgrace. But literacy in English—in "ABC" as he and his family say—also saved his life. What drew his editor, Claire Chik, into his narrative and keeps all of us enchanted is the delight and freshness of his phrasing. He has written an ode to the English language that shines through like poetry. As the editor of his book of folktales remarked:

His use of the language has powerful attractions. Some of his sentences make one smile out of mere quaintness: "Every now and then they were often found to be short of this or that." These instances I have, sometimes regretfully, removed. Just as often, his English has the freshness of our first taste of something new. No native English speaker would have translated the monk's injunction to his novices in "Green Dragon Pond" into He Liyi's tumbling monosyllables—"Just go, go, go, both of you go down to buy."—and no native English speaker could better them. His texts were remarkable most of all for their rhythmical felicity, and for their manipulation of sound. In "A Stone Sheep," for instance, I could not bring myself to delete his line, "Her feet were seriously pierced by stings."[1]

Mr. He also loved two women. He recounts long conversations, letters, and arguments with both Guihua and Cuilian, the heroines of this story. They order him around. He tricks them and reasons with them. They stick by him as his troubles grow like weeds in his rice field. They are separated, then magically united. Rarely are we privileged to witness the interactions of a Chinese man and woman locked in such intimacy. I am impressed by the respect they pay to and earn from one another. And I am astounded by the daily neverending work they do; physical, emotional, social, and political work; work that nurtures, sustains, and drains. By the end of the book it is also his wives' stories Mr. He has told. The turbulent events that submerged a quarter of the world's people overshadow neither the personal qualities of these women nor his remarkable relationships with them.

Throughout the narrative we are ominously aware of how Mr. China in far-away Beijing translates his national policies into regional actions. Local administrative units control people's lives in random but telling ways, sometimes helpful but more often frustrating and tyrannical. Again and again Mr. He mentions the policies, their pettiness, and the permission he must get just to pursue simple activities. The presence of external and cold officialdom lurks in every chapter.

Yet also embedded in this autobiography is the richness of ordinary Chinese culture and life, of foods eaten, of customs explained, of rituals performed. No anthropologist could have done as much justice to the daily patterns of Chinese culture. For example, in Chapter 9 Mr. He describes why his family celebrated the Torch Festival in 1964. In fact, accounts of the Torch Festival appear in the earliest historical records of Yunnan Province. For many years the Communist Party tried to suppress this kind of local ethnic ceremonialism. They called it "feudal" or "primitive." More recently, however, the government has co-opted parts of these ceremonies as lures to the lucrative tour-

---

1. *The Spring of Butterflies and Other Folktales of China's Minority Peoples*, translated by He Liyi. Neil Philip, editor (U.K.: William Collins and Sons/New York: Lothrop, Lee and Shepard, 1985), p. 9.

ist trade. Officials now proudly proclaim the integrity and antiquity of a Torch Festival that bears little resemblance to Mr. He's village celebration.

According to the legend behind this ceremony, an ancient king desired another man's wife and so conspired to kill him. He built a chamber of pine trees and invited his rival and other chiefs to a banquet. The wife, knowing of the plot, begged her husband not to go. When he insisted, she sent him off with a gift of a white iron bracelet. On the night of the banquet, under a full moon, the king set fire to the chamber. When Madame Wife received word of this event, she gathered her soldiers and armed them with torches. Too late to save her husband, she searched for his skeleton in the ashes. Finally she located the bones by the iron bracelet. But her fingers were burned in the process. When the king captured her and shipped her to Dali on a boat, she leaped from the railing to her death rather than marry him. On the anniversary of this tragic death, Bai women use flower dye on their fingers and men erect torches in homes and villages or stage competitions and other ceremonies to honor her bravery.

It is important to follow simple things throughout Mr. He's saga. Note the references, say, to matches, cigarettes, and lighters. For Mr. He such items were still a novelty in 1962. Human excrement, on the other hand, was a valuable commodity. And, indeed, the daily economies of poverty for the He family never ceased. I think we would be bored by a scholarly analysis of Chinese family income. But Mr. He's descriptions of their Family Congresses, of their debates and the outcomes of their votes, give insights into the very heart and privacy of his family life.

One of the most unswerving themes in this book concerns the suffering and redemption experienced through "education." Without giving away the plot, I want to note that sacrifices for having been taught in the wrong setting, or for striving to learn in the right setting, dominate the entire book. Ironies also abound. Mr. He's grandmother sold family land to pay for his father's career advancement; thus the son was branded as a "landlord." And "reeducation" camps were really about punishment and hard work. In them, however, Mr. He learned an astonishing number and variety of careers. Indeed, he appears to have learned from every situation and person he encountered. In the end, he hands back both knowledge and wisdom, surely the measure of education at its best.

It is not easy to write books and find a publisher when you live in rural China and have little access to technologies most of us take for granted. In Chapter 17, Mr. He recounts how he received a typewriter with the assistance of a young Englishwoman named Claire Chik. Fluent in Chinese, she was teaching English at the Kunming Institute of Technology. Claire had completed a degree in Chinese studies and history at the School of Oriental and African Studies of London University and, later, received a scholarship to study the language intensively at Beijing University.

Despite the typewriter transfer, the two of them had not talked face to face. They arranged to meet during the festivities of the third lunar month after the Chinese New Year in 1984. Claire walked into the lobby of the Er Hai Hotel in the town of Xiaguan, outside of Dali City (this is an auspicious location). She asked in Chinese, "Is Teacher He here?" Turning, she saw him standing there, wearing the blue cotton uniform of China, hands clasped behind his back. "Very proper, very much a gentleman," she remembers thinking.

Mr. He asked Claire to read what he called a "little autobiography." The publisher of the book of folktales had requested a short introduction about the author. And what Mr. He had written was completely captivating. But it was too long for his publisher to use and too short to be a book. Claire begged him to expand and elaborate; she offered to help. When she returned to her job in Kunming, they continued to correspond.

In 1986 Claire moved with her husband and daughter to southern California. As she was preparing to leave China, Mr. He gave her some completed sections of his manuscript; then the two arranged a system of further correspondence. He numbered all his letters and she dated hers. One round trip by mail usually took a month. Otherwise simple matters of checking facts and asking and answering questions became frustrating procedures when their letters crossed in transit. But only one letter and a package ever went astray.

Pages poured out from Mr. He's typewriter as he sent her episode after episode. The pages were single spaced, typed edge to edge in tiny print on flimsy onionskin. In this way he saved money on postage and conserved precious paper. When his ribbons wore out, he used the red side. The letters on his small portable machine eventually lost their alignment. Until recently he typed with old-fashioned carbon paper and wrote only one draft.

Claire typed the episodes into her computer and arranged the sections into the chapters you will find here. She remarks, "I was in a new country and I knew no one. Working on this manuscript kept me sane from 1986 on." Mr. He remarks, "She worked with the power of two tigers and nine buffaloes." Drawn to his words and style, Claire has brilliantly preserved the clarity of his prose. Despite the birth of a son who occasionally destroyed her computer files, she kept working on the book. Her biggest problems were cutting the sheer bulk to a manageable length and finding a publisher for it.

For my part, I am an anthropologist and a university professor. My dreams of visiting China materialized in the summer of 1990, when I accompanied eleven colleagues and friends from New Orleans to China on a Fulbright-Hays travel grant. At one point we were seated in the lobby of the Er Hai Hotel in the town of Xiaguan outside the city of Dali in Yunnan Province. Here is what I wrote in my journal:

> The road is washed out, a big landslide. I hate that dangerous highway but it is the only road in and out of Dali. No trains, no planes, no rent-a-cars, no alterna-

tives. The Provincial Governor said they can fix the road in only five days(!). What a mess—at the tender mercies of weather and Chinese schedules. While we were negotiating with the Institute of the Minorities in Kunming to send a bus to meet us on the other side of the slide, I decided to tell the group the story about the sailor and the manatee. We needed cheering up. The story was complete with proper gestures; the suspense built and I looked up to see a Chinese elder dressed in worn blue cotton clothes. He had the most intelligent knowing eyes and he was listening raptly to my naughty story. I hope I did not offend him. Wispy hairs. Thin. Like most Chinese of his generation he needs a good dentist. He looks overworked but his smile reminded me of a proud Sino-Pixie.

A Canadian couple, similarly marooned, introduced us to the man I came to know as Mr. He. I was intrigued by his fluent English. He wanted to know, "Where did you learn to tell stories?" We fell into instant trust and talked at every opportunity until the bus taking us out left the following afternoon.

Mr. He showed me the book of folktales he had collected, translated, and published. He explained how difficult it was to find paper, to make copies, and to post materials abroad. A copying machine had only just reached Dali; both the machine and international postage were expensive. With such elaborate tact and politeness that I almost missed the point, he suggested that I might be able to assist him with his little stories. We agreed to correspond. Mr. He added me to his international correspondence network and I began to receive additional, tantalizing pieces of his life story, one sent from Denmark and another from Australia. I was hooked and curious. I wrote him and fervently urged him to write the whole story down. Modestly, he replied, "Please practice patience, understand my limited resources, and contact Claire Chik."

I called Claire; he had already written to her about me. She sent me the manuscript she had just finished retyping. I stayed up all night to read it. The next morning I wrote Dean Birkenkamp at Westview Press to tell him how extraordinary was this manuscript. He agreed with me and the rest, as we say, is history.

## Being Bai

Mr. He and his family belong to the Bai People, one of China's largest minority groups. As he explains, "At home we speak Bai, not the official language of my country, Mandarin. In the past, because our contacts with outsiders were limited and frustrated by this language trouble, we were looked down upon as ignorant and backward. We never found it easy to compete with the Han people." Many of the following chapters contain references to this intriguing minority status. But what does it actually entail? Mr. He's tribulations were similar to those many endured under Mao's rule. His trials during the last forty years of transformation in China stem more from his "privileged" background and knowledge of a "dangerous" foreign language than from his ethnicity. In fact, the advantages and delights of being Bai intersect his life at key moments, as we shall see.

The story of "minority nationhood" in China is complex and confusing. Unless individuals expressly identify themselves as minority persons, it is impossible to tell. Members of the identified minority groups cannot be distinguished by physical traits or cultural habits from the Han nationality (that is, the ethnic Chinese). Although Mr. He is Bai, he must identify himself from the beginning. He wants us to know that "I am, of course, Chinese; however, I should like to add one more word: I am Bai Chinese. I belong not to the great Hans of Central China but to the Bai National Minority."

What Westerners call ethnic groups, the Chinese call *minzu,* meaning "national minorities" or "nationalities." Sixty-seven million people are grouped into fifty-five of these nationalities. The Han majority, 94 percent of China's population, constitute the fifty-sixth nationality. These minorities largely reside in a strategic frontier arc on the northern, western, and southern borders of the great landmass of China.

In the period from 1949 to 1957, the newly formed Communist government promoted what it called "cultural flourishing." This program included research on the pluralism and diversity within China's vast population. In 1956 teams of government officials, bureaucrats, scholars, and students spread out across the nation. Their task was to survey and define ethnicity for the entire country and to assign the status of "national minorities" to selected groups. The teams collected and recorded folklore and documented the linguistic, geographical, and historical distributions of these diverse peoples. Stalin's four criteria of "nation" or ethnicity guided them: *Minzu*s had a common language, a common territory, a common economic life, and common psychological dispositions (that is, cultural life and customs). More than 400 groups stepped forward to claim their status as minorities. Yunnan Province itself had approximately 260 claimants during this period of identification.

As a result of their work, the research teams certified the Bai as the second largest ethnic minority in Yunnan Province. This rugged land, part of the great mountain roof of Asia, is home to approximately one-fifth of China's minority groups. Bordering on Burma, India, and Vietnam, Yunnan has long been a crossroads of warfare, trade, and migration as well as a breeding ground of ideas, people, and groups. With a history as convoluted as their mountain homes, "national minorities" such as the Bai have crossed modern political boundaries. Evidence reveals that they are older than either the Han borders or the boundaries drawn by the Communist Party. In fact, the Bai people are referred to in the earliest archaeological records of the Bronze Age, as well as in later manuscripts written by Han historians. The 1982 and 1984 population censuses of China listed more than 1.2 million Bai; most of these, approximately 900,000, are concentrated in Dali Autonomous Prefecture, which has a special status because of its minority populations. For English readers, the most important contemporary and ethnographic work on this area is *Under the Ancestor's Shadow* by Francis L.K. Hsu.[2]

Dali has long been the capital of Bai settlement. This city, 400 kilometers from Kunming, is famous not only for its scenic beauty and delightful weather but also for its 500-year role as the political, economic, and cultural center of the Nanzhao and Dali kingdoms, which controlled Yunnan in the past. Indeed, as a place of strategic importance, it was a gateway for promoting cultural and trade relations between China and Southeast Asian countries. Much of the action in the present autobiography takes place in villages in the Bai homeland, in the Dali Autonomous Prefecture, and along a fabled road called the "China-India" highway. One part of this highway is the old Southern Silk Road. Another part is known by Americans as the Burma Road of World War II fame. Mr. He remarks on its "about-to-fall-down-rocks." I myself took queasy notice of its unmarked and ungraded curves, of the buses and trucks along it that used horns instead of brakes, and of the wrecks strewn at the base of its menacing cliffs.

Chinese officials are very careful to emphasize that before Liberation, minorities such as the Bai people lived in remote places and lacked schools, highways, telephones, and electricity. After Liberation, minority peoples had factory jobs and were involved in commerce and industry. As one Chinese Communist Party official described to me, "After Liberation, we introduced advanced culture and technology. We built hydroelectric plants and improved the rice harvests. We helped the national minorities make economic and agricultural plans." Some of this developmental zeal is reflected in the many jobs Mr. He masters in the course of surviving his country's policies. Of course, he sees those years before and after Liberation, and during the aftermath of the Communist Party's growing-up, from a very different point of view. He was at the bottom looking up.

Assertions of minority status have amounted to a historical roller coaster. At times it was better to deny or avoid what Han Chinese or Communists call "feudal practices." During the two decades of "national contradictions," or cultural homogenization, from 1957 to 1977, Chairman Mao stressed unity and pressed for an assimilationist ethic in politics. It was then that the Chinese or Han superculture superseded local ethnicities. But during the Cultural Revolution, radical officials prosecuted those who claimed minority status even in such simple matters as wearing ethnic clothing. The repression during this period also resulted in delayed publication of the voluminous reports on socioeconomic organizations, customs, and folklore of minority groups.

---

2. Francis L.K. Hsu, *Under the Ancestor's Shadow* (New York: Doubleday, 1967). Originally published in 1948 by Columbia University Press.

In 1978 the government began to ease up on minorities. State policy and funding promoted a new brand of ethnicity as a national treasure—in competition for tourist money. Coffee-table books, postcards of happy young women wearing "national costumes," and ethnic crafts such as embroidery marked this revivalistic fervor. More recent policies in China offer further advantages to minority-group members, such as special treatment on the national college entrance exams or exemptions to family-planning restrictions and the "one-child" policy. In a rush to gain recognition, many groups have sought reclassification. Even some of the Han aspired to a category of legitimate difference, which offered enhanced educational and economic opportunities, preferential status, and access to governmental channels. In the meantime, many individuals within China's minorities have married one another. For this reason and others, interethnic tensions have not been a problem, particularly relative to the broader difficulties of Chinese life.

In 1956, when the National Minorities Research Institute began to investigate the social history of the minority groups of Yunnan Province, it opened an office in Kunming. One of its first employees was Mr. He. Fluent in both Bai and Mandarin, he translated English materials into Chinese; at other times he accompanied groups of experts into a distant mountain area and acted as interpreter. (The researchers from Beijing were not familiar with the languages spoken in the native villages of the Chinese countryside.) Mr. He loved his work. "I rejoiced over the change," he writes. "I had been working in a government office building where an eight-hour day seemed like a sixty-four-hour day. As soon as I was transferred to do a translator's job, my work day passed by like eight minutes."

He Liyi had no political aspirations. Life seemed solid; working in Kunming offered more opportunities for him than did living in his village. He felt extremely fortunate to have such a good job as interpreter and researcher. He had a fiancée, some Christian friends, a portable manual typewriter, books in English, and the kind of plans that many bright and educated young men make for their lives. But in the summer of 1957, a year after he began his job for the National Minorities Research Institute, the great wheel of China shifted once again and took him with it. Mr. He begins his story at this point.

YUNNAN PROVINCE

# MR. CHINA'S SON

# PART ONE

# 1

# AN ANTI-PARTY
# RIGHTIST CAP FOR ME

**M**y ancestors settled in the remote mountainous area of northwestern Yunnan. I am, of course, Chinese; however, I should like to add one more word: I am Bai Chinese. I belong not to the great Hans of Central China but to the Bai National Minority. At home we speak Bai, not the official language of my country, Mandarin. In the past, because our contacts with outsiders were limited and frustrated by this language trouble, we were looked down upon as ignorant and backward. We never found it easy to compete with the Han people.

Early in 1956, something unusual happened. Under the direct leadership of the Beijing-based Academy of Social Sciences, a special committee—the Research Institute for National Minority People's Social History—was established in Kunming. Most of its personnel were from Beijing. Without delay, I was the first one selected to help in their investigations. Not only am I Bai, fluent in Mandarin, but I had also studied English at college. Sometimes I was instructed to translate English materials into Chinese for research use; sometimes, to join a group of experts and visit a distant mountain area. On these occasions I acted as an interpreter, since people from Beijing can't follow the language spoken by the native villagers.

I rejoiced over the change. I had been working in a government office building where an eight-hour day seemed like a sixty-four-hour day. But as soon as I was transferred to do a translator's job, my workday passed by like eight minutes. Opening my dusty boxes, I brought out my books. I began to think, I began to plan; I was going to use my English again.

But all at once, in the summer of 1957, a great political movement known to the world as the Struggle Against the Rightists started all over our country. In the beginning, people opened with statements like "We are living in Mao Zedong's era. Everybody is free to express his or her thoughts." The most popular saying was "Let a hundred flowers blossom and a hundred schools of thought contend." This was the policy set forth by Chairman Mao for pro-

3

moting the arts and sciences and for developing a flourishing socialist culture. Office work stopped. For several months we did nothing but hold meeting after meeting, where reports were delivered and documents chosen for discussion.

Then, in the autumn of 1957, came the second stage. This was called "Drawing a clear line between sweet-smelling flowers and poisonous weeds." Now we heard, "In order to protect our New China, to ensure its color doesn't change, everybody must boldly expose all the poisonous weeds. Chairman Mao states that 95 percent of the population are loyal to socialism, but 5 percent only pretend to serve the people in a false way. If you cannot find that 5 percent, you are blind." Right after this, the struggle began. In order to fulfill that number, the group members began to gather their strength and to reexamine and analyze all that had previously been said.

In our office, three people were being dragged out, found out, discovered. One was a fifty-year-old man, a returned scholar from America. Another was a young man named Gao, a classmate of mine from college, who was a talkative fellow. The third and last poisonous weed was I myself.

At first, face-to-face struggle meetings[1] were conducted in a friendly atmosphere. In some organizations, snacks were even prepared on the table. The activists criticized in kind voices and said, "Eat something soft." They offered you a cup of water or a cigarette. This was named "To struggle with pleasant wind and light rain." But as the movement went deeper, people used the phrase "To struggle with a bigger storm." They shouted at you, pointed at your forehead or pulled your hair. They were so furious that they banged the desks and chairs with their fists. They kicked the floor, as if the floor was an enemy. And finally they hit, beat, or even gave you a "helicopter ride"—tied your arms behind your back and hung you up by them. All these struggle meetings ended with a warning: "Let's stop here for this evening, but we have a tomorrow every day. Never, never retreat unless a final and complete victory is won!"

It was easy to accuse me. My family had been classified as "landlord." I had once said that although I admired the Soviets' heavy industry, their light industry was falling behind that of capitalist countries such as Britain and America. I remember saying, "If you go into a bookstore and pick up a copy of a Soviet magazine, it gives off a terrible smell. Can you find a strange smell on American publications? British and American portable typewriters are light and good-looking. What about Soviet typewriters? Ugly and too heavy." They also remembered, "You are a man who hates the Soviet Union and loves the enemy, America!" I had once commented that nowadays in China, as soon as you knew the beginning of a book, magazine, film, radio program, you knew exactly how it was going to end. For this they said, "You hate our new society! You hate our Party! No mistake—you are just the rightist we are all trying to search for!" If I made a little unconscious mistake in speech, they immediately seized the opportunity to do evil.

During the daytime we three were left in peace, but each of us had to write his own "material"—a written report expressing inner thoughts and giving convincing answers to hundreds of "whys" and "whats."

\*    \*    \*

One day, after we had entered the second angry stage, I received a letter from Wu Qiyan, a former girlfriend. I could hardly believe my eyes, because many of my friends, including my former old classmates, had started avoiding me after they learned I had become a poisonous weed. Earlier I had written to Qiyan in northeast China, telling her of my new job. Then, a little while before the Anti-Rightist Movement began, I heard she had returned to Kunming and been assigned to teach Russian at a middle school.[2] For a time I thought of going to see her, but when I reconsidered it, I gave up the idea. Following the invitation in her letter, that afternoon I ran as fast as my two legs could carry me. The moment her school building came into view I stopped, looked at the gate, and then exclaimed, "No, it's too late now! I am too dirty. Heaven will punish me if I go into that school and poison that teacher of Russian."

I ran home, knocked my forehead against the desk, covered my head with my hands, and then threw myself into bed and sobbed.

A knock came at the door. Immediately I wiped my eyes and listened. More knocks followed. I thought my colleagues were coming to fetch me for another struggle session, so I replied, "I am here. I have no wings. I cannot fly to Taiwan."

The knocking didn't stop. I tiptoed over, lifted the corner of my curtain, and looked out. It was Qiyan. She opened the door and came forward a step or two, looking around, as though we were playing hide-and-seek.

"Shuyi![3] Can you remember my name?" Gazing straight into my eyes, she approached nearer.

I couldn't control my tears. Her voice brought back memories from the past.

In spite of everything, Qiyan had taken the initiative and come knocking at my door. How kind and how great she was! I must offer her a cup of tea. I reached for my thermos, but there was not a drop of water in it. Formerly, the cleaning staff had brought me hot water regularly.[4] After they saw I had become a bad element, they stopped serving me. I ran out, intending to borrow some water from my next-door colleagues. People were talking inside, but they paid no attention to my knock. About twenty minutes later I did succeed in getting a thermos of hot water; I bought it from a tea shop.

As I was returning, four children accosted me at the main gate of my organization. One of them said, "Good afternoon, Mr. Lao You (Old Rightist)!"

Another boy asked, "Are you bringing poisonous water to your friend?"

The biggest boy came up to me like a top official and asked, "What side of the road are you walking on now?"

"I don't understand," I replied. "The road is public. It does not belong to your family."

"No, all of us are the masters of the road. You are a Lao You. As 'you' means 'right,' you must walk on the right side!" With a push he forced me to walk on the right side.

An old woman said, "Just listen to the children! Hereafter they will all become the leftists of our country."

The children followed me. I couldn't stop them. My only aim was to offer a cup of water to a special friend, but my head ached seriously. I found my door closed and nobody in. Luckily the window had been left open, and I climbed through. But at that moment I dropped the thermos. Glass and hot water smashed all over the floor.

Qiyan was nowhere to be seen. However, my room had changed while I was out buying water. There was no more dust on the desk. All my books looked in good order. A vase of straw-like flowers had disappeared. On my bed I noticed a blue-covered notebook. Upon opening it I found a little photo of myself pasted onto the first page. I was particularly touched when I saw a faded rose beneath it. Qiyan and I had once picked two roses from the same branch of a bush in a temple. Later we each kept one. I had been preserving mine in my biggest English-Chinese dictionary. As I opened the dictionary and looked at my rose, Qiyan came back. She put down a pail of cold water and took up the broom.

"Someone has broken a thermos."

"It was my fault. I forget everything when I am in a hurry. I haven't even a cup of water to offer!"

"It's all right. I know your present circumstances."

"Qiyan, you don't understand—I have become an enemy of the people. I am now a poisonous weed; even three-year-old children are trying to weed me out!"

"I *do* understand, Shuyi! It makes no difference. Exactly the same in our school!"

I heard voices and looked out the window. A group of my colleagues' children were looking back at me. One of them waved his hand and they repeated a new type of nursery rhyme. It sounded a bit like one I had read in an English book:

| | |
|---|---|
| *"One, two, three, four, five,* | *One, two, three, four, five,* |
| *We have caught a Lao You alive,* | *An inch the snake wants to move,* |
| *Six, seven, eight, nine, ten,* | *Six, seven, eight, nine, ten,* |
| *A strange lady brings him water again.* | *People will struggle him to death again!"* |

Qiyan closed the window and asked, "Do you have to get permission if you want to go out?"

"No. Big leaders up above haven't made a final decision. I am waiting for some sort of punishment now, but I still can go out and about in the streets."

"I'm afraid those little ghosts will bring you trouble. Shall we go for a walk?"

"But what if later someone says, 'You are playing with a wolf, a snake. …'"

"I don't mind."

"Just like your father! One day you'll become a famous lady-professor."

"You are wrong if you think my professor-father is great. As the earth turns round and round, everything changes. For a time he was called an important big-school professor.[5] But one day, my dear friend, there was a storm up above. He also received a cap—they say he is a fierce monster and demon.[6] In our present-day China, from north to south, from east to west, when anyone sees a weed which appears to be special or unusual, they say that weed is poisonous. They pull up everything. They destroy everything, no matter if it is poisonous or can be turned into a beautiful plant. Nowadays a father can do nothing for his children, and sometimes the children have to curse their parents. Anyway, I think both you and my father are in the same boat."

"So, according to your theory, I am a good man?"

"Of course you are! Otherwise I wouldn't have come to see you here. I have brought you a little gift. As I was dusting your bookshelf I found that familiar dictionary. That fully proved, after all, that you didn't forget me. Is there anything missing?" She put the two roses together.

"No, several springs and several autumns have come and gone, but nothing seems to be missing. Only the color has faded a little. But what about me? I have changed my 'color.' And Qiyan, you have not. You enjoy a sweet-smelling job. You are not involved in the present storm. Cherish it, protect it, and defend yourself. I am afraid I will spoil your bright future."

"I think the present movement today really is like a heavy storm. It's not easy to find a safe shelter. Thousands and millions of people can't resist this storm. In the past you seldom paid attention to the weather reports, and moreover there were holes in your shoes. You couldn't get a pair of rubber boots like important people with good connections can, but you still splashed about carelessly. Needless to say, all kinds of dirty mud got into your shoes. When the time came to examine each person's feet they said, 'Look at your feet! They're stinking!'

"But our weather is changeable. Don't forget that mud is washable, and one of these days a storm will come along and wash off your mud. Like many others, I believe you and my father will eventually see that day. So you must not be discouraged. How I wish I could take you to see my father, but, for the time being, it's raining heavily. It's better not to take a poisonous-weed friend to see a monster father!"

I opened the door and made sure no children were about. Qiyan walked ahead and I followed. As soon as we were in the main street we walked shoulder to shoulder, naturally. We drank, ate, and finally sat on a bench beside a lake. It was very late when we arrived at her school gate. Taking a lovely apple out of her bag, Qiyan said, "I saved this apple for you. It's from Shandong Province. It goes to foreign countries as well."

"You have it yourself or give it to your father."

"No, you must have it. My father has some already. All the way from Harbin to Beijing and then to Yunnan, I purposely kept one for you."

The apple passed to and fro many times. One of us missed and the apple rolled and rolled until it stopped just in front of the woman gatekeeper.[7] She at once cried out excitedly, "Ai, what a big apple! The biggest, the most beautiful apple I've ever seen in my life! Ah, I must enjoy it myself. ..." She smelled it and opened her mouth wide, making a funny show.

Qiyan and I exchanged glances. The old woman smiled and said, "Teacher Wu, I've been watching you from the very beginning of your 'apple ping-pong-ball game.' Very interesting. I guess you must be our Teacher Wu's Mr. So-and-so. Welcome to you. Now tell me, what do people call this fruit?"

"Everybody knows we call it 'ping guo,'" Qiyan replied.

"But what does the word 'ping' mean?"

"'Ping' means 'equal,'" I said.

The old woman cut the apple into two and handed half to Qiyan and half to me. "You make a lovely couple," she said.

Everybody smiled. We ate the apple. We didn't speak, but we understood each other's hearts. We hoped we would thereafter share joys and sorrows like we had shared that apple equally.

During the period when that violent political struggle movement was in full swing, Qiyan's visit to my room was a great comfort. In our organization's office, when I was forced to answer their criticisms, I had for a time thought that the only way out for me was to die. But now, when I thought of Qiyan's words and her kind concern, I felt my life wasn't over yet. She had given me a little strength with which to survive.

She dropped in at least once a week to see me. In order to avoid extra trouble, I never went to see her at her school. Each time she came she would bring me something special to eat or help a little in my room. On weekends we would go to see a film or walk for a while in a park. One afternoon during the Spring Festival holiday she took me to see her father. I was touched to see the old man, but it was not convenient to talk a great deal as there were many other guests.

By and by, my colleagues began to be suspicious of our relationship. When we met in our dormitory, some smiled a little; but inside that forced smile they often hid a sharp knife. I went about alone. The office director allowed me to go back to my desk as usual, but a decision had been made not to let rightists touch the work they normally did. He said, "You just sit and read newspapers, including those published in other provinces. The only reason you have been seriously criticized by all the comrades is that you didn't pay attention to politics in the past. You must make up for this shortcoming. The more you study politics, the higher your political level will be."

In the beginning of the struggle movement, when it stormed and rained hard I thought I would be drowned. As I studied the Party editorials, day after day, I slowly became convinced they would not order a man from a security organization to shoot me. But I didn't know what kind of punishment I would have to face and bear.

Meanwhile, Qiyan never said "I love you," and I never asked her "Do you really love me?" Nevertheless, we understood each other well. Shortly after the Spring Festival of 1958, our marriage proposal was approved by her father. At first we decided to get married as soon as I was permitted to go back to my work. However, when that would be was a top secret of the government. Later we made a newer decision: Get everything ready, as quickly as possible. Qiyan had to fill in several forms at three levels: the Communist Youth League, the school authorities, and the local people's government. It usually took a long time for everything to be processed smoothly.

One evening I was plunged into a state of terrible anxiety. How could I plan my life in my present uncertainty? I went to see our office director at his house. I told him everything about my past, and also about the true relationship between Qiyan and myself. At the end of our talk, he said, "Don't worry too much. Your problems have nothing to do with the law. Our Party is not going to send all the rightists to a court and then throw them into a jailhouse. Today we have big rightists, middle rightists, little rightists, and ordinary ones. There are many different types. You didn't secretly organize a group of counterrevolutionaries to destroy our society. You are perhaps only a little rightist. So the punishment for you, I think, will be a lighter one. You will be treated as an ordinary citizen. You'll receive regular pay from the nation. I guarantee you won't experience any physical harm."

The next morning I rang Qiyan and told her to double her efforts to hurry along her marriage forms. Three days later, all my plans and dreams were destroyed. It happened suddenly and swiftly. At eight o'clock sharp we were told to attend a short meeting in the office. Our director opened the meeting with these words: "Comrades, listen to me carefully. Our plans and prearrangements always fall behind the flying speed of our society. I thought we would have to wait for a considerable time to see the outcome of our great struggle against the rightists. But no. The formal note from a high level has come at last. I was instructed to declare it today in the presence of everybody.

"Closing the gate here we are a big revolutionary family. By mastering our great leader Chairman Mao Zedong's thought, using his thoughts as a mirror, we can see which comrade is true to our Party, and which is going to destroy our great cause of the proletarian dictatorship. In this organization, as we look in the mirror, we see three enemies. In the past, since we didn't pay enough attention to politics, we were all deceived by their sweetest words. But today, under the correct leadership of our Party, and with the spirit of persistently chasing the enemy, we finally succeeded in revealing their ugly faces as those of monsters and snakes and ghosts. We all know where they were born, their past family history, what they said and did to injure our socialism. It is all down in black and white. They can never deny a word. All their material will be put into a big paper bag and will follow each one of them.

"These three are not good-for-nothings. The Party has spent a big sum of money in training them. They are valuable state property. Later, they thought they were wiser than others, so they began to fire at our Party. They didn't know that real wisdom is in the hands of the people. Yet when the time came for the Party to consider their problems, it was lenient and forgiving. As bad as they are, we don't intend to shoot, to beat them to death. We'll let them have an opportunity to correct their defects and make a self-reform plan in the coming years. As soon as they realize they have been ungrateful to the Party and the people, the people will welcome them back to contribute to our nation's modernization program. I hope you three will consider and cherish this last opportunity.

"Finally, I want you three to understand this: If you had committed such crimes in the Kuomintang days, you would have had your heads cut off. You must be cheerful and rejoice because you are under the leadership of the Chinese Communist Party. Yes, we agree, none of you killed a person in the street, or set fire to a building—but your anti-Party thoughts and the words you used to attack our Party were fiercer than those who use a gun to fire or a TNT packet to destroy. They were not trifles. If we place your anti-Party problems on a big-principle desk, it wouldn't be an exaggeration to describe them as a case of treason. And you know the penalty for treason is death. Are we going to give you a death sentence? No. You'll live. You still have a great hope to join our big revolutionary family. Bear this in mind: Based on Marx–Lenin–Mao Zedong thought theory, all your problems belong to 'contradictions between the people and the enemy.' But our Party hasn't punished you in accordance with this rule. In order to give you a chance to correct your wrongdoings, our Party has turned a 'people-to-enemy' contradiction into a 'people-to-people' contradiction. Your problems are problems *among* people, not *between* people and enemies. You three are very lucky. If our Party had used the first to punish you, you would have died. Please treasure this lenient policy of our Party.

"The note we have received from above makes it clear that there is some difference between each of you. One will be sent to a distant county in south Yunnan. The other two will be sent to a small county not far from Kunming. Generally speaking, they are all state-owned farms. They are not concentration camps, neither are they labor-reform farms of the Security Department, nor are they under the control of policemen. They are very new farms, set up only several months ago. You are to receive a reeducation program through labor. There is no fixed date on which you will be able to leave. Two weeks, two years, or ten years—nobody knows how long you'll have to stay. You'll have the right to vote. You'll receive a little salary to buy soap, cigarettes, stamps. The country takes care of everything. Just pack your things right after this meeting and get ready to jump into a jeep."

Coming out of the office building, I thought of what Qiyan's school gate-keeper had said as we ate that apple. Would Qiyan like to share her future with a man who was going to reform his thoughts on a farm? I had to tell her the news, so first I ran to borrow one of our organization's bicycles.

"What for?" the man at the gate asked.

"Very important. I'll be back in a little while."

"No, just now I was informed not to lend anything to you but, instead, to watch you more carefully."

As I began to pack I was called to the phone. I rushed upstairs. Another hand stopped mine as I picked up the receiver.

"Not for you now. This telephone serves the people," the man said.

"Am I an animal?"

"How dare you say that! Before eight o'clock you could use this phone, but after the meeting. ..."

"Please, only this time, the last time. I won't talk too long."

"I'll have to ask the director first. Don't touch it until I come back."

My tears streamed down. The man returned and said, "What are you crying for? You're not only a rightist but also full of bourgeois ideas! The director says all right. But tell me what you want to say."

"Please tell the caller I am leaving before lunch. Tell her I am going to a farm, and ask her to come over and see me as soon as her class ends."

For fear they would not allow me to talk to Qiyan in person when she arrived, I dashed off the following letter:

*Dear Qiyan,*

*At the moment I am forced to pack in a hurry, and to make matters worse, so many thoughts are appearing in my head and I have a hundred things to tell and say, but I simply don't know where to begin.*

*Ridiculous things do happen every day. Here they say I am still a "citizen," there I am stopped from using the telephone. I will never be able to understand such policies. Didn't we feel hopeful about our future? Your father also said we should have a hopeful outlook. They hadn't drawn up the final curtain then, so we thought many things were within our reach. Today, when we look back at our behavior, I must say both of us were naive and childish.*

*A word about our future. I think, beginning from today, we must set an
example in being practical. Can we manage to get married? Can a schoolteacher
marry a criminal on a farm? Maybe you will say, "I don't mind!" Dangerous!
Do you know what "social pressure" means? Since the situation has changed like
this, I have no more courage to think of that which is out of my reach. If only you
consider the duration, because they didn't tell me how many years I would have to
reform on the farm, you will come to see my point of view.*

*It makes my heart ache when I recall our times together. What did we talk
about beside the lake? Remember? I said no matter what kind of fierce storm
might come I would stand by you. I am very sorry. All that's in the past. I hope you
will forgive me and accept me as a good friend of yours. Always take care of
yourself and write if your policy is "good friends." I hope I can keep on hearing
from you.*

*By the way, I leave three boxes of things at our gatekeeper's room for you to
collect. I am taking the typewriter and some books. Please take care of the rest for
me.*

*Shuyi*

Someone had begun hurrying me even before I ended my letter to Qiyan.
My room was in a state of disorder. Time was so limited that I could only cram
my belongings into several cardboard boxes. At about half past ten, Lao Li
(the returned student from America) and I were rudely forced into a jeep. A
crowd had gathered to watch. One of the children called out, "Look, ladies
and gentlemen, over there, Mrs. Lao You is coming to see her Mr. Lao You
off!"

I thought he was making fun of me, but upon looking out of the jeep window I saw Qiyan riding up on a bicycle. The engine started. I asked the driver
to wait for a moment, but the colleague who was responsible for taking us to
the farm stopped him, saying, "No, you must not wait. The political mission
is above all. No more love-making affairs for an anti-Party element who is
going to a reform farm."

Our jeep began to move. Qiyan was pedaling hard and had almost reached
us. We waved and called—but we couldn't hear each other. Her bike raced
forward into the cloud of dust rising up behind our jeep. I dropped the letter
out of the window but couldn't tell if she had seen it or not. Soon our jeep
pulled away, and she disappeared from sight.

We bumped along. The colleague escorting us just smoked and said nothing. The middle-aged driver offered us cigarettes many times and asked Lao
Li and me many questions. When he asked me how long we would have to
spend on the "reeducation through labor" farm, I said, "I am living in a
drum. That's top secret."

Lao Li added, "Heaven only knows the length of time."

The driver laughed, "*No* time means they have a lot of time to do whatever they want to do. What a wonderful flexible policy! To you, *no* time means *no* hope is left for you. You will have to wait for a long, long time before that *no* time comes."

## NOTES

1. "Struggle meeting." Here "struggle" is a translation of the Chinese *douzheng*, which means "to accuse and denounce." *Douzheng* is also used in the phrase "class struggle." Because all such political movements were in one way or another supposed to be manifestations of Marxist/Leninist class antagonisms, Mr. He often uses terms such as "struggle me" or "struggling them" in describing the process. For Mr. He, these terms range in meaning from mild verbal criticism to outright torture.

2. The Chinese middle school combines junior high and high school; the junior grades are known as *chuzhong* and the senior ones as *gaozhong*. Pupils must pass an examination in order to be admitted into the senior department. In the rural areas it is common for middle schools to offer just the three years of *chuzhong*. Only the better ones, located in the county capital or in larger towns, offer the three senior years as well.

3. Mr. He was born with the name Zhang Shuyi. When he married his second wife, he had to change his name to He Liyi. (See Part 2.)

4. In Chinese cities most places of work (known as work units, or *danwei*) provide living quarters, a cafeteria, in some cases even shops and recreational facilities, on site. A portion of the staff, primarily the unmarried members, lives in dormitories, often sharing rooms. As these are not equipped with kitchens, the cleaning staff boil water in a large coal-burning boiler, fill thermos flasks, and place one or two in each room daily. In some dormitories the residents help themselves directly at the boiler.

5. *Big-school:* university or college.

6. *Cap:* This comes from the phrase *dai maozi*—literally, "to wear a hat," meaning "to put a label on somebody." The phrase itself originates in the practice of placing tall, white, pointed paper hats on the victims of modern political movements.

7. Larger work units, including the living quarters, cafeteria, and so on, are almost always surrounded by a wall. Gate houses are built at each gate and a gatekeeper, usually an elderly man or woman, is employed to keep watch.

# A "GENERAL BUFFALO"
# AMONG THE RIGHTISTS

**A**n hour later, our jeep stopped in front of a new office building. Above the door we read: "Kunming Guangming Farm (State-Owned)."[1] One after the other, group after group, people of all sorts began to arrive. Lao Li and I were ordered to wait at a corner. After the necessary paperwork was completed, our jeep went away. A man took us to have a rest in a large room. There we saw more passenger-like people. We just looked at one another and said nothing. Many kept on drying their tears. Presently a boy came to sell cakes. Like the others, we silently bought some for our lunch.

At four, two horse-drawn carts pulled up. Handing a letter to one of the drivers, a young man said, "Take them to the Third Brigade. Some more will be arriving shortly. You'd better hurry."

We piled in. I was happy because I had my former colleague, Lao Li, to talk to. The cart went faster and faster, but after about ten minutes a bicycle caught up with us. The bicycle driver panted out, "Is there a man called Zhang Shuyi on this cart?"

Nobody answered. My face turned pale. Some unlucky thing is going to happen to me, I thought.

"A young man, under thirty." The cyclist's eyes rested on me. "Don't be afraid, it's a good thing. Many wanted it but were refused."

"He is Zhang Shuyi. We come from the same organization," Lao Li said quickly.

"Okay. Congratulations! Follow me," he said, helping me get my luggage down.

Lao Li and I waved goodbye.

The cyclist took me to a nearby restaurant. Seated at a corner table he began, "Don't be afraid, young man. My name is Debiao, my last name is Yang. I work in the farm's General Affairs Office. My cultural level is junior middle school, not qualified to sit on a chair and use a pen, but I know many people and hear countless interesting things every day. I know more than those who have a desk. We have perhaps twenty production brigades scattered around the county. At the moment about a hundred people form a brigade, but the number is increasing with each passing day. They say that more and more will be arriving. Very soon it's going to be one of the biggest reform farms in Yunnan Province.

"We have received many newcomers this week alone. Yesterday I took a lecturer, a man with glasses on, to the farm's small machinery factory. He was over forty, I think, according to our rules too old to work in a factory, but he was sent from a technical institute in Kunming. The director said he might be able to suggest something to speed up our production here. Therefore, they made an exception—let him join our machinery factory. This morning, oh, so beautiful, I saw a lady, very young, maybe twenty or twenty-four at most. Our doctor had been awaiting her arrival for some time. As soon as she got out from the white ambulance she was warmly received. Our low-level little nurses struggled to carry her things. The doctor greeted her, telling others that she was to be a head-nurse, a very, very good job. They honored her, but she didn't return even a little smile. She wept painfully as she was saying goodbye to a young man, possibly her boyfriend or her husband. Truly, this farm is all colors of the rainbow."

"May I ask how we address each other here?"

"Formally speaking, you should address me as Brigade Leader Yang, but being called 'brigade leader' cannot make me fat.[2] Among people who were sent here to be reformed just add the word 'lao' for an older person and the word 'xiao' for a younger person. You can call me Xiao Yang, too. Never use the word 'comrade.'"

"All right, Xiao Yang, where are you taking me?"

"The farm's brick and tile factory, only two *li* away from here.[3] All their jobs are very interesting. Everything is handmade. Young men around twenty-five are selected to work there. You are under thirty, so they want you to become a brick maker. You are lucky."

"Lucky?"

"Of course, very lucky. Gradually you will get to know the difference between you and those who were sent away on that horse-cart. They are agricultural workers. You are a factory worker. You belong to industry. Every day they carry a spade or a hoe and walk for several miles before they get to the field. For them the endless land is their office desk. The hot sun is their underwear. No radio broadcast, no music, no electricity, nowhere to spend their pocket money. Above all, for them it isn't an eight-hour working system."

"I begin to understand now. It's a farm, but for me, I'll become a factory worker."

"Right! In a way you are prisoners now, but not like the ones arrested by a policeman. You are what they call a 'new type' of prisoner. You are still a citizen. Later, when an election takes place in this county, you will be able to vote. That is a political right, and in the eyes of the law, you enjoy an equal share. Economically speaking, everybody will receive a regular payment at the end of each month. Those who were sent to be farmers get only a little, just enough to buy soap, toothpaste, or some stamps. That's because what they produce in the fields is very cheap. Factory workers' products are more expensive than grain, so they get more pay. Your monthly income is two or three times higher than those who work on a farm."

"Can a relative or friend come to see me in person?"

"Why, you are a citizen, of course they can! By the way, does your family know you were sent here to join this reeducation-through-labor farm?"

"Well, I was born into a landlord family. More trouble will follow if I contact my landlord relatives, so I haven't done that in a long, long time."

"You can speak English, I was told?"

"Oh, a little."

"How can a little English make a translator? I heard them talking in the office. Maybe you could teach me ABC, secretly. Don't be sad. Make friends and enjoy your new life."

Finally he said that in the factory people ate only twice a day. Meat was available twice a month. Bearing this in mind, we ordered some supper. Xiao Yang was kind enough to pay for the meal. Then he took me to the factory on his bicycle's "tail." This Brigade Leader Yang was a good young man, and I remember him well.

*             *             *

The chief director of the brick and tile factory led us down a corridor and into a big thirty-bed dormitory. Here he called together a twelve-member group meeting and said, in a serious manner, "This is Zhang Shuyi, from Kunming. Our farm's General Affairs Office has agreed to make him a group leader. Everybody has to respect him and listen to him. You must help one another to produce more bricks and tiles for our national reconstruction. More products mean greater progress in performing meritorious services to atone for your crimes. The more contributions you make, the earlier you will be able to leave here and join the biggest revolutionary family."

We were all "people with problems," nervous and sorrowful. In the beginning, even the question "What was your occupation before you came here?" made us hesitate. We had a talented young doctor in our group, but he timidly replied, "No, no, I only swept the floor at the hospital." There was also a librarian from Yunnan University. Once he secretly told me he had been to America. I was overjoyed to get to know another person who could speak English, but he was so fearful he refused even to mention the *word* "English"! For a time there was a very fat man. We were all interested to hear that he had been the personal cook of the provincial governor before Liberation.[4] He told us, "What was I? Nothing but a cook! I cooked the vegetables, boiled the rice.

I had no connection with the nation's important affairs. Oh, but, here I am. ..." Although in our hearts we gradually came to understand one another's troubles and problems, under those circumstances no true friendships developed. I made some friends, but they were all common ones, not heart-to-heart ones.

The factory was divided into three sections: One group dug the ground, carried the earth, and mixed it with a good-quality sand, then carried this mixture again and placed it into a round hole. Finally they added water to produce a mud-like substance. The next group mixed up the mud-like substance up with hoes and, after this, led several buffalo into the hole to mix the earth and sand into a good-quality mud. The last group was responsible for making damp bricks. The mud mixture was put into brick-shaped wooden boxes, and these were placed neatly on the ground to dry in the sun and open air. Finally, these half-made bricks were placed into a kiln, which looks like a small hillock with a chimney, and baked for several days.

I was assigned to work in the middle group that produced the mud. We were divided into six subgroups. A subgroup had twelve persons and six buffalo. Each person had to take off his shoes and spend six hours a day in that round hole of mud. At first, the buffalo walked quickly, but two or three hours later they were so tired they refused to walk. Some clever buffalo moved their feet into the footprints that other buffalo had already made. Therefore, we had to blindfold them!

Our main job was to follow the buffalo and fill in their footprints. When the animals were having a rest, we mixed and turned the mud ourselves. The worst part was watching the buffaloes' tails all the time. The mud had to be very clean, with no buffalo urine or droppings in it. If we noticed a buffalo was going to drop some terrible things, we pressed its tail tightly and shouted, "Oh, please be quick, bring me a basket!" Or if we noticed it was about to urinate, we would yell, "Quick! Pass me the pail!" If we were too late, we had to stop the animal and clean the droppings out with our own fingers.

When a batch of mud was properly mixed, we cut the mud and passed it out of the hole piece by piece, to be placed in a nearby shed for the next group. This last job was very heavy, but in a way it looked as if we were playing a basketball game. Everybody enjoyed it.

We were all "prisoners," but luckily Xiao Yang had made me a group leader. This gave me a few privileges. For instance, an ordinary group member had to obtain "double permission" if he wanted to go out to buy something. First, the group leader had to say "Okay," and then the brigade leader had to sign his name on a printed form. But if I wanted to go out, I just said a word to the brigade leader; there was no need for me to fill in that printed form. Only a group leader was allowed to get hot water directly from the kitchen.

I tried to be a helpful group leader. If I saw the mud was spoiled by a buffalo's watery droppings, it was I who took the lead to clean it up with my fingers. When my group members' wives came to visit, I gave up my spare time so they could be together for a little longer. Whenever I discovered some new problems in my group, I rushed over to see Xiao Yang. With his advice all the problems were solved smoothly. At an end-of-the-year rally, which more than 1,000 people attended, my group won a red flag. All our names were read out over the loudspeakers.

After the Spring Festival of 1959, I was instructed to work in the brick-making section. It took me a month to master the new skill. Then in March I fell ill. This sickness, common throughout the country, was known as the "water swelling sickness," edema.[5] People said that in certain poor districts half the population suffered from it that year. In my brick and tile factory, for a time, nearly 30 percent of the total work force suffered from this disease. Early in the morning the farm's clinic looked like the entrance to a theater. People showed their swollen feet or hands. Someone said the disease was caused by salt. Right away they stopped serving salt with our meals. But still we could not get rid of it. Symptoms disappeared on Monday, only to reappear on Wednesday or Thursday. I became too weak to make bricks. I was allowed to return to my former section, mud preparation, which was slightly lighter work. I bought several bottles of this medicine and that medicine in addition to the free clinic medicine, but I always found myself unwell.

\*       \*       \*

Throughout my years of reeducation through labor, I never forgot Qiyan, my last friend in Kunming. About four months after I entered the factory she wrote to me first, in June 1958. She hadn't, after all, missed my goodbye letter dropped out of the jeep window. She explained that she hadn't written immediately because the only information she could obtain was heard from other people, not acquired from an official document. This kind of labor-education-punishment was a new policy, and she wanted to wait and see how it differed from the punishment given by a court. The last part of her letter was full of encouraging words and clearly showed her heart: that she would still like to be my friend and was always hoping to hear from me.

We wrote to each other at least once a month after this first letter. Having made sure that the authorities didn't examine our personal letters,[6] each time I replied I wrote a long letter describing my daily life at the factory. In October that year Qiyan sent me a big parcel, containing something to eat, to use, and to read.

I made a special secret policy for Qiyan: to be fully aware that my once honorable seat in a state-run organization has been smashed by the movement. I have not the least skill for repairing that chair, nor any hope of doing so. It's a completely wishful and silly thought for me to marry a teacher of Russian. What they called "still a citizen" was false! But always be grateful to her, and tell her the truth. Look on her as an older sister, or at least make her a very special friend.

*    *    *

For a time while I was working in the mud-producing section, one of my daily musts was to drive our buffalo down into a nearby river to let the animals have a wash. One afternoon, while I was swimming and playing among the buffalo, I heard a small boy shout,

*"Look at that white shirt,*
*Off it flies with a three-hand!*
*Here I go to a white-capped policeman,*
*In a minute I'll see you repent!"*

I noticed my shirt was missing and swam swiftly to the bank. The boy whispered, "Hurry, over there, that woman three-hand has stolen your shirt. Look, disappeared now, at the back of that willow tree."

"Thank you!" I said, picking up my rubber whip.

The strange lady turned toward me and all at once I realized that she wasn't a three-handed thief. It was Qiyan. Her eyes looked straight into mine. Within three minutes her face changed several times. First, she gave me an angry look. Then she looked shy. Finally she looked sad.

I threw away my rubber whip. "You see, Qiyan, what am I? Oh, I took a friend as an enemy!"

"It's all right, Shuyi. I should have let you know before I came to visit. But as I was passing the bridge over there I saw some buffalo. They reminded me of your descriptions. I stopped to look and after a few moments saw you. I wanted to give you a surprise, so I waited behind a tree and then secretly took away your shirt. Well, nothing but for fun, a joke."

She put down my shirt, walked closer, and looked at me from all sides. She let out a sad sigh. "Poor Shuyi! You have changed from top to bottom. I would hardly have recognized you if we'd met in the street."

"Yes, completely changed. Those animals have forced me to change. Really change. But what can I do? I'm helpless, just like a buffalo."

"Your skin, the lung-colored sunburn, all look healthy, like a strong man at a sports-meet parade.[7] But your long hair terrified me! And only one button left on your shirt. I'm sorry I can't do much for you today."

"Oh, who has the pleasure to make himself look nice on this farm? My only companions are these buffalo."

We sat down under the willow tree. Qiyan said, "Well, life is long and a person's life covers many things. I have beautiful clothes to wear. I enjoy a regular share of the nation's money. At my school I am counted an outstanding teacher. But something's missing. A year has come and gone since you were sent here, but it's made no difference to me."

"Dangerous, Qiyan. I can never compare with you."

"Yes, I realize that too, but I still have more than a hundred 'I wonder this' and 'I wonder that.'"

After Qiyan gave me two cans of beef and two of pork, two bags of sugar, and several boxes of cookies, we took a rest at her bus stop. We ordered some tea, but before we could finish drinking the bus arrived. As I was shaking Qiyan's hand, she said, "Always take care of yourself and always remember to do your job well. I enjoy your detailed letters very much. Never forget to write again and again. Bye-bye."

As the bus began to move, she threw down a white envelope. Inside were 30 *yuan*[8] and a note: "A little pocket money. Please keep and use."

Qiyan's sudden visit lasted about two hours. We didn't talk about our marriage problem. By listening to her words, seeing what she had brought me, I came to the conclusion that she hadn't decided whether to marry me or not. She was still willing to be my friend. I was grateful, and I cherished her special friendship.

*    *    *

In April of 1959, the brigade leader of our factory "promoted" me. For almost half a year, everybody called me "General Buffalo." In the brick and tile factory we had forty-five buffalo, but only thirty of them were in good health. The other fifteen were weak or ill. One day I was luckily chosen to look after those handicapped buffalo. I did nothing but put them out to pasture. Within the four walls of the factory I was a prisoner. But as soon as I drove my fifteen "soldiers" out of the gate, I became a local peasant.

Every morning a cook prepared a cold breakfast and lunch in a box for me. My daily work began just as the sun rose. Grasping a long rubber whip, I followed my fifteen "soldiers." After leaving our factory gate behind, I had to walk for about two *li* along a main highway before turning off into the hills and fields. The moment I left that busy highway behind, I feared nothing. There was no one to scold or order me around.

The cook could only prepare something simple for my breakfast and lunch; but within two weeks many village children had become my good friends, and we often shared our meals. Yesterday I gave my breakfast to a cowherd and he gave me his mother-made lunch. Today I gave my turnips and potatoes to two girl shepherds and they gave me their corn and buckwheat cakes. For a time in the late fifties, ordinary villagers couldn't obtain rice to eat. But occasionally the cook secretly slipped some pure rice into my lunch. Then an excited bargain took place between me and the village children.

Once I discovered a clump of mushrooms growing in the grass. I offered them to the village children, and they ran home to fetch a pot, oil, and salt. Then we cooked and ate in a circle on the ground. Sometimes, after making sure that my "soldiers" would not damage any crops, I volunteered free service to some of the local peasants—I would join a group of them to weed or hoe. On such occasions, I was kindly invited to join their in-the-field lunch.

If I drove my buffalo a little farther than usual I came to many orchards: peaches, pears, apples, and chestnuts. In each orchard, the village head appointed an old man to look after the fruit. These orchard-watchers built straw huts in their appointed orchard, and would rush there early in the morning and return home late at night. If fruit was hanging from the branches, they slept in the hut, watching day and night. They always welcomed me, saying, "Pick as many as you wish every day when you return."

It was a tradition of the local people to use the orchard as a park, for relaxation and games. The children in particular had a lot of fun. As a rule, their parents instructed them to look after the family's domestic animals after school and during their vacations. As soon as they came out of their houses, they formed into groups of twos and threes and trooped over to the orchard, driving their pigs, buffalo, and goats before them to graze under the fruit trees. The girls went crazy in the freedom of the orchard. They liked to make a swing by tying the ends of a large rope between two fruit trees. I remember once a pear tree was so fruitful that they lay down on the ground and tried to eat without using their hands. The most popular game among the boys was "struggle the crickets." Two crickets were put into a box and made to bite, kick, and fight. The onlookers gambled on the competition, and it wasn't strange to see someone win a boiled egg, a hat, a mug. Unavoidably, some little ones returned home sadly, eyes filled with tears, because they had lost their favorite toy. In that case the old man would say, "You didn't win, but I still have the pleasure to offer you some peaches. Looking after the fruit is my main job, but I love to have all of you around here to be my good company. I don't want someone's parents to quarrel with me!" Life in a summer–autumn time orchard was most enjoyable.

Among the village people an unforgettable friend was a sixty-year-old man, Lao Wang. He had built a simple cottage beside a pond. When there was rain, his cottage became my shelter. When I was thirsty, his cottage became my tea shop. When I fell ill at the factory, he came to see me. Each market day he or his grandson would bring me fresh fish as a gift. I was touched by their special care.

When the villagers talked about him, they said that Lao Wang was their county's "Foolish Old Man." The foolish old man our Chairman Mao wrote about was the one who slowly moved away a mountain that stood in front of his house. Here, Lao Wang was the only old man who had built a private pond outside his village. Some villagers envied him, but most loved and respected him, because he himself had built this fish pond within ten years' time. Lao Wang was overjoyed when he learned I was a college graduate. His son had settled in a distant province and had sent him a large pile of books, one by one. But the trouble was that Lao Wang couldn't read. He made an exhibition of all these books for me to view. I knew nothing about raising fish, but I was particularly touched by his strong will in building that pond. I read some of these fish-raising books, and then we discussed them together. Combining my bookish theory with his practical experience, we seemed to gain a lot of knowledge in fish breeding. In his eyes, I was not only a foreign language translator but also an expert on fish culture!

*          *          *

During the daytime, playing outside with my "soldiers" and the boys and girls, or chatting with the orchard-watchers or Lao Wang, I forgot my bitter past and bleak present. But as I returned to the brick and tile factory at sunset, I became downcast and filled with anger. What heinous crime had I committed? At our evening meetings sometimes I did say "Yes," only because I was forced to, but in my heart I replied "No!" I began imagining all the people on the farm as dirty white maggots, the kind found in our public lavatories in China. Those maggots wriggle and squirm for days and nights, yet they cannot crawl out of the urine and shit. Like the maggots, we crawled fiercely too, but, from sunrise until sunset, month after month, year after year, we still found ourselves in the same spot. It was impossible to show any "outstanding good deeds" and persuade the farm authorities to free us at an earlier date.

One evening when I was alone, I combined everything in my situation together and made some secret policies for myself: (1) Listen and watch carefully. Do and say like others. (2) Completely give up the thought of leaving the farm quickly. Make the factory my second home. Bear everything and prepare for a stay of three to five years. (3) Don't force myself to perform "meritorious services," but also remember not to commit any new mistake. (4) Don't build too many castles in the air, and don't be too sad over the past. (5) Grasp today. Eat, play, and live as well as I can within the circle of the factory and the fields.

Never did I do a thing which ran against my secret policies. Never offended anyone. Praised others rather than criticized. Particularly, from the beginning to the very end, I tried to keep on good terms with the important people around me. Late in the afternoon when I returned home, I often brought back something special from the fields. Once I picked a basketful of mushrooms for the cook. In return he secretly slipped a little more food into my box. I brought back fruit for the buffalo-overseer. In return he secretly gave me some dried broad beans, originally prepared for the buffalo. Once, passing a valley, I picked a bag of red fruit, a kind of wild strawberry. I handed the whole bag to the factory leader's wife. My group mates, too, were pleased when I brought some treats back. As soon as I returned, they came to find me.

*          *          *

My days as "General Buffalo" had their peace and sweetness, but one evening in January 1960 another nine inmates and myself were suddenly called together. Our factory brigade leader said, "We received a name list this morning. No more brick and tile work for you for some time. Stay and move your beds together. Another twenty will be arriving tomorrow. Our farm's office is going to organize a 'study class.' All you thirty have various unclear or unsettled problems. Another new brigade leader and several others will come here to help from the beginning to the end. If everything goes smoothly, we shall close this study class within two or three months."

The next day two government workers arrived, looking ready to get down to business. They were accompanied by a brigade leader from the farm's General Affairs Office. A meeting was held at which one of the officials delivered a two-hour-long report. He began with something about the international situation and its problems. The second part was about our own national affairs. The last part was the most important: "According to our investigations, each of you thirty have secret crimes in your past. Of course, you have confessed some, but today many of you are still hiding some. The Party wants you to confess everything. Only by pouring everything out completely will you 'clean yourselves' and have a chance to be treated leniently. Therefore, we have organized this study class for you to make up what you didn't confess during the previous movement. Under the correct leadership of the higher authorities, our farm's office is going to carry out this class to its final end. We will never retreat until a final victory is won."

We were divided into three groups. In my group, the oldest member was fifty. We represented many colors of our society: a doctor, three schoolteachers, two government office workers, a radio-station reporter, two factory workers, and myself. No one was allowed to see an outsider, post a letter, or go out to buy anything. Guards took turns to watching us around the clock. At our daily group meetings, each group member had to make a detailed report of his past history. When your turn came, you began with "My name is. … I was born into a … family. My father was a. … As a child I went to school in. …" Sometimes it took two or three days to hear out one member's whole story.

Everybody hoped to please and flatter the officials who attended our meetings. The officials themselves never attacked us—but they pestered, and they mobilized all the group members to attack one another. "You must understand," one said, "why the People's Government made you gather here. The country hasn't forgotten you—it builds a great hope on you. Not only is this the right time, a golden opportunity for you to tell all your past wrongdoings and reactionary thoughts, but if you want to become perfect men, then this is also a good chance for you to reveal all you know about other people's wrongdoings. The policy is: Those who render meritorious service receive rewards."

Here, "render meritorious service" meant "be brave and expose your group members' questionable problems." Those who took the initiative in criticizing others were regarded as loyal to the people and the Party. On the other hand, if you kept silent the group members would say you were afraid. You feared someone would be offended and then reveal serious problems of your own past. Therefore, in order to make a favorable impression many began to attack each other violently. Even someone who showed no interest and seldom spoke would suddenly become very active as soon as he saw a high-level brigade leader approaching. For this reason the struggle at our so-called study class was fiercer than I had experienced in Kunming. People seldom spoke politely or slowly. One slogan of those times ran, "Do not treat an enemy with kindness." Nearly everybody shouted at each other, "You are a liar! Get down on your knees! You are simply farting! You are vomiting shit from your mouth!"

Sometimes the other group members forced you to kneel down on broken tiles for hours and hours. Or they tied you up or made you stand straight for a whole night. If you had a call of nature, you had to go with at least two other people. Day after day and week after week we did nothing but take part in meeting after screaming meeting. Sometimes the meetings lasted for days and nights together. If there was no meeting, then we had to write self-criticism reports. I lost track of time.

## NOTES

1. Mr. He explains, "The 'farmers' were all 'wrongdoers'; but the policy said they could become good people, so the farm was called *Guangming,* which means 'bright, full of sunlight.'"

2. *Cannot make me fat:* In a country where the majority were never far from the brink of starvation, fatness was considered a symbol of power and prosperity. This phrase means "cannot make me important."

3. *Li:* There are slightly more than three *li* to the mile.

4. The term *Liberation* refers to the Communist victory in 1949; it can also refer specifically to the arrival of Communist forces into the area where the speaker was living in either 1949 or 1950.

5. Malnutrition—specifically lack of protein—led to this illness.

6. Mr. He explains, "One day when we had been unexpectedly ordered to work on a railway line, I saw a local postman enter an office room. Shortly afterward, someone inside the office brought out several letters. The man called out the receivers' names. I stood by and heard my name. He immediately gave the letter to me. Therefore, I was sure that they didn't examine our letters."

7. *Lung-colored:* If anyone is looking pale, he or she will be advised, "You must exercise and every day go out for a while to let the sunshine burn your body. In this way very soon your skin color will change to that of a pig's lung."

8. In 1952, one U.S. dollar was equivalent to 2.5 *yuan*. in 1979, 1.9 *yuan;* and in 1993, 5.7 *yuan*. These figures are somewhat misleading, however, because they represent fairly arbitrary rates set by the government with foreign trade in mind and divorced from the domestic economy. Accordingly, they tend to underestimate the purchasing power of the *yuan*—especially given the simplicity of life in China. Thirty *yuan* would have been a sizable sum of money; as an example consider Qiyan's monthly salary, which, soon after her graduation, would have been about 50 *yuan*.

# 3

# I WAVE GOODBYE
# TO MY HOMELAND

This is my history, the real one, which I did not "confess" at the study class.

For a farmer, the most priceless property is the living land. Everything comes from the fields. More land means a happier life. But when my father was old enough to receive a higher education, my grandmother hadn't thought a bit about the priceless value of our private land. She had named my father, the only boy among her eight children, Shoushu, meaning "to receive a book," because she regarded learning as the "eye of the mind." In order to let my father become a useful man, she created all the favorable conditions for him to continue going to school. Above all, she sold some of our land. With the money, she sent him to Kunming.

On the eve of his departure she took him to bow before our ancestral tablet. "This is your father's name," she said. "A great mason of our county. Whenever people wanted to build something big and important, they came to ask your father to be their chief-director. You were only a baby when he left the house for the West.[1] You must be a good son and study hard."

The journey from Jianchuan County, my family's homeland, to Kunming was a long one. As there was no highway, let alone bus service, it took twenty-four days for my father to reach Kunming on foot. Soon after his arrival, he was lucky enough to be selected to study in a police academy. Later, in 1933 or 1934, the news that my father had become a police officer in Eryuan County spread like wildfire. The villagers said that my grandmother's "pain"—selling our priceless land—had turned into a huge "gain"—her bringing up a police officer son.

As for my mother, she was a traditional, simple country woman. She came from a village about a *li* to the east of my father's village. She married when she was very young, about sixteen or seventeen. I was born in 1930, as the second son; she bore four daughters, including twins, after me. Unfortunately, she and my masterful grandmother often fought and scolded each other. This got so bad that when I was three or four, my mother was forced to leave home and move in with another family in our village. After that, my grandmother looked after me.

One day, when I was five, my father's third sister carried me on her back in a bamboo basket to join my father and elder brother in Eryuan County Town, the capital of Eryuan County, some seventy *li* from Jianchuan. About a year later, in 1936, I followed my father to his second post in Dengchuan County. I was again carried in a bamboo basket, but this time I was given a mouth organ to play along the way. Eryuan was the first place I started learning to speak Mandarin. And it was in Dengchuan that I began learning to read and write Chinese characters.

That year while my father was serving in Dengchuan County, we met a miserable aged woman one afternoon in a market square. A little girl was crying beside her. A man introduced the old woman to my father. After a while, an agreement was reached. My father bought some rolls of cloth and gave them to the woman. In return she gave the crying girl to us. My mother had just given birth to the twins and was busy all the time; my father's aim was to let that woman's granddaughter help my mother. In a way this bargain looked like the buying of a slave girl, but after she joined our family we treated her exactly the same as we treated my real sisters.

None of our sisters went to school, nor did they go with us to join my father. Generation after generation, people looked down on women. I remember once my father wanted to let my sisters go to a primary school, but this suggestion was strongly opposed by my mother: "Not worthwhile. Marry a chicken, follow a chicken. Marry a dog, follow a dog. When they grow up they become the wives of other people and work for another family's interests. We get nothing."

While I grew from age six to thirteen, my father was sent to work here and there, all over Yunnan Province. People in those places all spoke Mandarin, not our Bai language. My father made a family policy for me: If I spoke only Mandarin for three months at a stretch, he would give me extra pocket money. But if I ran against his rule, he drew a circle in a corner and made me stand straight for several hours. By the time I was in grade two, I spoke Mandarin fluently. My ugly native accent had dropped away. Nobody believed I was born in Jianchuan. So, for me, the all-important language problem was solved at an early age.

In 1943, my father was transferred to a police station on the outskirts of Kunming. Instead of accompanying him there, my brother and I were sent to study at the Lijiang County Middle School about ninety *li* from Jianchuan. There was no highway at the time, so we went on foot; it took us two days. We climbed over several high mountains and carried a sack of rice, which we cooked and ate along the way.

Our school was ranked as the third best in Yunnan Province. It had both junior and senior departments and was run by the authorities in Kunming. Like most of the students, we boarded at school. They killed a pig or two each week, so we had a little meat. Before long, my brother was selected to study at a military institute far away in Sichuan Province. (Upon graduation in 1948, he was instructed to join an army unit in Shanxi Province.) All on my own in Lijiang, I felt rather lonely. Finally, in 1944, my father agreed to let me join him in Kunming.

Mother was unhappy about this. My grandmother had died and she had moved back into our family house in the village. Now she insisted I join her there. Mother's idea was to let me continue my studies at the recently founded middle school in my home county. She said, "You will have to make the journey all alone. You will go astray."

"Nothing is wrong with my tongue and lips," I answered. "I'll meet strangers all the way to Kunming, but I can ask and find my father."

After much persuading, she finally agreed to let me go.

*     *     *

I left my birthplace on a mid-autumn day. It was the very first time in my life I had traveled alone, and the journey, compared to all the other ones, was many times longer. My mother insisted on accompanying me for almost half a day.[2] Although for years now I had seen her only during summer and winter vacations, we were close, and of course she always worried about me. All the way she chattered interminably: "You must be careful. You must be polite. Be sure not to eat the little stones and sand in the rice when you go to a restaurant. Use the money sewn into your left pocket first. After that, open the right pocket. The money stitched into the outside pocket is little, but you'll have to be very careful, especially when you sleep in a hotel. You must listen to your father. ..."

At noon we got to a market-like village where traveling businessmen habitually stopped to cook their lunch. We rested under a big tree. Opening our bamboo-made rice boxes, mother and I had our goodbye lunch on the ground. My mother seldom used her money on ordinary occasions, but this time she bought extra food from a roadside inn. Really I couldn't eat much, but she frequently helped me to the best things. She herself just looked at me for a long, long time, and ate like a bird.

After lunch, she bought some ripe pears for me, saying, "You'll have to walk for several days. It's dangerous to eat wild fruit." Then she noticed a tear in my trouser leg and rushed in panic to borrow a needle and thread from the innkeeper's wife. Here she got talking to some traveling businessmen, and soon took me to bow my thanks for agreeing to let me join their traveling party.

"Take special care of your things. The new handmade shoes, tie them to your waist when you go to bed in a hotel. Write back as soon as you see your father in Kunming. Listen to everything the uncles say.[3] Always be a good boy." On and on, she repeated many, many other things. I was tired of listening to her. Finally, hanging the little bag on my back, she said, "Really, goodbye now, my son, take care all the way. ..."

I was then only a fourteen-year-old boy. How much worldly wisdom did I have? How could I understand her feelings?

It took us three days to get to Dali Town. I waved goodbye to those traveling businessmen and went on alone to Xiaguan, where I arrived at noon on the fourth day of my journey. Xiaguan at that time was smaller than an ordinary county town, but as it is located at an important mountain pass, all the trucks traveling in western Yunnan have to pass through it. We were still fighting against the Japanese invaders, so it was not difficult to meet a person from north China or Shanghai in the lanes of Xiaguan. All sorts of dialects and accents mixed together there.

I had heard a little about electricity during my first year at middle school in Lijiang, but before I got to Xiaguan I had never seen an electric light. It happened that the very day I arrived in Xiaguan was the first day the people there started using electricity. Large numbers of villagers flocked into Xiaguan, rushing out into the streets to enjoy this electricity. I stood among the crowd; I didn't know what was going to happen. An old woman asked, "Is there a god in Heaven to control the electricity, like the Fire God and the Water God?"

A woman with a baby on her back said, "Of course they have a god to control electricity!"

Just then the lights went out and someone shouted, "Look, the Electric God has become angry! Let's run home!"

In a flash the lights went on again. Then another woman said, "Don't be silly! There isn't any Electric God at all. They call him a machine engineer, a person like you and me, who opens and shuts the electricity in a room. They call that person 'Master Electricity.'"

At that moment a traveling match-seller, hawking his wares, passed by. An old man who had been gazing at a street light for a long time turned to him and asked, "Can I touch my longest pipe to that electric bulb and get a light?"

The match-seller struck a match and offered it to him. Laughing, he said, "No, that electric fire can't produce a flame for a smoker. You will have to buy my matches all year round!"

I slept in the dormitory of an inn that night. Around midnight, I was awakened by a roar of laughter. A man, absolutely naked, leaned over me and asked, "Is it all gold in your bag?"

"No, it's nothing but two pairs of handmade shoes, one for my father and one for me. My mother made them. I have another new shirt as well."

"Too funny! Can you sleep well with that bag's rough rope around your body?"

"Well, my mother said there were lots of thieves in Xiaguan. That's why I tied it on like this."

"No, no, don't be silly. Electricity is as bright as day. A thief usually goes to steal in the dark, understand?"

"Yes, that's right," added another man sharing our room. "When electricity is here, all the thieves run away. Electricity is just great! Today last month I was here in this same dormitory. That night there were thousands of fleas jumping around. I couldn't sleep a wink. Today, by the use of electricity, all the fleas have run away. Too wonderful to speak of! It's simply a miracle."

The next day, in a nearby restaurant, I noticed a group of young men standing beside a driver who was slowly eating his meal.

Finally the driver asked, "Why don't you sit down and order your dishes?"

"We have eaten, but we want to smoke," one of them answered.

"Yes," said another, smiling and showing his cigarette. "We also have matches, but we would like to try out a fire-machine. We noticed you had one in your pocket."

The driver laughed, "Oh, I am sorry!" He handed them his cigarette lighter. "It's nothing new to me. I bought it in Shanghai. It won't be too long now before you can buy one in Yunnan Province."

The group thoroughly enjoyed themselves with the lighter.

*          *          *

Our War of Resistance was on.[4] The pipeline carrying gasoline from Calcutta to Kunming was still under construction. There was a serious gasoline shortage, and most trucks had to use charcoal. Every two or three hours the driver had to stop and add more charcoal to the large gas producer attached to the truck. But there were nevertheless thousands of trucks on the roads, moving goods all over China. And Xiaguan was jam-packed with them. I had no problem hitching a ride with the lighter-owning driver.

That old master driver was an odd but kind man.[5] He came from another distant province and spoke with a strange accent. At first I could catch only half of his words. But like an actor he danced his hands up and down when he spoke, and soon I knew the other half. Since I volunteered to clean his truck and was the first passenger to offer help whenever he stopped to get water, I was allowed to sit up front next to him. The back of his truck was full of "yellow fish," the name given to on-the-way passengers who pay to hitch a ride in a truck. If a person looked rich, he demanded a lot of money. If the person looked poor, he wanted only a little. As for me, he kindly invited me to take all my meals with him, free of charge.

At a place called Yunnanyi we saw an airfield and airplanes in the distance. All the jeep drivers here were brown-haired, blue-eyed foreigners. They were U.S. airmen, stationed here for the purpose of training a Chinese air force. As we approached the airfield, my master driver suddenly pulled over and stopped.

"Watch my truck here until I get back. I'm going to try my luck again."

I was worried and warned, "Look, can you see the English letters 'M.P.' on their sleeves? That means they are policemen. They protect the airfield. I'm afraid they might arrest you!"

"Don't be childish. I've done this before. It's easy to make a profitable bargain here with some American soldiers."

He ran over to the entrance. Each time a jeep went by he stuck up his thumb and shouted at the top of his voice, "*Lao Mei ting hao!* (Old American very good!)" Some American soldiers also showed their thumbs and shouted back, "*Ting hao!* (Very good!)" Then I noticed our driver throwing several packets of cigarettes up into the air. A jeep stopped. He got in. After a little while he returned, all smiles. He was so wild with joy that he offered a cigarette to each passenger. As he passed them around he kept on repeating, "Sorry, only one for each. You must know it was made in America and came all the way from America. Look, there is a camel on the packet. Not easy, not easy!"

When I heard his cigarettes were from a foreign country, I also stretched out my hand.

"Not for little ones. But don't worry, I'll make it up to you later."

"Oh, Master! My father smokes. I'd like to let him enjoy a foreign cigarette."

"No, you are my helper. I won't let you down."

That night I slept in the same room as my master driver. After supper, we took a walk around the back of the truck station. We chatted, and many of the things we talked about remain in my mind as if it were yesterday.

"What does your father do in Kunming?" he asked.

"He's a little police officer. Is it great to be a policeman?"

"Well, it's hard to give you an exact answer. People have lots of nicknames for each profession. For example, if you hear someone say, 'I am a candle,' that means he is a schoolteacher. He burns to give others light, but in the end he destroys himself. If you hear someone say a 'blood-sucker' is coming, that means a tax-collector is coming to get money. ..."

"All right, Master. There are as many as seventy-two professions. I don't care about the others. I wonder what people call my father, a policeman?"

"If you hear someone saying, 'Be careful, a cat is coming!' that means a policeman is approaching. Oh, I envy you, having a cat-father in the city. You will become a 'little cat.' In a big city, all the rats offer cats presents. You'll see many, many rats bring piles of good things to please your father."

"Rats?"

"Ah, my boy, you really know nothing of the world. In a big city, all the thieves, the rats, organize themselves into groups. A rat doesn't want to become the meal of a cat. He wants to maintain his family. A group of rats want to make their 'king' cat rich, so they take turns to feed him."

"I don't believe that. There are lots of top officials in big cities, aren't there?"

"Oh, of course there are. Some people call a top official a 'tiger.' But all the tigers and lions and small animals, they are closely linked together. As soon as a cat gets something good, he secretly offers it to a bigger animal. When the suitable time comes, even a weak cat can make a big angry tiger smile and say, 'You are my good friend. Don't worry, I am not going to eat you up.' That's what the world is like today."

"May I ask what people call you drivers, then?"

"A four-wheeled truck has nothing to do with fish, but people give us the nickname 'yellow-fish catcher.' Nobody knows where this comes from. By the way, what are you going to be when you grow up?"

"I don't know yet. My brother is going to become a general. Maybe this time when I get to Kunming my father will tell me."

"You know, because of the war, I was forced to leave my Shandong Province and come to your Yunnan. As I travel around I have discovered that the sweetest-smelling profession in our China today is to join the International Route."

"What does that mean?"

"Well, English, English! You know, I didn't mean to get more, but while I was with the American airmen putting their cigarettes into my pocket, one of them saw the green stone bird on my neck-chain. Our faces and hands helped us to understand one another. Finally, he gave me a 10-dollar note for it. That airman was really a fool. He thought my stone-made bird was jade. The point of my story is to demonstrate that if you can speak English you can win a lot of money from foreigners. Can you speak any English?"

"Of course. I'm already a middle-school student. 'A, B, C, good morning, goodbye, how do you do?'"

"Oh, I never imagined you were a middle-school student![6] If I had taken you with me you would have got a lot of good things from that American airman. Now let me try. 'Gou tou bai.' Okay?"

"Well ... in fact it's 'goodbye.' The way you said it really sounded like the Chinese for 'dog's head waves.' That was absolutely Chinese-English, not the way to say it at all!"

We both had a good laugh.

My master driver's truck was an old-type truck. On a flat road it went steadily. And when it went downhill it seemed perfectly normal, as fast as a gasoline-run truck. But when it went uphill the speed was slower than a man walking! On the second day we had to climb over a huge mountain, so it took eight hours to cover about seventy *li*. On the third day, the road was quite flat and very smooth, but unfortunately we ran short of charcoal. It took the driver four hours to buy some more from a distant village.

Every day my master driver kept on talking and talking endlessly. I hadn't been anywhere before. Everything seemed interesting. On the fourth day, sometime after we had eaten lunch, the truck ran downhill steadily for about two *li* and rounded a bend. My master suddenly shouted out, "Kunming! Here we are. Little ghost, look, that is beautiful Lake Dian Chi."

*       *       *

Kunming. Kunming. I couldn't find any words to express my longing for this great capital city of our Yunnan Province. As I was growing up, my grandmother had talked about it again and again, and my young soul had flown to Kunming. Now, at last, I had arrived in person. Look at the tall buildings in the distance. Maybe my father lived in one of them. If my father's office was high up, I would buy a telescope and watch the fishermen catch fish on Lake Dian Chi every day.

"Master, is Bijiguan (Purple Chicken Pass) far from those reach-the-cloud buildings?" I asked the driver.

"Bijiguan? Why? This is Bijiguan," he said as he slowed down and brought the truck to a stop.

"Oh, thank you, Master! This is my destination." I was very surprised. Grasping my little bag, I jumped down and added, "My father's letter says he works somewhere near Bijiguan."

The driver looked pleased. Handing me a packet of American cigarettes, he said, "Here, my Little Master, take this to your cat-father as a gift from me. I'll miss you. We have had a good trip. Gou tou bai!"

The truck pulled away. I had no idea where my father's police station was. I looked around. Three strangers came by, but none of them could tell me where a police station was. Luckily the fourth stranger, a peasant, said her house was next door to one. I followed her, and a shabby temple-like house came into view. I was disappointed. It wasn't a tall modern building as I had expected. But I was very, very glad to have found my father. How big his eyes became when I said "Hello, Father!" He picked me up and cried out, "Oh, great! Coming to Kunming alone!"

Bijiguan belonged to Kunming County, but the big city was still fifteen *li* away from my father's station. Nothing was as I had imagined. The place looked like a village. There were no factories and no department stores. Each week a market day was held at which people came to buy and sell. The two dormitories for my father's policemen looked like dark prison rooms. There was only one window in the wall of my father's small bedroom. The room in the middle, their office, was larger and brighter, but behind a bamboo curtain I saw a fierce idol in the old temple wall. Apart from electricity, everything seemed worse than in my home county.

During my first month in Bijiguan, there was little to occupy my interest other than going out to see something new along the road. I watched carefully all the people in cars and trucks. I would follow a group of strangers for a distance and try to overhear a snatch of interesting dialogue. Sometimes I did hear a little, but in most cases their conversations were a puzzle to me. Apart from these solitary wanderings, my only pleasure was an occasional visit to Kunming City with my father.

Our War of Resistance had a huge impact on "Spring City," as Kunming became known in the forties, owing to its mild and lovely climate. This slow rural town, sitting on the banks of Lake Dian Chi and partially surrounded by mountains, suddenly became a hub of activity. Essential goods for the war—jeeps, trucks, gasoline, military equipment—had to be flown from India to Kunming. The sky above Kunming became crowded with all types of airplanes. On the ground, American soldiers and little green jeeps could be seen everywhere.

As the Japanese invaders' fire spread from province to province, Kunming, safely tucked away in the southwest of China, became swollen with refugees. Before the war, the population was about 150,000. There were only a few factories and a few middle schools. The highest educational institution was Donglu University (now known as Yunnan University). But as the war progressed, more and more people from all corners of China, mostly the rich and well educated, began arriving. The original public schools simply couldn't open their doors to all the newcomers. As a result, many private middle schools appeared. In the field of higher education, several famous institutes from all over China moved to the peace of Kunming. So many, in fact, that by the time the Sun Yat-sen University arrived from Canton, there was no more room for it. The staff had to move to the outskirts and turn an ancient, broken temple into a college.

Among these newly arrived institutes, the "Associated University of Southwest China" was the biggest and most famous. It was formed by three universities: Beijing, Qinghua, and Nankai. Between them they had many distinguished professors, but the new university had to be built in the simplest way. The classrooms and dormitories were all single-story buildings with roofs made out of dry straw, bamboo, or corrugated iron. The dining hall was an open-air one. This Associated University looked miserably poor, but its students were very talented, and many later became world-famous scholars.

One day, my father took me to Wenlin (Culture Forest) Street, not far from the Associated University. One side of that street was all tea houses. I had seen many tea houses in the city before. As a rule, all the tea-drinkers smoked tobacco, either in a water pipe made of bamboo or in a kind of long brass-made pipe. They played chess, sang ancient operas, or listened to someone's adventure stories. But the Wenlin Street tea houses were quite different. The master of the tea house made a big cup of tea and placed it on the table in front of each person. That was all. The tea-drinkers didn't play any games, nor did I see them talk or sing. They didn't even drink. They just read and wrote quietly and attentively. After paying for that one cup of tea, they could sit undisturbed. We stood beside their tables for a long, long time, but nobody lifted his head to have a look at us.

On our way home my father told me, "Those tea-drinkers are big-school students from Beijing. Because of the war, the country has no money to build a big library or a reading room for them. They pay a little and then they can read and write at that 'library' for as long as they want."

"Well ... they looked strange. Some were wearing those blue or black garments the old men wear at home. Others looked poor." I really doubted they were university students.

My father slowly replied, "No, my boy. Wearing beautiful clothes and knowing nothing is just like a pillow that is colorfully embroidered on the outside but useless dry straw on the inside. I want you to copy those tea-drinkers."

"Of course I wish I could become a big-school student, too. But I am not from Beijing. Do you think I can, coming from a Bai county?"

"It depends on you yourself. I only want you to remember the three most important things in a person's life."

"What are they, the three things?"

"If, for example, at the end of a term your school report is not as good as your classmates', then you must write out a hundred 'whys' on a piece of paper and think of a way to answer each. You must correct your mistakes, and make up what you have missed."

"All right, what is the second most important thing?"

"Time," my father explained. "You see, many things we can do again. A heavy storm destroys our house. We can save money, keep on working hard, and then build another house. But you can never gain back time you lose in the past. This year you are fourteen, next year you will be fifteen, not thirteen. Understand? Time is above all."

"I see. I think the third thing is work hard and be a good student?"

"Yes, of course you must do that. But you must put the stress on *asking*. You must ask, and ask again. But ask things carefully. A person's mouth is the creator of all problems and the entrance for all diseases. As the saying goes, 'Illness comes in from the mouth, and all troubles go out from the mouth.' Watch and observe with your eyes first, listen to people with your ears second. Open your mouth and speak last of all. If you do things in the wrong order, you will get into trouble."

*       *       *

Again I felt lonely. Every day I thought of my mother at home, and of my former village playmates. More than a month passed. Just as I was about to ask if I could go home and live with my mother, my father placed a new school bag and a set of new textbooks before me.

"You are homesick, I know. Cheer up! After breakfast I'm going to take you to a private middle school called Yude (Virtue Cultivation) Middle School. Most of the pupils and staff come from east China. Their principal is from Shanghai. People here call it the Shanghai People's Middle School. The staff have a rule not to accept local children and, at first, were reluctant to let you join them. But in the end they agreed to make an exception. Sometimes a school needs a policeman's help. You'll have a three-*li* walk every day. Don't be afraid. They are very nice people."

As we approached, I really wasn't convinced that those peasant-looking cottages were a school. The walls were made of bamboo and the roofs of straw. Not until I was taken inside to meet my thirteen classmates did I fully believe it was a school. Unfortunately, I was instructed to share a desk with a tall girl. I found this the strangest thing because in the countryside all my teachers had drawn a clear line between girl-students and boy-students. My father's words kept going through my mind: "Copy everything. Listen and say nothing."

All that first day, whenever I saw the teacher smile at me, I immediately smiled back. When my classmates clapped their hands, I straight away clapped a little, too. Once they suddenly laughed. I must have done something wrong, so I didn't copy their laughter that time. I really couldn't understand their Shanghai dialect, and sometimes just covered my head with my two hands. My girl desk-mate often whispered to me; but again, I couldn't follow all of her strange accent. I learned nothing that first day, and ran home right after the last period was over.

Hong Youying, my desk-mate, was the daughter of a small-factory owner. She came from somewhere near Shanghai. It took me a long time to tell her that I came from a distant mountain area and belonged to the Bai people. I thought she would look down on me, but strange to say, she actually seemed interested in me. Many other schoolmates also became my good friends after I told them I came from a national minority people's area. On Sundays they invited me to meet their parents and see their homes.

I asked my fellow classmates, "Did you know how to plant a rice seedling before you came to Yunnan? Do you have horse-drawn carts in Shanghai? Have you ever seen a Japanese? How many tall buildings are there in Shanghai? Can you stand straight in an airplane?" And they'd ask me, "Is it easy to catch a monkey near your house? Do you often see tigers in your village? Why are there some people here who have large necks?[7] How do Bai people kill a fat pig, by using a long knife or burning it in a fire? When are you going to marry your parents-chosen little wife?"

I showed them how to catch two crickets and make them fight in a box. I taught them how to cook rice in a field when there was no iron pot about, and how to catch eels in a muddy pond. I taught them my native Bai language and they taught me the Shanghai dialect. We had hundreds of things to exchange.

Hong Youying was a beautiful girl. She was also very good at singing and dancing. On Mondays she always gave me something special—a new book, a pencil, or something good to eat. Once she gave me a picture of herself. However, I didn't know how to be friends with a girl. One day the teacher wanted me to hold her hand while the whole class danced round together. Everybody grasped each other's hands and formed a circle. On my left side was a boy classmate. I took his hand as the teacher had shown us. But on my right side stood Hong Youying. Time and again I refused to touch her fingers. The whole collective dance couldn't go round. Finally the gatekeeper hurried toward us with a chopstick. She held one end and I grasped the other. Everybody laughed and laughed, but once in a while Hong Youying gave me an angry look. As soon as the dance ended, she broke that chopstick and threw it at my face. Thereafter, we still shared the same desk, but whenever I asked her something she replied, "I don't care!"

*       *       *

The driver's stories had left a deep impression on me. As soon as I entered the Yude school, I secretly began to watch my father's business. Week after week and month after month I waited, hoping to see some "rats" bringing good things to my "cat-father." I also wished I could have a look at a "city-tiger," particularly my father's boss. I had already been a "little cat" for almost a year, but I really hadn't seen any "rats," "tigers," or anything else out of the ordinary. Was my father a perfectly upright police officer? In China we say, "Is he as clean as a piece of white paper, like the broad masses of common people?" Truly, in all my father's time as an ordinary county-level police officer, he never ordered someone to kill another person. He didn't force several women to become his Number Two wife, Number Three wife. He didn't use his police power to seize a big sum of cash here and straight away build a beautiful house there. But as I grew from age fourteen to fifteen, I began to understand many things. How many people with a little power or money were as clean as a piece of white paper? All crows are black, as the saying goes. So it was with my own father, I discovered.

At that time, there were six police stations in Kunming County. My father headed one of them. According to his documents, it was an eighteen-member police station. In reality, it had only about twelve members, sometimes fewer. Yet each month the government sent the salary, rice, and clothing for eighteen people. My father "ate" at least six people's money and food. In old China, people called this "to scoop the oil from the surface of a nourishing pot of soup." This must have been the main source of my father's extra income.

Each month my father had to provide a written report showing how the money was used. To hide his secret, he always carefully prepared six false names. As soon as he heard that a bigger official was coming down to look and see how things actually stood, he hurried to hire some strangers and dress them each in a policeman's uniform. Once it happened that my father could hire only five extra people. It was getting late and there was no time left to find a sixth person, so I was made to be a "moment's little policeman." I stood at the end of the line when the big official came to call the roll. Unfortunately, I forgot the false name my father had assigned me, and didn't answer when it was called out.

"The total number of your brothers is correct, but one of them didn't answer." The official looked sternly at my father. "I smell a rat in this matter."

"Yes, sir, but he is a … little newcomer, sir." My father's face became red, but he forced himself to smile. Pointing at his ears, he added, "He is having some ear trouble this week. The other day we ordered him to stop a group of villagers who were fishing under the bridge with TNT. So. …"

My father explained slowly. The big official listened and studied me for a while. Just then another important colleague of his from Kunming dropped in hurriedly. They talked, and the danger was over.

If some villagers came to report a problem, both the plaintiff and the defendant had to pay all sorts of money. When the plaintiff related his problems, one of my father's policemen would say, "Nothing can be solved without a written form. Place your money on the desk. When we are not so busy we will send someone to bring you and the accused here." Later, another policeman was sent to summon them both to the police station. Besides enjoying a free meal at the plaintiff's house, that policeman usually demanded a sum of money to buy a new pair of grass sandals or shoes. When everything had been agreed and a set of fingerprints made on the paper, both sides were asked to pay another sum called "fee for signing your name."

My father presided over the trial: "Everything is here. How can you refute it? It's against the law. We must put you in prison for one year." And the defendant often said something like, "No, please, if you do, my children will go hungry, my wife will. …" The trial ended. Next thing, some policemen went to threaten the defendant. A little later, another went to talk to him in a sympathetic manner. In the end, a sum of money replaced the sentence.

According to the rules, my father had to write everything down in black and white. But if a 100-dollar fine was imposed, he frequently wrote down 50 or 60 dollars and quietly "ate" the difference. He knew that no serious problems would arise from his followers, because they could neither read nor write. Every few weeks he would say, "All of you have been working hard. So everything has turned out successfully. Behind the closed gate we are one big family. We share woe and happiness together. We must celebrate our success.

Here is some money. Get wine, fish, and meat. We must enjoy a big meal together."

On market days, three times a month, the policemen got up early, cleaned their guns, and tidied up their uniforms. All day long they wandered around, watching everything closely in the market. At noon, they would start exercising their power with their mouths: They accepted many cigarettes, cup after cup of tea, a bowl of cold noodles, several pieces of candy. Then they would enjoy an entertainment program for a while, again free of charge. Late in the afternoon, when the market-goers were about to leave, they began to use their hands. Everything was planned out beforehand. This policeman went to buy meat; that one, fish; and the third, fresh vegetables. At that time of the day, the bargain sometimes became a "I give the whole and accept only half the money" bargain. The policeman would approach the seller, saying, "Good afternoon, Master Yu! May you find lots of big money today!" The seller would usually reply, "Oh, yes. Thank you. All because of your protection. Here you are, just a little to show a bit of my heart."

Sometimes I lingered and heard things which made me sad: "I just hate those cats! I am a vegetable seller. I am not a rat. But I had to act like a rat. I couldn't help it." Once I heard a village woman say, "Well, what I was forced to offer was actually like a single hair from my head. But I hope all of them, including their wives and children, die like dogs." My father's policemen happily showed me what they had "bought" when they returned. I couldn't eat when I thought of that woman's words.

Although my father didn't go to the market and stretch out his hand in person, behind the curtain he was also an eater of those cheap things. One day I told him what I heard in the market. He just sighed and sighed. After a long silence he said, "I am very sorry, too, my boy. Yes, some of the things we do here are not fair. There are too many unreasonable problems, but, after all, neither you nor I are to blame. As you go ahead you will see much, much more which will make you sad and angry."

Once my father took me to see a colleague of his who was serving in a high-up police station under the direct leadership of the Kunming General Police Headquarters. There they had bright windows and shining desks, bicycles and motorcars. Learning that I was the son, that friend took me into a big room filled with boxes of all sizes, bottles of wine, and many other things which I couldn't even name. Everything looked colorful, wrapped in cellophane or red paper. I thought I was entering a special shop. As we were about to leave, the man pulled open one of the drawers and took out a watch. He said to my father, "I saved this one for you," and put his forefinger to his lips for a second. My father nodded knowingly and whispered, "Thank you!"

I was allowed to carry out as much as my arms could hold—cookies, candy, sugar cubes, and much more. My father said, "Remember, just eat it yourself, eat as much as your stomach can hold. Don't ask me nor tell others. The less you speak, the happier you will be. It's the Moon Festival. The policemen here just had cakes and wine. When the Spring Festival comes my friend will give you something else." It took me a long time to eat all those good things.

On Saturdays and Sundays all my father's policemen were extremely busy. About two *li* from our station there was a village situated in a most beautiful spot, right beside Lake Dian Chi. Next to the poor farm cottages there were several new houses, everything inside and out completely up-to-date. The owners of these modern houses were all top officials from Kunming or the Yunnan Provincial Government. A few were generals or military commanders. In the early 1940s the Japanese often came to lay "eggs" on Kunming, so they built this village as a safe shelter. By late 1944 the enemy planes had stopped bombing, but on weekends the "tigers" still came to entertain themselves here as happily as could be. My father's duty was to protect them. In order to please those top officials, he wore his uniform, shone his shoes, and even shaved. I was also extremely happy, because I could follow them and watch things.

All the policemen, including my father, knew absolutely nothing, but on such occasions they even pretended to know international affairs. They strutted up and down the road leading to the village, looking around as if they were searching for something. If anyone came into view they ran after and shouted, "Are you sick? Clear off! Don't you know a big-head is coming here to do important things for the country? This is a highway; it belongs to the government. You go on that little path over there."

Each time a car passed by, they stood at full attention and saluted. Once a passenger threw a cigarette butt out of the window. One of the policemen immediately ran to pick it up, crying out with joy, "How lucky I am to have found a big-head's cigarette end! No wonder this morning, as soon as I got up, two larks sang a greeting song to me."

Another policeman pointed to the trademark and said, "Look, nothing special, just ordinary ones."

"My friend, you are always too proud. Don't pretend you are a fat man when in fact your face is only swollen from a beating. Not all people can enjoy something from a car. It depends on your fate. My grandfather's grandfather is buried in a good location, so today I was able to pick up that big-head's cigarette end. You failed because your family grave is dirty; it's in a bad location."

Like my father's policemen, the local villagers viewed top officials from Kunming as very special, as a different kind of people altogether. No matter how strict the policemen were, the locals still came to see things. Once the cars had all passed by, they crowded around and asked lots of questions. I heard one woman ask, "Do you know them?"

"Of course I do!" replied one of the policemen. "It was these provincial top officials who invited the American airmen to help us fight against the eastern foreign ghosts.[8] With this military help from America we have won a series of victories. But we were told we still have enemies. ...."

"More enemies?" the woman asked, surprised.

"Yes, the Communists. Our big leaders in the city always teach us to be careful. The common people will suffer again if the Communists come to rule us. They eat from a big pot, use one very large quilt to cover all the family, old and young, in the same bed, and several men marry one woman."

By observing people's reactions, I could sense that they seemed at that time to have heard something about the Communists. By the end of 1945, and early in 1946, many things indicated that local Communists were making some secret preparations. Student associations were established at all levels. In Kunming, students spoke in the streets at impromptu meetings, or sang revolutionary songs and danced. Several student demonstrations broke out between 1947 and 1948. During one of these demonstrations, four students were killed. This became known as the December First Incident, and those four graves can still be seen today at the Yunnan Normal University (formerly Kunming Teachers College). A weekly magazine called *Democracy* sold like hotcakes. Most of its articles criticized the Kuomintang's reactionary rule. The articles were written by famous professors, and one of these, a poet-professor, was assassinated by the Kuomintang.

*        *        *

One Sunday morning in 1946, while we were still in bed, my father was urgently awakened and summoned to the top officials' lake-side village. Again I ran after him. Pointing to a wall surrounding one of the houses, a well-dressed man said, "You see it yourself! 'Down with Chiang Kai-shek! Down with all the corrupt officials!'"

"Oh, I. ...." My father couldn't continue.

"You must know Communists have come to your village! All the Communists are as cunning as foxes. They do not bear the label 'Communist' on their foreheads. They disguise themselves as tame sheep."

"Yes. ...." My father lowered his head.

"It's *you* who are responsible in this area. I give you one week to find and tie up the Communists who painted these reactionary slogans last night. If you do not arrest them, I'll send you to hell to meet your father and mother underground." With a bang he slammed the car door and drove away.

After that, my father was very worried and his face constantly wore a frown. Various meetings were held, and some young people were brought into the station for questioning. But the policemen couldn't find the men responsible for those painted slogans.

Three days later, my father showed me where he kept his money and told me to take down some names and addresses from his notebook. He said, "I don't think they will shoot me in Kunming, because the problem was only a couple of slogans. But it is too easy for them to give me trouble. If I'm arrested and don't return within half a month, post the money to your mother first. The second thing is to write a short letter to your elder brother. With the name list, you two can go to see our friends in Kunming City. Try and get them to help."

I was frightened by my father's words. The following Monday he was taken to Kunming by car. I hated that car. I wept as I saw the driver start the engine. For days and nights I felt great anxiety about my father's absence. All the other policemen looked sad. Nobody knew what ought to be done. On the eighth day my father returned, wearing a woebegone expression. In the presence of his brother policemen, he said, "We had a big important meeting in the city. I am all right. No problems at all."

In the evening before we went to bed, he told me a different story: "Had it not been for that watch, which I took along, I would have been put in prison."

"The watch?"

"Yes, that watch saved me. We didn't find the men who painted those slogans, so they put me into a separate room and ordered me to write a long self-criticism report. I handed in my report four times, and each time their answer was, 'Do it again!' One day another man, perhaps a secretary or a kind of director, entered and asked me many details. He seemed not so bad. I offered him a cigarette. He saw the watch and appeared to like it. I thought and thought. Finally I gave it to him, and asked him to see you if something worse should happen to me. Unexpectedly, on the seventh day, he dropped in and said he had succeeded in persuading his fellow policemen to free me. They punished me only by recording a big demerit in my personal file."

"What did he do with the watch?"

"Well, how do I know? The dealings of these top officials are very complicated. Once we have given the thing away, forget about it. Don't mention it again. Life is like that: You gain something here, and over there you have to give it away."

**NOTES**

1. *The West:* The Pure Land school of Buddhism teaches that after a person dies, his or her soul goes to the Western Paradise, or Pure Land in the West. Mr. He explains, "The aged people always advise the young, 'If you do good to other people, you shall go to the Western Paradise and enjoy a comfortable life in Heaven. If you do many unkind things, you will go to the underground world and suffer miserably.'"

2. Unhampered by foot-binding, which is not a Bai custom, Mr. He's mother was able to accompany him.

3. *Uncles:* the traveling businessmen.

4. The War of Resistance was the eight-year war fought against the Japanese invasion and occupation of China from 1937 to 1945.

5. *Master:* This is the nearest English equivalent to the Chinese *shifu,* meaning "master craftsman" (as distinct from "apprentice"). It is a term of respect given to carpenters, cooks, tailors, bakers—anyone with a special skill. Even today, only a tiny percentage of the population in China can drive, so this is considered a "special skill."

6. Shortly before the Japanese invasion, Kuomintang statistics indicated that 13 to 15 percent of children of school age attended elementary school. Once the six years of elementary education were completed, those wishing to continue at middle school had to take a competitive examination for the limited number of places available. Edgar Snow states, "In old China even primary education was so rare that any graduate was considered an 'intellectual.'" (See Edgar Snow, *Red China Today* [New York: Vintage Books, 1971], p. 235.) No wonder the driver was impressed.

7. *Large necks:* Yunnan is an inland province where, in the past, lack of iodine sometimes led to goiters.

8. *Eastern foreign ghosts:* This phrase is a translation of *dongyang guizi,* a derogatory term for the Japanese.

# 4

# AN EXECUTION AND AN
# EYELESS VILLAGE GIRL

The eastern foreign ghosts surrendered. In all corners of Kunming, celebrations lasted for several weeks. Hundreds of archways, woven from fresh green fir or pine branches, were put up over roads and alleys. People wore their finest clothes and sang and danced for joy. Some dressed up as well-known characters from operas or walked about on stilts. Cinemas presented free movie shows to primary-school pupils. Department stores held sales. Slogans to celebrate the victory of our eight-year war could be seen everywhere.

With the coming of the final victory, however, everything seemed to change. Conditions became very unstable. Inflation was terrible. The price of gold and rice rose rapidly. One day it was suddenly announced that new notes issued by the Central Bank had become good-for-nothing paper. All we could do was to paste the gray-green notes onto our walls, or weave them into hats for children to play with. In every marketplace, people refused to accept paper money. Only silver coins would do.

Not long after the Japanese surrender, the Burma Road—or the China-India Public Highway, as we called it—was formally and joyfully reopened to traffic. For some years now the Japanese had controlled the Burmese section of the road, cutting the land route between China and India. A very big and special welcome was prepared for a unit of American soldiers who had driven all the way along the Burma Road from a military base somewhere in India. The arrival of the first group of American soldiers into Kunming was quite unforgettable.

It happened that the Burma Road ran past my father's police station. It also happened that at the back of my father's station there was a big square. The night before the Americans triumphantly drove their trucks and jeeps into Kunming, their leading officers camped out in that big square. My father was instructed to keep guard. All the common people and their curious children were forcibly kept at a distance, but since I was the son of a police officer I could follow his steps wherever he went.

I watched every move made by the American soldiers with wide eyes. At meal times they each had a box and yet, very strange to say, they did hardly any cooking at all. Some had a little portable stove, but most simply ate what came out of that cardboard box. Cookies, candy, butter, cheese, and meat were packed into all sizes of boxes or into closed metal containers with openers attached. (The Kuomintang soldiers usually cooked their meals on an open fire, and they often forced the common people to offer them firewood.) When it was time to go to bed, I saw some sleeping in a flexible bed that could open and close up, and some—in a net.

Just before bedtime, an American officer gave us one of those big cardboard boxes. Back in our room, we unpacked wildly. Among the contents were several little packets which we could not make out. "It's soap, soap, I know that," my father said. "You must not waste them. We'll save them, take them home to use if we go to a special party."

(When my father was out, I secretly opened one of those little packets and washed my hands with it. I was disappointed. I rubbed and rubbed, first with cold water, then with hot, but not a bubble was to be found. Several weeks later, I showed one to a friend of ours in Kunming. He ate it as soon as I took it out of my pocket! "Chocolate, they call it," he told me.)

Early the next morning the American soldiers began their departure for Kunming. We rushed to see them off. Everyone in Kunming stopped working. Hundreds of peasants from nearby counties came in flocks to watch. Again they all put on their best clothes, and many carried the flags of our two countries. Everybody said over and over, "It's the first time in my life!" The procession was a river of American trucks and jeeps. A river of people. A river of flags. It was so huge, a dragon of vehicles. The head had reached Kunming, but the tail was still moving in our Bijiguan fifteen *li* away. The moment the head arrived in Kunming, a cloud of smoke from thousands of firecrackers covered half the sky. In the city center, a big open-air ceremony was held at which top officials from both countries spoke.

After this, jeeps and military trucks passed by our station four or five times a month. The Americans were still helping Chiang Kai-shek in his war against the Communists. Airplanes, too, continued to bring in all kinds of equipment. One rainy night, an American airplane crashed into the top of a mountain not far from my father's station. The news took three days to reach us. I followed two policemen to see the place, but we found nothing except broken engine parts. One of the policemen turned everything over and over and uncovered a bracelet-like object under a heap of ashes. Several English words were inscribed on it. "What's the use of this?" he asked. "We cannot eat it." Saying this, he threw it away. I ran after it. Later I showed it to my teacher of English. She said, "The words indicate a person's name, and maybe an address in America. Possibly it belonged to an American airman who was burned to ashes in the crash. Maybe some day they will come and look for it."

A short while later, a second airplane crashed into the same mountain. This time, my father was ordered to guard the wreckage. Two hours after our arrival, a helicopter landed. One of the passengers was a Chinese man who could also speak English. My father was questioned for a long time. I was asked to show my bracelet-like thing. The moment the pilot saw it he smiled and patted me again and again. "*Ting hao, ting hao!* (Very good, very good!)" He gave me some chewing gum and my father a packet of cigarettes. Our policemen each took a little piece of the airplane's wing.

About two weeks later, a band of thieves climbed over the wall of a house in the lakeside village, opened a gate, and stole a radio and a refrigerator. My father was accused of having close links with a large number of village thieves. But even before this case could be cleared up, another problem arose. A man suddenly arrived by car and harangued my father: "We received a secret report the other day. They say you have made a huge sum of foreign money out of the recent air crash. You and your brothers have 'eaten' the remains of the plane. Do you know that was part of our nation's public property? Your working ability is too low. Many, many foreigners are here to help us. What do you know about ABC? You are not qualified to work in Kunming. Just get ready to leave!"

My father wanted to say something in reply, but the man turned his back and ordered the driver to start the car.

That was how my father ended his career in Kunming County. In the summer or autumn of 1946, he was forced to leave Bijiguan for a post in a small county located in eastern Yunnan. Initially, he had been sacked altogether; but he sold all he had and secretly offered everything to another top official. Through a back door, police headquarters assigned him this lower job. He didn't like to work in such a faraway district, but with a view to letting my brother and me continue our studies, he said he would be pleased to bear all hardships under any circumstances.

The night before he left Bijiguan my father talked the whole night through. He smoked his stick-like pipe thoughtfully and told me, "To be frank, I do not want you to become a top official or a rich man like those who live in that lakeside village. I only wish you to enrich yourself to the best of your ability. Learn to talk and do things like the educated Han people. The language is our enemy. Sometimes we can do better than any of them, but they make you line up and wait and wait.

"The war seems to have ended now. It appears to me that English is very popular and very useful. Everybody says English smells best, but I don't believe people like we Bais can master that foreign language and go abroad to study. In the days ahead, if you find it is too difficult, never mind. Our country is big. You will enjoy a good job and lead a good life on condition that you can learn our motherland's tongue well."

* * *

My father departed for eastern Yunnan. I was left alone in Bijiguan. Shortly after my father's departure, my Shanghai middle school closed its doors. Through an examination I was luckily selected to study at the Kunming Kunhua Technical School. I was not very enthusiastic about math and physics, but this school had other attractions. It was a public school run by the Department of Industry. The school authorities paid for food and all textbooks. We lived in a big dormitory, and this too was free. Moreover, after three years of training they were said to offer a job. So I moved to that school in Kunming City.

Right after the War of Resistance ended in 1945, the War of Liberation followed closely.[1] Everyone had wanted to fight against the Japanese, to drive them out of China. But, after all, the Communists were quite a different matter—they were our own Chinese brothers. In some areas Kuomintang soldiers began to run away when they were sent to fight the Communists. In this instance, my father was not a bad man. He pitied those soldiers and, during his service in both Kunming and eastern Yunnan, secretly helped many Bai soldiers flee home. From time to time he even gave them traveling expenses.

By the time he went to work in eastern Yunnan, local guerrilla forces led by underground Communist organizations had increased all over the province. In many counties they were secretly planning to fight against the local-government departments. One evening while my father was out on business, about twenty men rushed into his station and seized all the guns. The head of the county became furious. He made a false report about my father, accusing him of being a member of the local underground Communist organization, and of running a station that was "actually a nest of soldiers who refused to fight the Communists." He handed that report in to the Provincial Police Headquarters. So, within four months, my father had lost his job once again and returned to Kunming—penniless. My father's permanent rice bowl had broken into a hundred pieces.[2]

It was impossible to repair that bowl again. He did odd jobs here and there, but no longer had a regular source of income. By now my elder brother had become a platoon leader, but his unit was in another distant province, and moving all the time. He seldom wrote to us, let alone sent money. I continued to live in my dormitory at the technical school, and my father moved into a cheap public house that belonged to people from our Jianchuan County. We became poor in Kunming.

By early 1948 the Communist troops were advancing by leaps and bounds. There was no doubt that the whole of Yunnan would become Communist very soon. Thus it was out of the question for my father to buy another policeman's job. All the while he was planning to return to our home village. For a time he tried to force me to burn my books and return home with him. Toward the end of 1948, we had a father-son Family Meeting. He said, "I know the world much better than you do. Listen to my words: A golden nest, a silver nest, an earthen nest is best. To dig the earth is the happiest job. I want you to give up Kunming and return home with me."

"No!" I protested. "You are my father, but today, in this case, I'm not going to consider your proposal. Entering a college is not easy. I am going to become a teacher of English anyway."

"All right!" he got angry. "Hereafter, never call me Baba again! You go along your sunny, wide road while I go along my poor, dark, single-planked, narrow bridge!"

Shortly before our conversation I had made a very kind friend in my technical school. Her name was Miss Xue, and she was my English teacher. She came from Shanghai and, after escaping to Kunming during the war, had attended the Associated University of Southwest China. Occasionally Miss Xue gave me a little sum of money, and this I used to buy soap, toothpaste, paper, and ink, as well as needle and thread to repair my old clothes. I could keep on studying at school even if my father gave me nothing. Therefore, I shouted back, "I am not going home with you!"

*      *      *

Because I had left my familiar Bai homeland at an early age, and because I felt cut off from the mainstream of Han culture, my thoughts had always gone beyond Yunnan Province to life in other distant lands. From the time I had met that truck driver on my way to Kunming, so many living examples had taught me the importance of learning a foreign language. When I thought about the main reason for which my father had been forced to leave Kunming County, I said to myself, "You must learn English to make up where your father failed. Work hard at English and then show something great to let everybody know." After this I forced myself to "eat" English whenever I had a good opportunity.

One day in 1948, I heard church music and Bible readings on the Kunming radio station. I wrote a letter, in Chinese, asking for detailed information. Two weeks later I received a letter from an American missionary, a Mrs. B. Meter, inviting me to join her English Bible classes. She had rented a small house and turned it into a chapel called "Baptist Church in Kunming." I went to the chapel and was treated kindly. Thereafter I often joined the Bible classes as well. Three months later, I became a Christian.

After Mrs. Meter's departure, another American missionary named Mrs. Nance arrived. This Mrs. Nance had four children, and gradually I became a special friend of theirs. Their Chinese was worse than Mrs. Meter's, so every week I went to help with the Sunday school. Mrs. Nance learned some Chinese from me, and I learned some oral English from her and her children. In this way, English began to come alive for me.

As the days went by, I gradually realized the true importance of mastering English. I didn't ask a librarian to show me any actual reading material. I just used my own eyes to watch what I saw in Kunming. Along the way, I made a simple comparison between a Kuomintang soldier and an American one. My country was too poor! How to make this poor country rich was a big question in my mind.

After we won the war, many important people expressed their views in the newspapers. Students at all levels in Kunming also launched a series of movements to discuss national problems. Everywhere, people demanded peace and democracy. Kuomintang inefficiency and corruption were attacked. Everybody opposed civil war. Everybody wanted to build a New China. For myself, when I asked the question, "Why has our 5,000-year-old China fallen behind several-hundred-year-old America?" the answer came back, "The main trouble is that too many people in China can't even read their own names. The most pressing task is to train a group of good and qualified teachers, set up more schools, work toward universal education. In particular, if we had a lot of scholars who could use English as a weapon to fire at other countries' advanced experiences, my country would march forward with high speed."

\*            \*            \*

One Sunday morning, Miss Xue took me to pay a visit on a Professor Wu, a Christian from Canton. He was a former teacher of hers at the Associated University. It was on this occasion that I was introduced to Professor Wu's youngest daughter, Qiyan. Miss Xue said, "I know both of you are crazy about learning English." At that time Qiyan was already a freshman in the English department at Kunming Teachers College. On yet another Sunday, the Wus invited Miss Xue and me to spend the day at a hot spring outside Kunming. In fact they kindly included me in all their gatherings and outings after that first meeting. I thought to myself, "Study hard, reach their level, and then realize that ambition of becoming an English teacher."

As it turned out, my first step toward realizing this great goal was very successful. It happened just before Kunming's liberation, in September 1949. According to the policies at that time, students from my technical school were not allowed to study English at the college level. They had to study math or some other technical subject. But Miss Xue insisted that I take the university entrance examination and put my emphasis on English. Before the examination, she wrote out a 200-word passage in English and ordered me to memorize it. The passage expressed my strong determination to devote myself to the study of English. She said, "After you have answered everything on their English examination sheet, just add this passage at the back of your paper. Maybe the officials concerned will be happy to make an exception and select you."

I did just as she suggested and, in the end, found my name among those selected to study English at a private college called Kunming Wuhua College. Every time I thought about becoming an English major I felt as proud as if I had become a top official of Yunnan Province. It was one of the happiest days of my life.

In 1949, before Miss Xue left Kunming for Shanghai, she gave me a pile of English books, saying, "I've taught English at several schools in Kunming, but nobody could correctly pronounce the word 'faith' and the word 'enthusiastic.' You pronounce these words all right. If you keep on studying hard, I believe you'll certainly succeed in going abroad to become an expert. That's why I've been treating you like a younger brother of mine. As for the Cantonese girl Wu Qiyan, maybe she's a little older than you, but that doesn't matter. You can learn a lot from her and her father. I don't think I'll come back to Yunnan again, but I look forward to hearing from you in the distant future. Goodbye for now."

During my first term at college, I lived with my father at his public house. He was still jobless, and we were very poor. The college wanted me to pay 80 silver dollars as a school fee. My father sold some of his old clothes and gave me 20. A friend of mine from a rich family stretched out his hand and gave me another 20. A very kind Christian friend, a Mr. Ye, gave me the remainder as a congratulatory gift. Through this friend I also got a job in the evenings teaching two young boys English. Somehow I managed to make ends meet, but again my father urged me to give up studying at the college and return home to become a farmer for the rest of my life. It was a constant struggle between us.

In December 1949, Kunming was liberated.[3] My private Wuhua College was forced to close its doors owing to a lack of funds. A series of negotiations began between our principal and the provincial government. Finally a decision was made: Let all the students from the English department of Wuhua College continue their studies at Kunming Teachers College.

In the beginning, Kunming Teachers College was only a small department attached to the Associated University of Southwest China. When the Associated University began to move back to north China in 1947, Kunming Teachers College spread out into the vacated school site. The classrooms and dormitories were still the same straw-roofed buildings, and I began living on campus in one of them. Our long dormitory was divided into four or five smaller rooms, with two students sharing one room. Shortly after Liberation, the "library–tea houses" in Wenlin Street disappeared. A real library with a large reading room and rows of desks was set up in our college. But I preferred to study in my own quiet room. We had electricity twenty-four hours a day, a luxury never before experienced. Every day I ate three free meals in that open-air dining room.

Most of our classes were conducted in the mornings, from eight to twelve o'clock. Of course we had not a single radio or tape recorder, but I nevertheless enjoyed all my English courses tremendously. Perhaps in my third year, World History and English Literature were added. We also had to study politics, and this I hated. I just couldn't see the relevance of it. Whenever I missed a political study class, other students would jump to criticize me.

Between 1950 and 1953, the years I studied at Kunming Teachers College, the total student-staff population remained only a few hundred. Just over eighty young students were selected to study English in 1950. Many couldn't swallow the language. After a year of study, a large number retreated. Some more ran away to study other subjects during the second year. Finally, only seventeen remained. I was one of those seventeen.

*   *   *

One day in January 1950, my brother unexpectedly returned to Kunming. My father and I had assumed that he'd fled to Taiwan the previous year.

My brother told us the true inside story of his return: "Chiang Kai-shek's Kuomintang army was really a good-for-nothing army. All our top military officials were too corrupt, too selfish, too cruel, worse than animals. I hate them from my bones. Each one of them did nothing for the country, just ran after money, women, and higher positions so they could ride on people's necks. Chiang Kai-shek had an army of millions and millions of soldiers, all with modern American equipment, but what was the final outcome? A big egg, zero. At first they said that the Japanese kill all, burn all, and grasp all. We must watch our doors so as not to let the Japanese rule over us. Later, they said Communist soldiers were as bad as the Japanese. This is not true. I have seen proof with my own eyes. In Shanxi Province, the common people ran away as soon as they saw a Kuomintang soldier approaching. They welcomed the Communist army. The truth is that Chairman Mao's army, although small in number, has the support of the people.

"What was the use of being a soldier in Chiang Kai-shek's army? More and more facts taught us we were wrong. So some of our important commanders had a secret meeting. We all had the same desire: to become soldiers in the Communist army. We joined an uprising. We were warmly received by the Communists. A top commander of the People's Liberation Army delivered a report to us. His words struck a chord in our hearts. Our conditions improved a great deal. We had not the best quality, but enough to eat and enough to wear and some money to spend. It was only in the Communist army that we felt we were real brothers. All sorts of worries disappeared.

"Finally they said everything was up to us; Stay and be a People's Liberation Army soldier or, if we liked, go home and produce more grain for the nation. I thought and thought about this problem for several weeks. I thought of father, brother and everything in our home village. Every bird loves his nest, as the saying goes. They also gave us enough money for traveling expenses. So, I said goodbye to them and safely returned. I have been a soldier for a long time, but I am still a healthy man. Hereafter, I am going to be a farmer."

My father had long ago come to the same conclusion. But a few days after this, the military representative of our Street Government Office came to see him.[4] He wanted my father to write a detailed report of his past history, and also to explain what he hoped to contribute to the Communist cause. Two weeks later he returned and said, "It took us several days to discuss more than 200 people's problems. Your name was quickly passed among the qualified list. The new government has agreed to give you a chance to reform your reactionary thoughts. Take this note and report to the Political Office of Yunnan People's Revolutionary University. After three to six months of studying the ideas of Marx, Lenin, and Mao Zedong, you will become a new man and be offered a job serving the people. Chairman Mao, our great savior, needs millions to help build New China."

My father hesitated. In the end, however, he concluded, "Our house and land in the village are large enough to support several generations. In Kunming I have to obey other people. At home I am my own boss. I long to be able to begin a day's work when the sun rises and return home to eat and sleep when the sun sets. Isn't that a freer life than being an old student at the People's Revolutionary University?"

Nothing I said would change his mind. So he and my brother packed up and returned home to our village together. Again I was left alone in Kunming.

*                    *                    *

Sometime in 1951 I received a letter from home. It was a letter of pure sad news. After arriving in Jianchuan, our local county government had a lot to do with both father and brother. My brother was too naive. At first he tried to protest and defend himself. He pointed out that although he had been a Kuomintang platoon leader, he had joined an uprising. This was a great deed of merit. He had won honor. He had contributed to the New China. He showed the document that had been given to him by the People's Liberation Army Headquarters. But as things stood at that time in the countryside, this formal document was about as valuable as toilet paper. The Land Reform Movement was raging all over China.[5] The local Land Reform Work Team didn't even glance at his document. Instead, they took him into custody. For a long time my sisters had to take him his three daily meals. He was full of regret. If he had stayed on and become a member of the People's Liberation Army, he would have been all right. He realized that he had chosen the wrong way—but it was too late!

In relating my father's problems, the letter said that his fate was worse. He was arrested before the Land Reform Movement began. At first my father was sent to do hard labor on a state-owned farm. As soon as the movement began, he was forced to follow a group of local landlords, tyrants, counterrevolutionaries, and bandits from village to village. Then he was forced to kneel down on an open-air platform. It was said that he hadn't committed any intolerable crimes in our own home county, but for many, many years he had been a reactionary policeman of the Kuomintang. He was supposed to have done a great deal of harm to people in other counties.

Our family was classified as "landlord"; indeed, we were called one of the biggest landlord families in the area. Did we own hundreds of *mou* of land?[6] No. The reason was that my father had been a Kuomintang policeman. Our house, furniture, farming tools, and 80 percent of our vegetable garden were all confiscated.

A little later, the only son of my fifth aunt was sent to study at the Yunnan Minorities Institute in Kunming. One afternoon he came to see me. We had supper together and then chatted for an hour in my dormitory. He suggested we take a walk at the back of my college. Finally he made me sit down under a tree and gave me a little piece of paper. On that paper I read:

*I am all right. Don't worry about me. Pay attention to your main subject—English. Mother tongue is also very, very important. Never neglect Chinese.*

The handwriting was my father's, and the note had obviously been written to me. "Why's there no receiver's name and no writer's signature?" I asked my cousin.

He replied slowly, "Well, it's like this. The folks at home thought this news would be the heaviest blow on you. All the relatives agreed not to tell you. But sooner or later some other people will tell you everything."

"What everything?" I shook his shoulder.

"Your father was executed earlier this year. Only your mother was allowed to see him for about ten minutes. He told her that his death was like a cup of cheap cold water that had been knocked upside down. A useless old man was going to die, but that man's young son had succeeded in entering a national university to study a foreign language. When your mother went to bury him, she found this unfinished note in one of his pockets."

When I thought of the miserable outcome of my father and brother, I couldn't control my tears. When I thought of myself in Kunming, I was happy. I was the youngest, but the road I had chosen was the correct one. No doubt, 100 percent, if I had listened to my father's wrong advice I would have had to wear a landlord's cap in Jianchuan.

Late in 1951, all students were required to fill in piles of complicated forms. The authorities wanted a record of everybody's past history. When it came to my father's and brother's occupations, I left a blank. A month later, I was told to see an important official at our College Office. After answering a lot of questions relating to my family background, I was forced to fill in a new form. In the two blanks the man told me to put "Police Officer of the Old Regime/Landlord" and "Reactionary Kuomintang Soldier."

Seeing me walk out sadly and silently, the man called me back. He smiled and said, "I can see what you are thinking. Don't worry. Nearly 80 percent of our students belong to landlord or capitalist families. Your father is your father and you are you. Our Communist government draws a clear class line between a landlord and his children. It was your parents who exploited the poor common people. They are the target of our revolution, not you. Under the leadership of Chairman Mao, you are a builder of New China. The school authorities prepare everything for you. In winter, if you are cold, we will give you a coat. If you are sick, we will give you medicine. Don't worry about anything; just study, study, and again study. Cut off all contacts with your family and establish a firm thought: Serve the people. China belongs to you. ..."

I returned the man a forced smile, but in my heart I objected to the words "reactionary" and "landlord." Our entire village and all its surrounding land didn't equal the holdings of one single big landlord in the Kunming area. For a time, I wanted to go back and argue with that man, but many of my friends warned me not to offend the officials in our College Office. One said, "Be clever, particularly at a time when our country is changing each passing day. The people in our College Office are like tigers. If you dare to touch a tiger's buttocks, he will welcome you to enjoy a trip to his tummy." So I didn't say a word about this problem.

From 1950 until 1953 I got only that one letter from my home village. That was all, nothing else. Four years' worth of rice and vegetables were given me by the college authorities. As was a free bed in the dormitory. That was a big help. During my third year I taught some of the teachers' children in my spare time, and so earned a little money for daily necessities. In my last year I began to write articles reporting the changes taking place in Yunnan for an English monthly magazine in Shanghai. The editor sent me a small sum of money. That was how I got through my college education.

But as I think back to all the reasons for my successfully studying the English language during those tumultuous years, the most important was another unforgettable teacher. His name was Mr. Chen, the dean of our English department. He was a graduate of Beijing's Qinghua University and had studied for three years in the United States. During the anti-Japanese war, he had served as an interpreter with the Flying Tigers when the American air force was helping us in Kunming.

It was during my sophomore year that I became good friends with Mr. Chen. Determined to learn all I could from him, I often knocked at his door on Saturday evenings or Sunday afternoons. In addition to English questions,

I was always asking him to describe what he had seen abroad. He had four young children, and after he had helped me with my questions I would play with them for a while. I volunteered to sweep the floor, or to go out to buy and then carry back the coal brickets we use for cooking in Kunming. Gradually I became part of the family. It was not unusual to see me eating at their table, making a cup of tea in their kitchen, or going to see a film together with them all. It was Mr. Chen who taught me how to use a typewriter.

If Miss Xue and Qiyan were like my sisters, then Mr. Chen was something like my father. Those two ladies taught me to look at the whole country, but Mr. Chen taught me to look at the whole world. Miss Xue and the Wus made me face the English language; they brought me to its door. Mr. Chen was the man who opened that door for me.

While at Kunming Teachers College I occasionally received a letter from Miss Xue. But after my graduation in 1953 we completely lost touch. Miss Xue had gone away, but she had lain a good foundation for me and Qiyan to become close friends. We often helped each other with our homework, and I spent most Sundays at her home. Every now and then we would say a few words about getting married. She said she would wait another year for me, even a little longer. Miss Xue had written from Shanghai, "It is not easy to find a girl who shares your same interests." Yes, quite true! I had learned that before she taught me, but things turned out differently.

Upon Qiyan's graduation in 1952, instead of assigning her a job as a teacher of English, the college authorities sent her to study Russian in northeast China. More and more evidence showed that the English language was not as popular as it had been in previous years. It was now called "the language of Paper-Tiger American Imperialism." Qiyan had no desire to learn Russian, but the trouble was she had joined the Communist Youth League. She had to obey any decision made by the college authorities. Finally we said goodbye. Our correspondence continued for several months and then stopped abruptly.

*     *     *

About three months before my graduation, my cousin again came to see me at college. He had recently been back to our home county to attend the funeral of an important relative. He shook my hand warmly, saying, "Congratulations on your coming graduation! It will be so great a thing in our county. You are the very first college student in our village. Everybody is proud of you. Let's go and celebrate right now."

"Where?"

"To a restaurant, in a hotel. I'll show you the way; it's not so far from your school here."

"A restaurant? Well ... you know I'm still a poor student. How can that be?"

"Never mind. It's my treat. I'll enjoy your banquet later."

"But today you are my guest here. Allow me to invite you to a simple dinner in our college canteen."

"Oh, don't say simple or complicated! Don't worry about money," my cousin insisted. "She has prepared more than enough money. Let's hurry and warm her heart. Like a chick just coming out from its shell, she is a bit nervous and sometimes trembling."

"What are you talking about?"

"Just go, go, go. You'll understand everything. She must be getting anxious by now."

"I really cannot imagine who is waiting for me."

"Well, my cousin, polite, smart, and good-looking, too. A very nice girl, but she is wearing our national costume, quite different from the city girls. People like to stare at her all the time, and they make her sick. And then she can't speak Mandarin fluently. You must make her feel at home, and remember, speak our village dialect."

Now I knew who the girl was. My brother had mentioned her in that one letter, but I had never imagined she would come to Kunming.

Within ten minutes my cousin had made me sit down at a table in a corner of a nearby restaurant. Then he rushed out. In another five minutes he came rushing back, followed by a girl who was wearing the dress and apron of our Bai women. My cousin was the first to speak: "Here you are at last!"

"How do you do, Guihua," I said to her.

She replied nothing, only glanced at me shyly.

"Now I have fulfilled my duty in bringing you two here to form a special family of our times," my cousin said. He rummaged in his bag and pulled out two or three letters and some money.

The girl's name was Li Guihua, the second daughter of our next-door neighbor in Jianchuan. We had been childhood playmates, and had often climbed a hill at the back of our village to collect firewood together. We had loved each other, too. When we were perhaps ten years old, some gifts—a pair of earrings and two jade-green bracelets—had been sent to Guihua's family. That was our marriage engagement, carried out by the parents on both sides.

When I went to Kunming in 1944, neither side had said a word. Everybody considered it a joke. Years went by; we forgot about it. And after 1949 we all knew that this kind of engagement was wrong. In the new society everybody got married in accordance with his or her own choice. Today, one of the letters brought by my cousin was from our village head. It said:

> It looks like such an engagement doesn't go with our marriage law today, but
> there is an important difference in this case. All these years you said nothing, and
> this was just the main reason why your Guihua has refused countless marriage
> proposals. She and her parents are very good, and a respectable family in our

*village. They want to enjoy a good name, so they have been waiting for you faithfully. Now the right time has come. In Kunming, people will naturally ask you a lot of questions. You must tell the truth. You were engaged in the long past, but now in the new society both of you agree to get married. Everything will be all right.*

On the whole, Guihua was really a nice girl. Every now and then I would glance at her, but she continued gazing at the floor. When my cousin or I asked her something, her answers were very short. From beginning to end she volunteered not a word herself. When the waiter brought us some dishes, she turned away, never daring to help herself. She just ate what we put on her plate, slowly and quietly.

After my cousin left, I was the only person to take care of her. A typical village girl coming to a big city for the first time was bound to encounter innumerable difficulties. I told her, "I still have to go to classes. You know I can't watch you all the time. What are you going to do hereafter?"

She replied simply, "My mother said do nothing but all you order me to do and eat whatever you bring me."

"What on earth can you do here? I go to study a foreign language and you don't even know how to speak Mandarin!"

"I can wash your clothes and take special care of you if you get sick."

"You must change *your* clothes! Any money left about you?"

"Yes, my father gave me some. Other relatives gave me some, too." As she said this she tore off two hidden pockets sewn onto her blouse. "They wanted me to give it to you as soon as I saw you, secretly. You keep it, but dress me like the Han girls of Kunming."

This was the most troublesome problem I had ever encountered in my life. What on earth was I going to do? Lots of serious problems would arise in my home village if I sent Guihua away. On the other hand, it would be difficult for a college student to organize a happy family life with an illiterate village girl. To tell the truth, I didn't love her as a husband should love his wife, but I pitied her very much.

I rented a small room for her in a house shared by ten families. It was near my college in a lane called Wenhuaxiang (Culture Alley). The room was so narrow and so short that I had to put the chair under the bed, but it was all I could afford. I stayed on at my dormitory. Twice a day I brought her meals from our college canteen. Later we borrowed a pot from this friend and a pan from that one. Finally I bought her a simple set of kitchenware and she began to cook for herself.

Oh, she was such a trouble! Once, when I had taken her to my college dormitory, I asked her to go to the boiler room and fetch some hot water.[7] She should have returned in less than five minutes. After ten she was still nowhere to be seen. In the end I ran after her. There she was, looking at the boiler.

"What's the matter with you?"

"Nobody in the room. I haven't seen a boiler before, so I was planning to let someone use it first, but nobody came. Now you show me how to operate a boiler."

She had drawn water from a well or fetched it from the river all her life—but had never turned on a faucet.

One Saturday evening I took her to see a film. At the cinema entrance I bumped into a friend who wanted to ask a question. As the film had already begun, I gave Guihua a ticket and told her to go in first. When I got to our seats five minutes later, people were shouting at her. They would have driven her out if I hadn't arrived at that moment. The chairs in the cinema had flip-up seats that had to be pushed down before you could sit on them. She had never seen this kind of chair, so she just perched on top of the flipped-up seat. Of course the people behind couldn't see and started yelling at her.

She did many more stupid things. What I have mentioned is only a bit of a mouthful. No matter what she did, she brought me nothing but trouble. All my teachers and classmates talked about my "good-for-nothing" village girl. Mr. Chen said, "I think she is a nice girl. How do you explain the word 'stupid'? I don't agree with those who say she is stupid. In a country girl's eyes, everything here is new. She hasn't even *heard* of many of our city things, so it isn't strange to see her make mistakes. That's the reason she makes us laugh. You must be patient. Observe her from all sides. Every day you must think of something new with which to test her."

I was seriously troubled by the problem of my village fiancée. I thought about it for days and nights. After summing up all the viewpoints and advice, I made a decision: No. The talk had begun when we were little. The situation had changed now that we were adults. I said, "You are very good, but we cannot get married. You must go home and look for another man." Instantly she began to cry and fell ill the next day. Two weeks later, I bought her a ticket to Jianchuan and wrote a detailed letter to her parents. Again she became seriously ill. She wept so painfully that she couldn't eat for three days.

At last she said that she wanted to see the principal of my college in order to settle this marriage question. Well, it was a personal affair. There was no need to see a principal. Instead, I took her to see Mr. Chen. In his sitting room she wept bitterly once again. Through her tears she said, "Well, all I want is that you make an on-the-spot investigation of my history. I am not the most beautiful girl in the world, but I assure you I can do everything at home. Many people, including Party members, office workers, and schoolteachers, all asked to marry me, but in my heart I always thought a big-school student must be stronger and know everything on earth. So, one by one, I told them all to go away. I hoped you hadn't forgotten me. If I had forgotten you, I would've been married a long time ago, and by now I would be a mother.

"Now you look down on me. Kunming is a big modern city and I am what they call a country cousin. Yes, obviously I am a village girl, but I am not blind or lame. I need to look at things first, and sooner or later I'll learn. However, you want me to go home. To say is easy, but most painful to do. Why didn't you tell me earlier? Everything would be easy to correct if I hadn't come here. Can a village girl be the wife of a college student? I still have my doubts. It is questionable. Truly this gap between us is too wide and too deep to speak of. But what can be done now? Too late, a hundred times too late! Don't you think that each person has a 'face'? If you force me to go home, where shall I place my face? The whole village will talk, and those who failed in marrying me will laugh. Oh, I could never bear that.

"I didn't harm others; I didn't steal or do anything bad either. I've been a good girl. My sister was married early, and now she is the mother of three children. My mother often gets sick, although father is all right. They love me, but soon they will die. I only look forward to marrying you. I know nothing of the world but you. I want to give and help with all I have and all I am able. I prefer death if you don't want me. I would like to jump into Lake Dian Chi and take a long rest earlier."[8]

All was quiet in the sitting room for a long time after Guihua's speech. There was much truth in what she said. In conclusion Mr. Chen said, "Getting married is a serious problem for us all. We must reconsider it again and again. An English proverb says 'Look before you leap.' Don't go home yet. Stay and love each other; help each other as usual."

So the question still remained unsettled.

\*          \*          \*

The year 1953 was one I can never forget. Not only did Guihua arrive, but it was also the year I left college and began my career. Unfortunately, a nationwide political campaign to learn everything from the Soviet Union was launched throughout the country at this time.[9] Of us seventeen graduating students, seven were sent to study Russian in northeast China. This was considered the best option. I was always at the top of my class, yet they said my political behavior was not so good: I hadn't taken part in the political activities of the college; I would read an English book while an important official was delivering a political report; I refused to fill out a form to become a Communist Youth League member. And on top of all this, I had taken a village fiancée. For these reasons, the college authorities crossed my name off the list of those to be sent to northeast China.

The Provincial Personnel Department assigned me, along with nine other students, to work in Yunnan. Of these, six students whose English was not particularly good, but who were very active in political movements, were selected to work at the Kunming Railway Bureau. Another student went to work in a factory. Yet another was assigned to work at the Kunming zoo! Together with my classmate Gao, I was assigned to work for a committee attached to the Yunnan Provincial Government. We all had jobs, but none of them had anything to do with English.

The name of my new organization sounded very great and powerful. In the minds of the common villagers, all those who worked there were "top officials of the province." "A thousand congratulations!" Guihua's father wrote to us. "I am exceedingly happy to have you married to my daughter. The whole village was overjoyed to hear the greatest news of your new post. Many envy you. You will bring us honor."

As a matter of fact, since I didn't wish to work as a government office worker, I was bitterly disappointed. It was the heaviest blow of my life, even heavier than the arrival of a poor village girl who knew nothing. Well, we understood that it was a dangerous thing to refuse a job offered by our country. All my English books were locked up in a box. Times had changed. Swimming in what was called the most beautiful Soviet Sea, how could I go against the violent tide and tell people I wanted to further my knowledge of English? That movement washed away my dream of using English.

As for the village girl Guihua, sometimes I hated her, but at the same time, especially when I put myself in her position, I pitied her and loved her very much. After all, she herself was not the person to be blamed. All these troubles were caused by feudal ideas or, let us say, by the backwardness of the countryside.[10] I worried very much about her life. If something bad should happen, how could I face her parents? I stopped thinking about driving her home. Right after I was informed that I had to work in a government office, shortly before my graduation, I made up my mind to marry Guihua.

*                    *                    *

Our funny wedding was arranged on a weekend. Neither of us wore anything special. We just washed our old clothes the day before. Early on the morning of our wedding day, we went first to a hospital. Taking the health certificates they issued us, together with a document given by my college authorities, we went directly to see the man at the marriage office. It took an hour for us to answer his questions covering all kinds of problems. Finally, the man just smoked and scratched his head. It looked as if he had no more to ask, but he still seemed unwilling to use his pen.

"The engagement was settled by our parents. That's true. We were still young at that time." I knew what he was considering, so I said this slowly. "But today, we are not children. We are marrying in the new society, both agree to. ..."

"Yes, yes," the man said. "But your case seems quite new to me. A college student marrying a village girl! Hundreds of couples have been passed by my pen, but this is the very first time for me to see a big-school student marry an eyeless village girl.[11] Well, sorry, I am only a little office worker. There are many more bigger ones in the office. Please wait for a while."

With these words, he phoned someone else, and then rushed up and down to see all his colleagues. We waited for another hour. Finally, handing over the wedding license, he said, "It's still okay. Here you are. Congratulations!"

On the way home, instead of going to fill up a large bag with good things at a department store, we bought a few packets of candy, cigarettes, cookies, tea, and sunflower and pumpkin seeds at a little shop. Our simple wedding party was held in a classroom in the foreign languages department. Apart from a bunch of fresh flowers brought by my girl-classmates, we had nothing special, not even a "double-happiness" red-paper poster pasted onto the wall. A cup of hot water or tea, a handful of candy, seeds, or cookies—these were our wedding banquet.

About twenty people attended, including Mr. Chen, his wife, and my cousin. We put the teacher's desk in the middle, but there were not many wedding presents to place on top. The most valuable gifts were a thermos flask and an enamel wash-basin. My classmates gave us a mug, a bar of soap, a comb, a toothbrush. After singing a Bai folk song, Guihua just sat there, accepting one or two if someone offered her candy or seeds. She understood very little of what the guests were talking about, and her face became red when anyone tried to start a conversation with her. I smiled a little, but I felt sad in my heart.

My college days ended. I began working. The committee I was attached to was the Committee of Political and Legal Affairs, an important branch directly under the leadership of the Provincial Peoples' Government. In addition to fulfilling my daily office tasks, I was mainly kept busy in helping my village wife. She continued to live in that small room I had rented for her in Culture Alley. I moved into the office workers' dormitory provided by my new work unit, sharing a room with some of my unmarried colleagues. Our dormitory was about a *li* away from Guihua's room, and I was always running back and forth. My plan was this: Take advantage of the city, make her master something which she could not learn in the countryside. If I could teach her some useful skill, she might even become a permanent worker in the city one day.

We two made several regulations. The most important was: Try always to speak in Mandarin. Her inability to speak, read, or write Chinese was the most serious problem. We began with recognizing and writing her own name.

Very early in the morning she was employed to sweep the streets for about two hours. She said to me, "I enjoy it. All the streets are paved in good order, so it's easier than when I used to sweep at home. Nobody knows I am the wife of a government worker. When they come out to work, my job is already done. But you must remember, *don't* tell this to anyone at my home."

During the daytime she volunteered to clean the yard in front of the house where she lived. Sometimes she offered to carry the next-room mother's crying baby. She earned a little money by washing clothes or sometimes embroidering a piece of cloth. Then she would wander about the streets aimlessly, using her eyes to watch this for a while and then her ears to listen to that for another while. In the evenings she went to join a group of housewives, and they taught her how to handle a sewing machine and cut a piece of good cloth into a beautiful dress. She selected a great number of modern designs for future use. She made a friend who was a cake seller. That woman taught her how to make various cakes.

For my part, whenever I had a chance to leave the office I went to help her learn to read and write. Often I arrived in a hurry and also left in a hurry. In the beginning progress was slow. I remember lesson two of our textbook mentioning something about Beijing. In Chinese, *shou du* means a "nation's capital city." But *shou du* also sounds like *shou duo,* which means "hands many." She was so silly that she asked, "Do you mean that people in Beijing have many hands?" But we didn't give up. In less than one year, she was able to recognize about 600 Chinese characters and had even begun to read some of the headlines in the newspapers. To my surprise, her Chinese improved so rapidly that she was soon able to write a simple letter using her own words. Under my regular direction, she learned how to use an abacus as well.

*              *              *

Fortunately, in December 1954, a permanent job supported by the government was offered to her in the preschool attached to my work unit.[12] The principal assigned her to be a cleaner. She came from the countryside and hadn't been trained formally, so to be a cleaner was the only suitable job for her. By using her eyes and ears, she learned something about looking after children, such as how to cook meals for infants, which medicine to give them, and how to inject a baby. Above all else, she learned to speak Mandarin fluently, with a little bit of a Kunming accent.

Guihua had changed. She could go everywhere in the city and do everything by herself with confidence now. When she changed out of her native clothes, she looked like an ordinary girl of the city. Homesickness was a thing of the past. She loved the city and enjoyed her job. What Mr. Chen had said was true. Guihua was a nice girl, a clever village girl. She had adapted quickly.

Underneath her city exterior, however, some feudal thoughts inherited from the countryside were still lurking. She accepted new knowledge rapidly but was unable to change her traditional, backward ideas for a long, long time. Several months after we got married, all kinds of rumors from all directions came to our ears. Many people from Jianchuan lived in Kunming, and news passed quickly from one to another. A letter from Guihua's father arrived:

> *You are a bad daughter. You haven't behaved as we taught you to at home. You are washing the dirty clothes of other people's children. Why not wash your own children's clothes first? Don't you know your husband is a college student and a government worker serving in the highest organization of our province? You do not want to protect your face. You just bring shame to your husband and the whole family. That's a slave-girl's dirty job. It would be much better to be a beggar in the street. We do not want money or to eat meat and fish every day. What we want is a good name for the family. We want you to bear children and honor our ancestors. As soon as you get this letter, I want you to stop going to wash and clean dirty things of other people's children. Immediately stop being a slave-girl and try to be a good wife and a good mother.*

She showed me the letter and began to cry. This was a serious problem. The political system could be changed relatively swiftly, but for us distant minority people it was very hard to get rid of such feudal thoughts within several years. And Guihua, being a traditional girl, took her father's criticisms to heart and obeyed him. Soon she stopped going to work at the preschool. She was very quick at learning new things, but she failed to learn the most important lesson of our times: that a modern girl should work so she could stand on her own two feet. That was the first step. To bear a child was the second step. Besides, it was considered a most precious thing to have a family that was *shuangfu gong*, meaning that both husband and wife are earning government salaries. Really, I couldn't support two or three people on my limited wages. But in order to be a "good daughter," she changed her mind suddenly. She turned a deaf ear to my suggestions and ignored her golden opportunity. Before long, she was sacked from her permanent job. I wept when I heard this news.

She again started sweeping the streets. So I said, "To sweep the streets is also a dirty job. How do you explain that?"

"That's different. First, I put a mouth-cover on to shadow my face.[13] I usually sweep very early in the morning. Nobody knows me. Second, I get through with my duties within two or three hours. In the preschool I have to keep on staying there for eight hours. Third, my parents and my relatives don't know what I am doing."

I looked at Guihua. She was beautiful and really very nice—only her traditional ideas were too strong to destroy. We talked and argued, but nothing resulted.

One day, afraid to hurt her feelings, I tried to be tactful: "It was a bad thing for you to give up that job. I feel very sad. Nevertheless, I love you much more than before."

"Well, I am still the same person. I still have to learn a lot from you and from other people."

"No, your success is great. You are no longer a silly village girl, but a girl of the city." I said this and then came to the point: "What do you say if I ask you to return home?"

"Ho, do as you please!"

"Are you going to jump into Lake Dian Chi if now I tell you to go home?"

"No, I'm not. Life is precious and I am young and can do many things in the world. Really I shall be happy to go home. I am confident I can manage everything well in our village if you really think I just get in your way and bring you trouble."

"Don't talk like that. I need your help." I paused for a while and then asked, "Shall we both go home?"

"Oh, no, that's wrong! That's just where the difference lies. You must bear every hardship and stick to your present work. Our country has spent a lot of money to let you receive a higher education. The Party wants you to serve the people. You cannot use the English you have learned in the college, but you can serve the people just the same. I am an ordinary village girl. I can hardly do anything here. Now I shall be glad to go home."

"How will you explain it to your father, and what would you say if the villagers should ask why you do not want to be the wife of a government worker, but prefer to return home to hold a hoe?"

"Well," she thought for a moment. "I can say this: His goal is high and the destination is very far. At present he is preparing to go to a foreign country. I must not bother him. I am a farmer. Our country needs more grain. We farmers ought to do our best to grow more grain. So I returned home. Is that right?"

"A wise answer. But suppose you stay at home for years and I keep on working in Kunming permanently?"

"Then I'll tell them he is coming back soon or I'll be going to Kunming soon."

"It sounds rather unusual."

"It doesn't matter. After all, everybody has a home and everybody has to return sooner or later. I don't believe you will stay in Kunming forever. Oh, home, sweet home. ... Can you sing that song?"

"Yes, everybody has a home. But besides a home, we must be very careful in planning a happy life. We must consider everything further and further, from all sides. Life doesn't mean eat, work, and sleep. We need something more."

"Oh yes," she said quickly, "we need a boy or a girl. They make our life more beautiful."

"Still, it isn't the best way. For the benefit of both sides, in order to make things easier, I think we must get a formal divorce before we separate and say goodbye."

"A divorce!" she shouted at me. I thought she was going to cry again, but she didn't. After a while she said thoughtfully, "Last year you didn't want to marry me. I couldn't do anything. I couldn't speak Mandarin, much less read or write. Later, we got married. A thousand worries disappeared. Then I learned something about everything, and that was my second great victory. Now I can earn a living all by myself even if you do not give me a cent. Anyway, the situation this year is not the situation of last year.

"Of course, some problems still exist, like a baby and what you call a permanent job. But I think the real trouble is that you are a college student and I am a village woman. I respect you and love you, but the gap between us is a deep and wide one. At the present stage, really, it's me who is giving you all the trouble. Maybe your own business is more important than mine for the time being. As long as your business is going on smoothly, both of us will be all right in the end. I don't think things are as serious as you do. You think a divorce is necessary, but I think we may separate and go in different directions without a formal divorce document."

Two weeks later, after we had talked three times, both of us agreed to divorce. In order to avoid trouble that might appear in the distant future, we also got a formal document, a real one. Everything went by smoothly and peacefully. At the office of the district court, we didn't sit opposite each other angrily as usually happens. We sat on the same bench and related our personal information slowly, neither of us shouting or scolding the other. The court workers were all surprised to see the calm way of our divorce. They all smiled. Coming out with the document in our hands, we walked shoulder to shoulder, just like a newly married couple.

It was a funny divorce. She had her system of thinking and considering things. I had mine. We seemed to understand each other, but sometimes we still suspected each other. Her father might criticize me, her relatives would say I was cruel, but anyway, Guihua wasn't a three-year-old child. I had the document in my hand. I thought she would weep for several days, but she didn't. Sometimes it seemed as if nothing had happened.

To begin with, I couldn't pay the money the court had instructed me to give her. All my colleagues lent me money, and I finally gave her three times the sum they had fixed. I felt for her and wanted to make up a little to her, so I made a gift of many things she had seen in the city and wished to have. I bought her a set of easy-to-read books. I also bought her a special fountain pen, and asked an expert to carve my name and some meaningful words on it. In return, she made me a special gift. It was a silk pillowcase. On this pillowcase she embroidered two ducks, one female and the other male, with the words, "We loved in Kunming."

The days before her departure were the happiest days of my life. We did nothing except go around the city to visit here and there. We had some pictures taken and ate our meals outside. The last day was spent in a park. She now nodded at whatever I explained.

"Let's wait and see, or just wish and hope. If I really use my English again in the future, one day we will get remarried."

"Yes, that's just what I was going to say. May Heaven help us to realize that. Our so-called divorce was a special divorce. We'll just use it as a 'cover' for our separation, so no friends or relatives will gossip. You have left an unforgettable impression on me and I still love you. I do not blame you. It was our parents' fault. Do trust me and believe in me. I'll keep your advice in my mind, and I swear to learn more new progressive ideas of our times. Certainly, a hundred certainlies, I'll wait for your return at home."

The morning we said goodbye at the bus station neither of us could control our painful tears. The bus began to move. As she waved, she suddenly threw out a big envelope wrapped in a handkerchief. The bus moved on and on. Guihua's last words were, "Thank you. Thank you for everything. I'll wait for you. ...."

In the envelope I found some money and a short letter:

*1. Don't tell people we are divorced. Please keep it as a top secret.*

*2. Don't forget me, never, never. I'll wait for you in the same way as I waited in the past.*

*3. Return the money to your colleagues right away.*

*4. I have a different kind of money, not in my purse, but stored safely in my head. With your help I learned to speak Mandarin. I can even write this letter myself. I can read a newspaper and use an abacus. I can operate a sewing machine and give an injection to a baby like a doctor. I can pronounce ABC too. These will be my money-tree in our village.*

*5. Don't worry about me, but always take care of yourself and do everything well.*

                                                              ***Guihua***

I was particularly touched by her letter. Straight away I returned the money to my colleagues.

*           *           *

That year, 1955, I was in a bad way. No time to study English for one thing, and no good friend to go out with or talk to for another. In a way my divorce was like unloading a heavy box from my shoulders, but at the same time I felt as if I had lost something so lovely and dear and valuable. I was greatly annoyed and frustrated by my office work. I thought of learning the Russian language, but it was not so easy to find a good teacher. There were some who asked me to teach English as a private teacher, but something bad might happen to me if I agreed to teach people the "enemy's" language. I was completely thrown into a state of great sorrow.

Then I was hired at the Research Institute and began using my rusty English once again. I thought my luck had turned. I was wrong.

## NOTES

1. After Japan's surrender in August 1945, the civil war between the Kuomintang and Communist forces began in earnest. This conflict is referred to as the War of Liberation.

2. *Rice bowl:* a phrase that, when used in this context, means "job" or "livelihood."

3. In the case of Kunming, the governor of Yunnan Province declared his support for the Communists when their victory seemed a certainty. Mr. He says, "Yunnan was self-liberated. Not a shot was fired in Kunming."

4. Sometime in 1950, a network of "Street Government Offices" was established in Kunming. Approximately 100 to 500 neighboring households made up each "office." They were responsible for such tasks as street cleaning and fire prevention, health and vaccination programs, arbitrating disputes, implementing government policies, and reporting criminal and political behavior.

5. During the Land Reform Movement the rural population was grouped into five categories: landlords, rich peasants, middle peasants, poor peasants, and landless laborers. An Agricultural Reform Law of June 1950 divided the property of landlords and rich peasants among the rest without indemnity. Mr. He says, "After the Land Reform Work Team arrived in a village, they visited poor people from house to house. In this way, they got to know the history of the village, urged the poor to stand up and fight against the class enemy, and helped them to recall bitter and enjoy sweet. Then mass meetings began. The landlords stood in the center and people began to reveal their past crimes and misdeeds. What followed were public-trial meetings, more horrible than ordinary struggle meetings in a small village. A public-trial meeting was many times larger; thousands came from several villages. At that time a death sentence could be decided at the county level. As a rule, the local authorities planned to sentence only a few to death, but all the landlords had to kneel on the platform. They didn't tell who was going to die. Sometimes timid ones were frightened to death."

6. *Mou:* One acre equals about 5.7 *mou.*

7. As noted in Chapter 1, dormitories are not equipped with kitchens, so hot water must be brought up in thermoses from coal-burning boilers.

8. *Take a long rest earlier:* die young.

9. Mr. He writes in a recent letter: "In 1950 Chairman Mao paid a visit to the Soviet Union. Right after his return, the whole country began crazily learning everything from the Russians. The waves of this movement reached their peaks between 1953 and 1958."

10. *Feudal:* Since 1949 the government has used this term, loosely and with a negative connotation, to describe the period before Liberation. It has carried over into everyday speech, and people often use it to describe conservative traditions. Arranged marriages, preference for sons over daughters, and patriarchal authority are all referred to as "feudal."

11. *Eyeless:* illiterate.

12. Mobility from countryside to city has been restricted since 1949 by the fact that the government controls almost all jobs and housing in the urban areas. It is an arduous, in most cases impossible, process for people from the countryside to find a city work unit to accept them. Thus, although Guihua's job is menial, Mr. He uses the word *fortunately* because she has succeeded in becoming formally attached to a work unit.

13. *Mouth-cover:* a mask, much like those worn by doctors. Masks are routinely worn in China when the weather is cold or if the area is dusty; they are also worn by individuals with a cough or cold.

# 5

# THE POLITICAL
# TYPHOON CONTINUES

It took half a day to relate my entire history to the group members of my study class, and several days to explain all the details. After a series of face-to-face struggle meetings, many of the events seemed all right; but each time I came to "confess" my Christianity problem, nobody believed it. I told them everything in great detail, but they just said "No!" Hundreds of times they asked: "How much money did the foreign monks and nuns give you before they returned to their countries?" "Where did you hide their radio receive-send machine?" "Who else joined your secret group?" "When are you going to contact them?"

In conclusion they said, "Under the leadership of the Chinese Communist Party we have become masters of our country, but you are still a foreigner's running dog! You have helped foreign monks and nuns to poison our people with their foreign Heaven Master. The Party never shoots an arrow without a target. One hundred percent you were a secret spy, planted before Liberation. The Party is offering you a golden chance to confess, but you remain indifferent and turn a deaf ear to the Party's good advice."

I couldn't bear these words. I was angry and told them to cut my body into a thousand pieces if they could place some facts on the table. They became furious and said I had gone mad, adding, "You are a die-hard. You obstinately cling to your reactionary position. Your head is cheaper than a dog's head; it's not worthwhile to end your life with a bullet." On many occasions I was made to sit up for the whole night "considering my problems" and then to write them all down one by one. The other group members took turns to watch. My Christianity problem lasted for two weeks but remained an unsolved "mystery."

There were several other people who had troubles similar to mine. Some wanted to die, but they couldn't find a way. For several days I was hovering between life and death. Night after night I slept on a tear-soaked pillow. I became weaker and weaker. If I killed myself, or if they made me die, later people would think I really was a secret spy of the foreign missionaries. A kind of temporary solution had to be considered.

Well, I knew that to make up something out of nothing was wrong; but finally I made up my mind to try it. A popular slogan of that time ran: "Leniency to those who confess their crimes and severity to those who refuse." As soon as they thought I was confessing something "important" or "new," they might stop troubling me for a while. In this way I made up false stories. My false material covered several pages. I put the stress on two problems.

The first related to my father's police business. I said that for a time I had been a Kuomintang reactionary policeman, one of Chiang Kai-shek's "knives." I had an active hand in helping my father oppress and exploit the common people. This was one of my biggest crimes. Second, I said that I had helped the missionaries poison the clean minds of our children with Bible stories. I had even taken some of my classmates to attend their Bible classes. Then I added that the books, shirt, and pencil-sharpener given to me as goodbye gifts by the missionaries were in fact bribes to continue anti-Communist propaganda. After their departure we exchanged several letters—meaning that I gave the missionaries secret information about China.

It wasn't a joke. I didn't want to die. Under such circumstances, this was the only solution I could come up with to keep on living for some time. After I handed in my false report I thought they would arrest me. I had lost touch with my family. Qiyan was my last friend in Kunming and I pinned my last hope on her. As I had no way of sending a letter, I scribbled a brief "will" to her in a notebook. I explained about my "confession" and ended:

> *If the previous struggle movement in Kunming was a storm, then the present study class is a typhoon. Thunder and lightening start together. I want to see how the present world goes on, so I finally did as they forced me to do. Right now I cannot imagine what kind of a death is waiting for me. Today you are the only friend who understands my past and present. If they are going to punish me mainly based on my being "a missionary's spy," I pray you can find a way to clear up this error for me. I never thought such a thing would happen to me this year. I don't know if I can keep on writing to you or see you again in the future, but your special friendship will stay in my mind as long as I am still living in the world.*

One day in April we were instructed to write a personal "thought summary." Everybody assumed that the farm would organize a big rally to punish us in public, but strangely enough, nothing serious happened. They gave us a two-day holiday to take a bath, have a haircut, and do some cleaning. Then one after the other, we returned to our original brigades. I hoped my factory brigade leader would let me look after those buffalo again, but he didn't mention it, and I was in no position to ask for my old job back.

Before I was forced to join the study class I had been an optimistic fellow, always forgetting that I should be reforming myself. After the class ended, especially when I thought of my false report, I felt disheartened. I took a gloomy view of everything. My mind was filled with grief and indignation. I had plenty of time to read, but I had no heart to read anything at all. Every month a mobile film team came to show us two films. In addition, our farm's own traveling recreational troupe, made up of inmates who showed talent in singing and dancing or had previously worked in a theater, came to give performances. Again I never felt like enjoying myself for a single minute. Later I could run to the post office, but I was too embarrassed to write to Qiyan. I didn't tear up the "will" in my notebook, but I didn't send it either. My mental burden became heavier each month. Until I was quite sure of the consequences of my false report, I would never write to her. She knew my past, but perhaps it was better not to tell her what I had made up.

Before the study class, I had held a permanent job. After I "graduated" from that class I became a mobile toiler. In May the leaders at the brick and tile factory wanted me to sift cinders. In June they wanted me to carry water to the kiln. Sometimes I became a purchasing agent: Taking their money and a list, I went out to buy daily personal necessities for many people. Sometimes they changed my job twice a month.

One afternoon in October 1960 I was suddenly called to the factory office and introduced to a middle-aged man. Our brigade leader said, "This is Master Wang, a famous barber from town. Our farm's office has invited him here to help us train a barber."

"How do you do, Master Wang," I said, nodding politely.

The brigade leader went on, "This is Zhang Shuyi, your new apprentice. We think perhaps he is the right man to learn your skill within a short period of time. The farm's office has approved."

As he said this, he handed me a wooden box and added, "Everything is new. You are to take responsibility for the whole set. If something is missing, you must pay for it out of your monthly salary. Listen and watch your Master Wang for two weeks. Try to start cutting during the third week. On this day next month you must be an independent barber. One *jiao* per head.[1] Turn in your money to our accountant once a week. Do you have any questions?"

"Well ... it's quite new to me," I replied slowly. "I don't know if I can do a good job. Maybe you could find someone else who would do it better."

"No, they suggested several others, but the office meeting approved none except you. Don't worry too much. You just try it first."

"All right." I had to agree. He was the leader. I was under his rule.

I began wearing a barber's white uniform the following day. During the first week I just watched my master cut and shave. My duty was to bring hot water and wash the customers' hair. On the tenth day, a young man wanted to cut all his hair off. Only a razor was needed. It seemed simple so I began my

first try. A week after that I started to use a pair of hair-clippers. I began performing the craft all by myself within a month.

But who would have thought it—my career as an independent barber lasted
only three days! A big change took place on my fourth day. A huge meeting
was called at which one-fourth of the inmates were ordered to leave the brick
and tile factory. Similar decisions were made in other brigades all over the
farm. My name was on their list. I returned my tools right after the meeting
was over. We were not allowed to ask any questions. The factory brigade
leader just said, "A new job is waiting for you. Everybody get busy. Pack all
your things and get ready to leave at any time."

Some jumped for joy. Some began to weep. Maybe they are coming to arrest those who attended the study class—this was what I thought. Right after
supper that evening I rushed over to see Xiao Yang. He secretly told me,
"Don't worry, it has nothing to do with those who joined the study class. It's
a big change. Not only some from our farm, but several hundred from other
places will follow."

I asked where we were going, but he wouldn't tell me that. As I was running back to pack my things, he called out, "You have got another bowl—being a barber is a good trade. Be happy and don't forget me. Goodbye. I hope
you throw off your cap soon and come back to see me."

Judging from his last words, I was sure we would be sent to reform in a different place. But where?

*        *        *

A few days later, after our five o'clock supper, all of a sudden we were ordered to leave for the railway station. I had to hurry. Clutching our untidy
luggage, we were made to line up. An official walked up and down, counting
us. All were present, so we set off for the railway station in twos and threes,
group after group. No armed policemen followed us. As we approached the
factory gates, Lao Wang came into view. He was the only one of my former
village friends to come and say goodbye to me. I was deeply touched. We said
goodbye reluctantly outside the factory gates.

Approximately 300 people were already gathered there when we reached
the station. A group of government-like workers told us to sit on our luggage
and wait for the train. One of them said, "Hereafter you have nothing to do
with this farm. Tomorrow, all of you will become railway builders. Our country has prepared everything for you. Don't worry, the country takes care of
you all the time."

Everybody now knew we were going to reform in a different place, but not
a single soul knew where. Nevertheless, most of us looked happy as we
boarded the train. Many got excited when we stopped at a Kunming station.
People whispered, "Maybe they want us to reform in Kunming?" Too bad!
Twenty minutes later the train began to move again. The day was just dawn-

ing when we were finally ordered to get out. Someone said, "Oh, here we are. I have been here before. They call it Songming County."

The sun rose. The land was white, covered with frost. It was colder than before. One of our new brigade leaders took ten of us to a nearby village to borrow four iron pots and buy several bundles of firewood from the local villagers. Another group went to collect stones. Within an hour we were taking turns drinking out of a mug of boiled water. We added some simple buns, and this was our breakfast.

While we ate, one of the leaders said, "Our destination is behind those mountains over there."

"Is it a factory or a farm?" someone asked.

"It isn't a farm; not a factory either."

"Oh, does that mean we have to carry heavy stones?"

"No, no, no," the new brigade leader smiled. "You weren't sent by a public security bureau. Carrying big and heavy stones is for criminals who are sentenced to reform in a labor-reform farm. People there are forced to work. Yours is different. We call it 'reeducation reform through labor.' You are citizens. All you have to do is to chop down some trees and cut grass, then build sheds along the future railway line."

"What for?"

"To house the railway workers who will be coming soon. The new railway will link up with the main line. There is rich coal inside those mountains."

At eleven o'clock everybody began to climb over the hills. At one we saw a small hut beside a zigzag path. A third of us were ordered to stop. Half of the rest stopped at another hut farther on. The last hundred stopped at about five o'clock. At each stop we saw local villagers building cooking stoves in the open air. Inside those newly built huts we saw bags of rice, potatoes, and dried vegetables. Nearby, hundreds of hoes, spades, and axes were piled high.

My group stopped at the third location. We were named the Third Brigade. From now on, everything went from bad to worse. There was nothing in those mountains and valleys. Living conditions were the poorest. Before we put up a shed we had to sleep in the open: under a big tree, in a small cave, or, after we cut down a few branches, in a little shelter. We washed in the small streams that were everywhere.

During the first week we were only a hundred in number. Another hundred new victims were added within a month. At the brick and tile factory, most of us had been sent from various Kunming-based organizations. Before becoming "enemies of the people" we had all held government jobs. What was more, most had received a good education. Year after year, people had seemed to understand and treat one another in a friendly manner. We had borrowed and returned things kindly and helped each other every day.

Now everything changed. About forty of the newcomers were from the Kunming area. The trouble was that the remaining sixty were formerly unemployed people. They were sent from the county level, and some were hardened village thieves. Though not anti-Party elements, they stole public property, secretly ran after young ladies, robbed people at street corners, and organized a group of gangsters. A few of them were very young. Some couldn't read their own names. Many didn't even know what "socialist" or "rightist" meant.

Our general brigade leader didn't care about a person's former occupation. Sixteen people were haphazardly organized into a group. Three groups made a team brigade, four team brigades made a big brigade. Every group was a colorful mixture, coming from various trades, covering all walks of life. Some made a large circle of friends in an hour. Some made enemies in five minutes. Some slept next to each other and followed each other to work but never exchanged a word in a week. Some drew the interest of other people with their "stealing adventure" stories. Some even taught others how to pickpocket in a bus or at the entrance to a theater. From early in the morning until late at night, hundreds of problems appeared among the group members. If anyone forgot to lock his box, valuable things flew away, without wings, in a flash. Sometimes there was fighting, sometimes weeping, sometimes laughter.

Every day we worked in the open air. Our daily tasks were to chop down tall trees and select long grass. The trees were used as supporting poles and the grass was used as thatch. The mountainsides were covered with grass, but it was troublesome finding clumps that were long and thigh-high. As a rule, tall, straight trees could be found only at the top of the mountains. Various bushes grew all over the slopes; dragging the felled trees down was always a problem. Sometimes ten people were sent out early in the morning but couldn't manage to bring back a single trunk at sunset.

The main thing we grumbled about was a shortage of food. Each group had a scale and all grain was carefully weighed. According to the government's ration policy, the country supplied manual workers with about fifty *jin* of rice every month.[2] But since we had to climb up and down several times a day, this quantity was insufficient, and most of us felt hungry all day long. Later, more potatoes were added, but after each meal everybody still felt something was missing. It was almost impossible to get meat or a little piece of candy. Although each person had some money in his pocket, it was useless, as nothing was available for purchase in those empty valleys.

In each brigade we had a man who was appointed to act as a doctor. He carried a Red Cross box wherever he went, but he could do nothing to heal those whose legs were constantly swollen. Upon receiving letters from our relatives, we learned that this problem was the same everywhere. The common people in the villages were having a most miserable time as well. A strange movement to smash all the individual, private cooking stoves was launched all over the countryside in 1958.[3] Over the radio we heard: "Too much precious time is wasted on cooking our daily meals. True happy communism means not only working together but also eating together from a big pot, like workers and students in the cities." All peasants, old and young, were ordered to eat their daily meals together, usually in the village square or in a temple. Moreover, our country had just launched a drive to increase steel production, and a call went out for people to donate their iron and brass pots to local furnaces.[4] In many villages, groups of young "activists" were organized to search from house to house. People were not allowed to keep any edibles at home or to make a fire. If you refused to accept this policy, people said that you were re- fusing to follow the masses to enjoy a happy socialist style of life.

Because of this policy, millions of peasants had to give up raising domestic animals. Fewer people went to market. Everything had to be done secretly. People later called it "The period when we had to eat big-pot rice." That was the time when getting something to eat was the Number One problem under the sun. That was the time when a hen cost much, much more than a baby pig normally costs. That was the time when you couldn't buy an egg in a several- hundred-person village. Nobody knows how many people died of hunger and the swelling sickness.[5]

It took us about forty days to build eleven large sheds. Each shed was big enough to accommodate twenty people. Each time we completed a group of sheds, we were ordered to move on to another valley or new mountain cor- ner. Each time we moved, everybody had to carry his own belongings and trudge through the undergrowth. Unfortunately, it happened that I fell ill when they ordered us to proceed to the second construction site. Being too weak to carry my possessions, I was forced to ask others to help. Each time I asked, I had to give out some gifts. My old portable typewriter was really a trouble; I gave a short-sleeved shirt to another worker who agreed to carry it for me.

The others walked faster. I moved very slowly. When I got to our destina- tion, I discovered they had burned more than half my books. The weather there was too cold to describe. Snow covered everything and people were hungry as wolves. The man who had carried my typewriter said, "A fire looks like a meal. We were forced to burn your books to make a fire; otherwise we would have frozen to death."

After we settled down at the first stop, I wrote a letter to Qiyan briefly tell- ing her about all the changes that had occurred. A month went by, yet I heard nothing from her. Maybe she, too, was facing some troubles, I thought to myself. Unexpectedly, a week after we started on the second construction site, I received a note and a postal order for 10 *yuan* from her. She said that her fa- ther had retired and that she would accompany him back to Guangdong Province sometime soon. That was why she had taken so long in replying, but she promised to keep in touch in the future. Again I began writing her de- scriptive letters about my days.

*          *          *

One evening in January 1961, our group leader told me to go and see the general brigade leader. My heart leapt to my mouth when I heard that sudden order. I thought, "Something bad is going to happen to me. Possibly they are planning to punish me because of my false report created at the study class." But I was wrong. The general brigade leader showed me a seat and offered me a cup of tea, saying, "We had a look at your personal file. On the whole, you have been behaving yourself well during the past two years. As you know, we have four big brigades, about 800 people, working on the line. But we have only three barbers, not enough to cope with the situation. A telephone reply from the farm said you had been trained to do a barber's job. We were pleased to hear that. I was told to tell you to leave this brigade and go to work as a barber in the Fourth Brigade, which is just a stone's throw away from our railway headquarters."

"Then you mean I'll have to move again?"

"Yes, you leave here tomorrow morning and report to the Fourth Brigade. Look, everything has been written quite clearly. They have put your name in the Third Group of the Fourth Brigade. You get your pay in this Third Group, share the same dormitory, and also eat with this group. Everything is the same as the others. The only difference is your job. You will have to cut the hair not only of the 200 people in your brigade but also of those who work at the headquarters."

"How far is it from here?"

"About thirty *li*, I think. A new set of tools is waiting for you there now."

Well, thirty *li* wasn't too far. Walking at normal speed, I could easily reach my destination within four or five hours. Apart from bedding and several tattered clothes, I had only my portable typewriter and two thick dictionaries left to carry along. Before I took my leave, the general brigade leader told me to follow the red marks made by the Kunming Railway Bureau's surveyors; then he drew a rough map on the ground.

"Yes, yes," I repeated. "You can be sure that my mouth is all right. I can ask people. You may trust me. I'll get there safely."

I said goodbye to all the members of my group. Since the Fourth Brigade was stationed close to our headquarters, everybody envied my transfer. They thought living conditions there would surely be better. Many asked me to buy something sweet for them.

One kindly cook secretly gave me two bowlfuls of cold rice wrapped up carefully in a piece of newspaper. I was particularly touched by his farewell gift. During that period the question of eating was of top importance in our daily lives. It was said that in the villages a spoonful of rice was now more precious than the most efficacious medicine.

The sun had just risen when I turned back to have a last look at our half-built sheds. At first I tried to follow the general brigade leader's advice, but because I was carrying my personal belongings on my back it was impossible to chase those painted red figures through the trees and bushes. I had the cold rice in my bag, so I wouldn't go hungry if I missed the most direct route. I was a newcomer. I didn't think the Fourth Brigade would organize a meeting to struggle me.

I got lost at noontime. While I was having a rest under a pine tree, two girls suddenly appeared. I thought they were looking for firewood, but the bamboo basket they carried was a very small one.

"Comrade, are you from the railway line?" one of the girls asked.

"Yes, I am a railway worker."

"Great! They say railway workers have too much rice to eat. If they cannot finish their rice at a meal, they just throw it away. Is this true?"

"Who told you that? I never heard of it."

"Well, tomorrow we will climb over that mountain and go to collect some rice or something else to eat."

"You were fooled. I myself just came from there. There's nothing, absolutely nothing." I looked at her basket and asked, "By the way, are you collecting mushrooms?"

"Mushrooms? Funny!" the girl smiled. "Where can you find mushrooms on a winter's day?"

"Oh yes! Mushrooms grow only in the rainy season. But what's that in your basket?"

"Why, don't you know?" the girl was surprised. "It has many names. Here we call it pine-tree-tip flowers. Actually they do not look like flowers, but people select them only from the tops of young pine trees."

"What for?"

"Well, we take them home, dry them in the sun, and bake them in the fire. Later, we mix them with other things and eat them."

"Eat? Very good to eat?"

"Not so good to eat. But when we can't get enough from the village's big pot, this mixture seems okay."

Further on I met another group of boys and girls. Some of them were digging up the roots of unknown plants. Some were collecting the leaves of a kind of wild vegetable. At lunchtime I came upon a small three-household village next to the road. I entered, hoping to find a fire and then eat my rice with hot water. Not a domestic animal could be found near those houses. Two of the three gates were locked. I walked through the third and quietly entered a room.

A seventyish old man stood up as soon as I came in the door. He looked at my typewriter box and said, "Welcome, comrade. Sit down. We have been waiting for your arrival."

"Waiting for me?" I wondered. "Have you eaten?"

"Not yet. My grandchildren will bring the lunch back soon. She is running a fever this morning. I'm afraid she's going home."

"Oh, Uncle, I'm sorry. I dropped in to ask for a cup of hot water."

The old man looked disappointed. "I thought you were our commune's village doctor."

"No, no. This isn't a doctor's medical box. It's a writing machine."

The grandmother was sleeping inside. As I was about to start making a fire, two children came in. Immediately the old man asked them, "What did they give you today?"

"Watery porridge, pumpkin soup, just the same thing," answered the boy.

"Let me see." The old man took the bowl. "Oh, false porridge! I can hardly see any rice in it. More than half is potatoes and beans. The quantity seems larger, though."

"No, grandpa. The same spoon, the same quantity. We told them you were not feeling well, too weak to go down and eat there. So they finally agreed to let us take yours home."

The two children had eaten their share at the village, but again they ate half the food they had brought for the old couple. All that remained for the two old people's lunch was a little soup. I gave half of my rice to them. The old man was touched. He said, "It's very kind of you. I haven't seen a bowl of pure rice for a long, long time. May God protect you all the year round!"

At about five o'clock I came to a small village at the foot of a hill. My Fourth Brigade was stationed to the north of this village, and our railway headquarters office was located in a temple to the south. I went south to report at the office and ate a hurried supper in their dining room; then a blue-uniformed man took me to see the Fourth Brigade leader. Without delay I was introduced to the Third Group.

The whistle for evening group discussions had already been blown before I finished setting up my bed. That first evening I sat between two groups, listening to both. My group was discussing a "group self-reform pact." The group leader read a few sentences from his notebook and then asked all the group members for comments. Another man, secretary to the group, wrote down what the others said. They sat around a burning fire, talking reasonably.

Our neighboring group also sat around a warm fire, but they were shouting at a young man who was made to stand straight in the middle, very close to the fire. They put out dozens of questions for him to explain: "Why did you sing a love song?" "Why didn't you listen when the group leader was reading an article from the newspaper?" "Why did you refuse to tell anyone how much money you had in your pocket?" "Why don't you speak at group meetings but gossip a lot when we are working?" Yet the young man didn't move or speak.

Before my group meeting ended, all the members signed their names. Each person was to copy the pact into his own notebook and learn it by heart. The pact began with these words: "We are broken brass and rusty things of society. The Party headed by Chairman Mao is our great Savior. Under his brilliant leadership we believe each one of us can reform ourselves to become useful men. In order to take away our caps at an earlier date, we have made up our minds to carry out the following points: Never return from work unless our fixed job is completely finished; report our inner thought-activities to the general brigade leader once a week; say not a reactionary word; protect public property and waste not a grain; take the lead to criticize oneself first and seriously criticize others next; expose all wrongdoings and bad speeches; respect and help others; and never forget to contribute more good services to the people in order to become a qualified citizen in the not too distant future."

Well, my group seemed not so bad. I had a corner in a dormitory shed to sleep in. The living conditions and food seemed neither better nor worse than those I had left behind. Anyway, good or bad, this was to be my new home.

**NOTES**

1. The Chinese unit of currency is the *yuan*. There are ten *jiao* to the *yuan*, ten *fen* to the *jiao*. In most provinces the term *mao* is used instead of *jiao*, but the Yunnanese prefer the latter and hardly ever use *mao*.

2. *Jin:* One *jin* equals about half a kilogram (1.1 pounds).

3. The background to this movement was the Great Leap Forward of 1958, an economic, political, and social program designed to increase industrial and agricultural production on a vast scale within a few short years. Throughout the countryside People's Communes were established in which land, tools, and livestock became the collective property of the communes. Henceforth, all peasants were to work on the communal land and eat at the communal canteen.

4. Also as part of the Great Leap Forward, a call went out to double the output of steel, the "marshal" of industry, in one year. A campaign was launched to establish "backyard" iron and steel furnaces in every collective unit.

5. Estimates vary from 20 to 30 million.

# 6

# A BIG MEETING FOR TAKING OFF RIGHTIST CAPS

**O**n my second day at the Fourth Brigade, I restarted my job as a barber. I didn't much like cutting hair, but when I compared myself with other victims of the movement, I felt very fortunate. I was given a white uniform. I was the only person allowed to travel from this group to that. I could enter the kitchen and enjoy a cup of hot water whenever I liked. The top officials at headquarters also asked me to cut their hair. Sometimes I was allowed to eat a meal at the headquarters canteen. I didn't have a Sunday, but I had plenty of time to rest. I could go and read newspapers for a while at the headquarters reading room. "Cut two more heads? Or shall I stop now?" It was up to me. I was free to arrange my daily life all by myself.

Wherever I went to cut they called me "Master Zhang." As soon as I took up the clippers, a cup of tea was placed beside me. When I had finished, they gave me a cigarette. My reputation as a master barber spread. Under an agreement made by the leading officials at headquarters, I was instructed to offer my services twice a month in the nearby village. An old lady came to invite me to cut her one-month-old grandson's hair. In return she gave me two sweet eggs. A rare treat. Another young man asked me to cut his hair the day before he and his bride went to register at their commune's marriage office. Later, they invited me to join their simple wedding party.

One customer I shall never forget was the man who slept in the bed next to mine. He was sent to reform himself two weeks after my arrival at the Fourth Brigade. While I was cutting his hair he told me the reason he had been forced to join us: "One day I was working on my private land, trying to find out why so many of the young corn sprouts were dying. I scratched with my fingers and dug out some of the corn-plant roots. I found that the sprouts died because worms came to eat the new roots under the earth. I collected some corn sprout remains, planning to give them to my hen to eat. I had only one hen left. Now the private plots in our village are all linked together. It happened that at the very moment I was gathering up my dead sprout remains, my neighbor came along. I hadn't touched her dying corn sprouts, but she said it was I who had damaged them. We have always hated each other. So she rushed to see the village head, and as she was reporting she added some more false details. My secret hen was found. All because I wanted to keep one hen at home I was labeled a production-saboteur. I had offended the village head and so one day I was sent here to reform myself."

"You didn't eat supper the day before yesterday. And I noticed you were sleepless last night. Was that the cause?"

"No, misfortunes followed one after the other," he sighed. Then he told me his second sad story: "I was the breadwinner of the family. At home I have a mother, wife, and two children. The biggest one is eleven. The young boy was only two years and four months old. After I came here my mother and wife could hardly maintain the family, and we often went hungry. One afternoon my wife carried the younger child on her back and went to the next village to see her mother, all because she wanted to get something to eat. Her family was not so rich either, almost the same as we were. She ate a meal there, nothing but vegetables. Her mother gave her some potatoes to take home.

"Well, a few potatoes were not enough for four people to live on for several days. It was very late when my wife and the young child set out for home. On her way she passed our village school, and remembered the plot of wheat the teachers had planted at the back of their classroom building. Every day the school arranged for two men to watch their wheat, but those two men were nowhere to be seen that night. She put the child down and, taking a scarf in her hand, went to steal their wheat ears. Alas, while she was grappling with the wheat, she suddenly heard a scream. Grasping her scarf she rushed back, but the child was nowhere to be seen. A wolf had taken him. She ran about in the field. There was no moonlight that night. Someone in the school eventually came out and organized several men to run after the wolf, but it was too late. All they got back was a cap and a pair of shoes."

*         *         *

One day I was instructed to meet the wife of an official who worked in our headquarters office at the nearest railway station. In my pocket I had the 10 *yuan* Qiyan had given me and some grain coupons.[1] I had planned to treat myself and enjoy a big meal, but to my surprise I found I couldn't buy anything in the restaurant. The lady server returned my grain coupon and said, "Sorry, sir. You must show me your other certificate to prove you are now traveling from place to place on official business. I cannot sell any cakes, buns, or anything connected with grain unless I see this certificate first. It's a new law."

So instead of a treat I went hungry!

Two hours after that, the lady I had been waiting to meet got down from the train. She had one of these new "traveling passenger's certificates."

Within five minutes she happily came out of the restaurant with eight steamed buns wrapped up in her handkerchief. She sat down in front of the restaurant entrance while I went to buy some water.

Strange! The official's wife suddenly began running after an old woman. I followed, running hard. Instead of the eight hot buns in her hand she now held a most beautiful new silk quilt. A wonderful dragon was embroidered on one side—a very expensive quilt from Hunan Province. I took the quilt and caught up with the old woman at the other end of the station. The woman knelt down on the ground and kept saying, in a painful tone of voice, "Gentleman, please have pity on me. My highest official, please let me go." Her head knocked many times on the ground. "That quilt cover was sent from Hunan Province two years ago. My husband worked there. A hundred times more expensive than your eight steamed buns. At this critical moment my young grandson's life is more precious than anything in the world. You see, grain coupons, I have many; but they demanded another note. I am a local woman here. Where can I get a traveling permit? My only grandson will go to the West if I do not produce something for him to eat."

I turned back to search for the young lady. I saw her waving, but couldn't make out what she wanted me to do. That poor old woman was nowhere to be seen when I turned back.

"Don't be sad, young man," the official's wife said as she came up to me. "Did she tell you her name and where she lives?"

"She escaped the moment I turned back to find you. I can return your grain coupons and the money. Her quilt is beautiful and special, but you cannot eat it."

"Oh, forget about it. You see, there we lost some buns but here we received a beautiful quilt in return. A good bargain we have made!"

\*         \*         \*

The question of eating kept on causing trouble. Thefts occurred one after the other. And more than ten of the younger men ran away after we went to bed or while we were working outside. The number of these deserters increased each week. A company of blue-uniformed railway security policemen arrived. With a view to preventing people from running away, two important measures were declared: (1) While working outside, when there is a break, we have to sit in a circle. Late at night, if someone needs the toilet, he has to call another two people to accompany him and then ask a blue-uniformed policeman as well. (2) Each group has to elect a special secretary. All of us have to open our boxes, bags, and pockets. We have to write down everything we own, even down to our toothbrushes. Nobody is allowed to keep his own valuables, including cash. All such valuables have to be handed in to the group secretary. If you need anything, you have to ask the general brigade leader's permission.

For myself, I handed in my typewriter, my dictionaries, a watch, two fountain pens, and several hundred of our nation's construction bonds. Qiyan's 10 *yuan* and some remaining grain coupons I hid in my underwear, sewn inside.

One windy night in March, a big fire broke out in our sheds. Nobody knew how it started. The guard whistled. In a flash all the people ran out. There was no fire brigade in the countryside and no river or pond nearby. The sparks flew off in all directions. Flames lit up the sky. We were all forced at gunpoint to stand in a circle. The property of two hundred people was burned into a heap of ashes. At dawn, four men were found burned to death in their beds. The next afternoon, when the roll was called, a further seven were found to have deserted.

A rescue party arrived from Kunming on the third day. Each of us received a new quilt. We were also given some sugar, but the quantity was limited to only two or three spoonfuls each. As to our personal belongings, including the valuables we had turned over to the group secretary, nobody said a word. That was the end of my old typewriter and my dictionaries. From that time on, I had nothing more about me in connection with the study of English. At least I had run out wearing my underwear—with Qiyan's 10 *yuan* and the grain coupons still safely sewn inside. With that money I bought a jacket, a pair of trousers, and a pair of shoes, all secondhand things. That was the extent of my personal property after the fire tragedy.

More and more blue-uniformed policemen arrived in our Fourth Brigade. Every day, right after the sun went down, no one was allowed to go outside our sheds. Formerly, I had been particularly independent in my daily life. But after the fire, I had to do whatever my group was ordered to do—sometimes cutting trees and grass, sometimes carrying stones, sometimes digging the earth or carrying firewood.

Upon hearing of my losses, Qiyan sent me a bedsheet and some clothes. I felt puzzled because her letter contained only a few sentences:

> *My father is not feeling well recently. I am planning to ask the school for a transfer to Guangdong Province. Immediately write a denial relating to the false report you were forced to make up at the factory's study class. Do this right away. The quicker the better. Always keep your mouth shut but never forget to keep your ears and eyes open.*
>
> *Qiyan*

Very possibly she had learned some important news in Kunming. I did exactly as she said in her letter. After I handed my denial in to the head official at headquarters I thought I might be questioned. But my written denial was like a heavy stone, falling down into a deep sea. They didn't ask me anything at all.

\*       \*       \*

Maybe in late May or early June of that same year, another big change took place. One day we were told that the country's plan for building our railway line had been called off. Statistics showed that the coal in that area was not worth the building of an expensive railway line. For this reason, the Regional Railway Headquarters had to make a speedy plan to arrange new jobs for more than a thousand people.

Our Fourth Brigade was dispatched to work at the sixth pit of a coal mine called Kunming Siying Coal Mine, also located in Songming County. For several years now, all the miners at Siying Coal Mine had been real criminals, under the supervision of the Public Security Bureau. People classified it as a "labor-reform mine." But in 1961, the classification of Siying changed to "reeducation-through-labor-reform mine." More than half the original criminals were either released or sent to other labor-reform farms. A few of them kept on working there as before, but they had become legal citizens of the country. It was these old miners who taught us how to work in a mine pit.

In my homeland, Jianchuan County, "mine pit" meant "hell." A coal mine was seen as the home of dead ghosts who were under the rule of an underground-world god. Being a miner meant working with ghosts. When a day's work was over in a mine pit, a miner's face would be sooty and filthy. Anyway, it was considered a very dangerous, terrible job. But oddly enough, I enjoyed the change. We slept in a big dormitory. We ate three meals a day in a dining hall. We could buy things at a store. The local nearby villagers often came to sell their eggs or their private vegetables. If we succeeded in producing more coal for the country, they added a little more money to our basic salary of 25 *yuan* a month. We saw free films once a month and opera performances on special festival days.

In each pit we were divided into three eight-hour shifts, working around the clock. The night shift was given an extra cake to eat. We rotated shifts three times a month. Each shift, in turn, was divided into several groups: Some dug coal, some repaired the tunnels, some pushed carts, some moved the coal with bamboo baskets. I did all of these jobs while working there, but for the longest time I was ordered to repair the planks that lined the ceilings in the underground tunnels. Life inside the mountain was really very uncomfortable. We were given a free piece of soap each week, as we did indeed emerge covered in soot.

One day in August, the whole mine stopped working. We were told nothing but "Everybody must go to a meeting today. It's going to be a very big meeting, very, very important." Most of us thought, "Possibly they are going to arrest some wrongdoers." After breakfast we all walked over to the fifth pit. That morning more than a thousand reeducation-through-labor people gathered there. As soon as we saw the red decorated platform and the big-character slogans, we knew it was a "good-news" meeting. We soon discovered that it was "A Big Meeting for Taking Off Rightist Caps"!

"I don't think the number is going to be a big one," many whispered. "At most ten." I thought, "We have at least a thousand rightists and all sorts of bad elements in this mine. Ten people once in a 365-day year. Dear me, I will have to wait for many, many years before my turn comes. ..."

The head of the mine delivered a long report. Several four-wheel top officials from Kunming spoke one after the other.[2] Then another important man opened up a red-paper packet containing a name list and read out, one by one, the names of those whose cap had been taken off. He began with the first pit and gradually worked up to our sixth pit.

After he began announcing the names I felt happier, because the number was above our expectation, many times bigger than ten. But for myself I was still not very optimistic. As soon as a name was heard from the loudspeaker, many people began to talk and comment. It was very noisy. I heard a name that sounded like mine, but I wasn't sure. A cigarette hit me. Another person threw a piece of candy at my head. Finally those who sat around me shook my hands. "Congratulations! You must buy a sack of sweets and invite us to eat your 'take-off-cap' candy!" I returned a smile to each of them, but in my heart I only half believed.

It took almost half an hour to read out the names of the lucky 200 people. After they had finished, a familiar important official from our sixth pit rushed up. In his hand he waved a piece of paper. As he passed by I pointed to my face. The man nodded and smiled, "Yes, yes, you too!"

We "capless" people were called upon to line up on the platform. Each of us had a big red-paper flower pinned onto our chests. Thousands of firecrackers were set off. More than a thousand people clapped their hands to greet us as we came down from the platform. As we walked we shouted, "Thank the Communist Party of China! Thank the people!" The others shouted, "Long live Chairman Mao! Long live the People's Republic of China! Learn from the people whose caps have been taken off! Let's increase our production and work harder to take our caps off earlier!"

The man who had read out the names finally ended the rally with the following words: "Congratulations! All these, for a time, were anti-Party people. However, that is a thing of the past. We Communists judge a man not from his dirty history but from his present behavior. Concrete statistics and practical actions show that these 200 people have been reforming themselves very well during the past three years. They have set model examples for the rest to learn from. We have spent more than a year reexamining their past history and conducting a series of careful on-the-spot investigations. According to our new policies, they are now fully qualified to throw away their caps. This decision has been formally approved by the highest authorities of our Yunnan Province. From now on, they are true citizens of our country. It's up to them: Leave for their home counties or stay on here as ordinary miners."

I wrote two letters, one to my brother and one to Qiyan. Qiyan's reply came first, but it was not very long:

> *After learning of a recent report, everybody in Kunming knows the present situation in our country has changed. Some more changes will follow. However, there's no clear indication of what's going to happen in the near future. I'll let you know as soon as I hear anything significant. For the time being, the most important thing is not to be too anxious to leave the coal mine. You must consider the long-term view. In order to offer more service to our country and lead a happier life in the distant future, you must bear some temporary hardships at present. Just be patient and stay on at the mine and wait for luck. If you do things in a hurry, you will spoil your future. Just wait, wait, hope, and hope quietly. Sooner or later there will be a day for us to meet again.*
>
> *Qiyan*

This letter was short, but each word was heavy with meaning. Reading between the lines I could see she was telling me something very important: Possibly all rightists and other bad elements would be allowed to return to their original work. If I went home, I might miss the chance to go back to my work unit in Kunming.

The second letter came from my brother and an aunt. My brother described many things about my divorced wife Guihua. He also told me the sad news that my mother had passed away in 1960. He wanted me to give up my job as a miner. My aunt's letter was shorter. She said nothing but "Come back, come back, and again, come back."

You see, one wanted me to stay and the other two from home wanted me to return to my village at once. Two roads for me to select, but which road was wider and brighter? Which road would lead to my happiness? My old aunt now took the place of my mother, but she was an uneducated village woman. My brother had received an education, but he wasn't living in a big city. Of the three, I thought Qiyan's suggestion was the best. She knew many things of the world. In the end, I made up my mind to stay on quietly at the coal mine for some time.

Half a year passed. My dirty cap had been taken away and I had become an ordinary miner of the country, but the name of my coal mine didn't sound so good: The whole society still looked down on people who worked in Siying Coal Mine. In April 1962 I wrote another letter to Qiyan. She didn't reply. I wrote again in May—but, again, no reply. It seemed as if I had lost everything on earth. Should I stay on at the coal mine? No! The situation had changed. My previous motto—See more and wait for a while—was no longer valid. A country always changes its policies. So it is with a person. I would be sorry if I didn't change my personal policies in time. Time is money, as the English proverb goes. I was over thirty. I had no wife, no children, no parents, no friends. For me, time was not just ordinary money but gold, yellow gold.

In this way, a new policy was made. I decided to say goodbye to the coal mine and—go home.

\* \* \*

I left Siying Coal Mine in June 1962. I planned to have a short stay in Kunming and then go home directly. The moment I got off the train I rushed to see Qiyan at her middle school. The gatekeeper was the same old woman who had cut the apple for us several years before. I was desperately disappointed when she told me that Qiyan had already gone back to her home province of Guangdong. The old woman gatekeeper took me to her house and pulled out a dusty cardboard box from under her bed. "It's yours," she said. "On the eve of her departure Teacher Wu brought it here to keep until you came. She said that you had told her to collect three boxes, but two of them were missing when she went to see the man at your former organization. Someone had stolen them away."

Yes, someone had stolen most of my books right after I was forced into that jeep. However, I was grateful to Qiyan. She had kept a few book seeds for me.[3] What was more, I found Guihua's goodbye gift, the embroidered pillowcase, tucked away among the things in the box. But Qiyan was nowhere to be found in Kunming. At midnight I turned on the light in my little hotel room and read my brother's letter once again:

> **Dear Younger Brother,**
>
> People said you had died on a farm, but now we are happy to hear you are still living in the world. They have taken your cap away. That is good news for us all.
>
> Elder sister passed away in 1959. Mother followed early in 1960.[4] We have had a hard time all these years, but on the whole, we are all right. Our remaining sisters are fine, and everybody welcomes you home. Uncle Li also welcomes you.[5] Guihua in particular is getting excited. I guess she is waiting eagerly for your early return.
>
> By the way, all these years we were in the dark as to the real truth about your relationship with Guihua. One year they told us you were divorced in Kunming. The next year they said you didn't do that. We also heard many rumors about Guihua. She herself didn't tell us the truth. Even her own father couldn't make it all out. It remains a puzzle.
>
> You might be surprised to hear that Guihua is not the same Guihua as before. She is no longer a backward village girl, but an advanced medical worker. She is in fact something like a highly qualified nurse or a doctor, especially in the countryside. She often comes to our house and asks about you. We ourselves do not know the truth, so we cannot say much. If you are still single, you had better hurry back—the earlier the better. I am afraid she is going away to study somewhere for

*a long time. But if you have married another girl, you bring her home. We will*
*welcome her just the same. Come back earlier and settle your marriage earlier. You*
*are not so young now.*

*Elder Brother*

For the whole night I couldn't close my eyes. I began to imagine my life in Jianchuan and fancy everything in the countryside. My future in my home village wouldn't be a good one. Formerly a college student, now forced to return home to shoulder a hoe—with a stain on my character. And what about Guihua? Formerly an illiterate village girl, now described by my brother as an "advanced medical worker"! I simply didn't know how to face her. She was flying higher and higher up into the beautiful sky while I was crawling further and further down into hell.

My father had once said, "East, west, home is best!" In my case, I didn't think home was best. But after all, what else could I do? Kunming had changed. More buildings, more beautiful parks, but I had no share. There were thousands of people walking in the streets, but nobody knew me. My old dean, Mr. Chen, had also been criticized in the movement and was powerless to help me in any way. What organization would like to offer me a job? There was only one way left open—to return home and struggle with the earth.

After paying a goodbye visit to Mr. Chen, I bought a ticket for home and returned to my hotel room. The next morning I got up early and went downstairs to have a quick breakfast. I forgot to lock my room. While I was gone, a heartless thief seized the opportunity to steal two of my traveling bags, including my ticket. The thief left the biggest bag for me, containing my quilt and Guihua's pillowcase. I fell down on the bag then and there. The girl in charge of my room came in at last. She suggested I see a policeman, then helped me up. I followed her slowly, carrying my quilt. All of a sudden I fell down and tumbled from the top stair, over and over, down to the very last.

When I was able to open my eyes again I found myself in a hospital bed. On the third day after that accident I recognized the man standing next to my bed as Mr. Chen. On the fourth day, Mrs. Chen and two elderly women came to see me. They brought with them sugar, money, and clothes. I refused to accept, because I couldn't recall who those two elderly women were.

"Xiao Zhang," one of them called first. "Do you remember Miss Xue of Shanghai, your middle-school English teacher?"

"Oh ... it's you, Aunt Li." My tears ran down. I couldn't speak. It was too painful in my heart. I suddenly remembered many things from the past.

"The best student of Xue. She said he was most promising and loved him very much," Miss Xue's former housekeeper said.

"Yes, I knew him at Professor Wu's house. At the college, Professor Wu's daughter meant to marry him. But now everything has changed."

As soon as the other woman mentioned Professor Wu I remembered that she had been the Wus' cook for many years.

I spent two weeks in the hospital bed and another week at the Chens. Had it not been for these two women and Mr. and Mrs. Chen's loving care, I would have died in Kunming, or at least would have become a beggar in the streets of that city. They cared for me, nursed me, and finally bought me a ticket for home.

## NOTES

1. Grain coupons are issued by the government as a means of rationing rice and wheat. Peasants are not entitled to grain coupons, as they are supposed to get grain directly from their own commune. In order to buy rice or wheat from a government grain shop, a person must produce a grain coupon. This used to be the case with restaurants as well, but since the early eighties customers can choose either to use grain coupons or to pay a little extra for rice and buns.

2. *Four wheel:* The officials came by car.

3. *Book seeds:* Here Mr. He means that the books will provide a means (albeit a modest one) from which his former learning can grow once again.

4. Both his elder sister and mother died of "hunger and the swelling sickness." Mr. He explains, "After my real oldest sister died, my adopted sister took her place; and everybody in the village recognizes her as the oldest daughter of our family."

5. *Uncle Li:* Guihua's father.

# PART TWO

# 7

# A BROKEN MIRROR
# GOES UNREPAIRED

After eighteen years of absence I arrived back in my homeland, Jianchuan County. In 1944 it had taken four days on foot from my home village to Xiaguan, and then another four days by charcoal truck to Kunming. By 1962 the time had been shortened to two days and five hours on a public bus. Toward the end of my homeward journey I was greatly surprised to see that the new, highway-like road extended right to our county's capital town, Jinghuazheng. Somehow I never expected to see these modern changes in my out-of-the-way Jianchuan.

I got off at the bus stop nearest my village. I felt nervous, sad, happy. I was happy to be in my native place. Happy, too, that despite all my sufferings I was still alive and healthy. I could work with my two hands and legs. But some feudal thoughts made me feel sad. When people leave home to work for a long time in a faraway place they are supposed to "Go out empty-handed but return with a fortune." True, I had gained a title: Big-School Student. But that was useless. In my pocket I had only a few *yuan*. My luggage was light. I had been punished on a thought-reform farm. Anyway, I was back where I had started.

My home village was four or five *li* from the bus station. I remembered that my great-aunt's family lived nearby. My great-aunt had died quite some time before, but her son and daughter-in-law still lived in the old house. They didn't recognize me when I first entered their gate. We stood face to face for a little while, smiling and exchanging a few words. I left most of my luggage at their house and walked on toward my home village alone. I met several people along the way, but all were strangers.

In the distance I could hear the loudspeaker's voice coming from my village. I remembered that in 1942 or 1943 my father had bought a secondhand phonograph. At that time it was just a mysterious wonder. People called it a "foreigner's singing machine." Everybody from far and wide came to see and hear it. Today people enjoyed a loudspeaker in the fields. Formerly, when I was young, only the rich in town could buy a box of matches. Ordinary villagers had heard about a match-fire, but none of them could afford to buy a box. We were said to be among the rich, yet we never bought a box of machine-made matches. As soon as a meal was over, we covered our "fire seed" with some ashes to keep it smoldering. When we smoked, we lit our cigarettes with a spark produced by two little stones. But today I saw many young people smoking cigarettes and using *lighters.*

I stood still for a while, observing my village. Beside the river, the wooden water wheel that used to turn two huge wheel-like stones in our flour-grinding mill was nowhere to be seen. The villagers had begun to use a machine-run grinder. At the edge of the village, an ancient temple had become a small factory. And straw-roofed houses were disappearing.

Suddenly a bicycle rider approached. "Hello, Xiao Shu, can you recognize me?" the rider stopped to ask. "I met your great-aunt's daughter-in-law in town. She told me the news of your return."

"Sorry, too long to recall everything exactly." I tried and tried, but really couldn't recognize him.

"Let me see your right hand. Is the scar still on that finger?" The man pulled my right hand toward him and then pointed to a nearby wall: "Today the peach tree built into that wall has disappeared, but the wall remains the same. Just think, who gave you first-aid after you and me climbed over it?"

"Oh, I remember now. Uncle Wang gave me the medicine. Are you Xiao Wang Fu?"

"That's right. I am Wang Fu!" He patted me and offered a cigarette.

Xiao Wang Fu began to relate his own story. He had studied for only one year in our county's middle school. Since his father had once been made a model farmer, he had seized this golden opportunity to become a postman. After two years of postal service he was recommended to join a short-term class in Kunming. Here he was trained to use a projector. Half a year later he became a member of the county's film projection unit. Now he had been promoted to head of a film projection team. Finally he said proudly, "My room in town is No. 24. You are welcome to visit me and see all the films for free. As soon as you mention my name they will let you in."

"Thank you very much. ... Do you remember once we took a blanket and went to see an open-air *silent* film?"

"Yes, as Chairman Mao teaches us, we must never forget our bitter past. How funny to think of that. Do you remember, in that silent film we saw a group of horses racing toward the audience. Everybody ran in four directions and we lost the blanket and had to return to find it later. It was already dawn when we got back to our village! Ha, ha!"

"And now you are a *sound*-film worker. Great, isn't it?"

"Yes, without Chairman Mao and our Party how could I have become a sound-film worker? Everybody has changed, but still nobody can reach your big-school level. Your doctor-wife is Number One in our village."

I knew whom he meant. I was just going to explain my bitter story when Wang Fu put in, "By the way, did you meet her on the way? She has been waiting for you for many, many days. The whole village knows that."

"No, Wang Fu. Let me tell you the truth. Our mirror broke a long time ago in Kunming."

Fortunately, at that moment my elder brother came up to meet me. I said goodbye to Wang Fu and followed my brother. I longed for a cup of cold water from our well, and for a rest under the pomegranate tree that grew beside the well. So I ran ahead. As I was about to step past our main gate, my brother pulled me back.

"It's been a long time," I said, "but I can still remember in which direction our house faces."

"My young brother, you forget this is 1962. After the Land Reform Movement, that is no longer ours." My brother whispered the word "ours." "Three poor peasant families live there now. We must go in at the small side door."

"But our great-grandfather's grandfather built it. ..."

My brother silenced me and led the way to a small wheat-straw-roofed house, once used as an animal shed, standing to the east of our old house. That evening, many villagers came to visit me there. The next day all my four sisters and other close relatives gathered. They pitied me very much, so they came to see me and sit near me and around me. We talked for two or three days, for hours at a time, deep into the night. Oh, I had too many questions to answer. They also related many land-reform-time tales. We wept as we spoke because the stories from my mouth and from theirs were bitter and sad.

While I was living in Kunming, I often read articles which said that we must not confuse the "landlords themselves" with the "children of the landlords." The nation's policy was to treat the children of landlords just like other ordinary people's children. But when I returned to my birthplace I saw with my own eyes how terribly my family had suffered, all because they were the children of a "landlord." After our house and most of our land had been confiscated, all that remained for our family was the little house my brother now lived in and a tiny plot of land. It was not nearly enough to house and feed the remaining members of my family.

My poor sisters! At the time of the Land Reform Movement three of them were old enough to marry. However, people from all walks of life had begun avoiding landlord families. In the countryside, people always say, "It doesn't matter if a man gets married early or late. But this is not the case with a girl. As soon as a girl is old enough to marry, the parents have to settle her marriage problem." My sisters were growing bigger and taller every day. And besides, our land couldn't support them. No food at home. Finally, the three eldest married, not because they loved the boys but because they wanted to survive, and especially because they wanted to let my mother lead an easier life at home. Of course my mother got not a single penny in dowry money. Everything was carried out in the simplest way. My three sisters looked like mourners following a funeral procession at their weddings.

My youngest sister hadn't yet married. I found her living with my brother and his wife and son when I returned home. In a way, he treated her like a servant. Shortly after my homecoming someone came to propose marriage to her, but my older brother wouldn't allow her to go. He said, "You just wait for some time until I find a girl to be my son's wife." He wanted to see how much money he would have to pay to get a wife for his son, and then make my sister's suitor pay the same amount for her.

All my sisters were earthrepairers. They had to shoulder a hoe every day. What else could poor, uneducated Bai women do?

My main trouble was that I had returned poor. Money, money! Formerly I used to say "Money is not everything," but now it seemed a little money could do a lot, and I had not a farthing in my pocket. As the days went by and my elder brother discovered I was penniless, he became cold toward me. He allowed me to use one room in his house, and for this I was grateful, but he had no mind to genuinely share with me what little he had.

*          *          *

My sisters returned to their homes. My former divorced wife Guihua had left for Kunming several days before my return. I was happy about that. On perhaps the sixth or seventh day, Uncle Li invited me to spend a day at his house.

"Welcome home!" The old man grasped my shoulders. "Let me have a good look at you. Yes, about twenty years, a little boy then, now taller."

"I'm sorry, Uncle Li."

"What did you call me just now?" The old man made a long face.

"My ears are getting too aged to hear things now. Will you please say it again?"

"Uncle Li, I'm very sorry," I repeated.

"Oh, you college student! I thought you would call me Father."[1]

"Didn't Guihua tell you what happened?"

"No, nobody could figure it out. She said this in the morning and that in the evening. It has been a difficult riddle for many years, but judging from her actions she is still yours."

"No, you are wrong, old man. She has been fooling you all these years. We were divorced in Kunming."

"Really?" he scratched his head.

Fearing that this news might make him change his attitude, I thought it best to leave. But before I could turn around he went on, "Well, anyway, we are still good neighbors. Let's go in and have a long chat today. I still doubt this news."

"No doubt at all, really. We were divorced formally, several years ago, in a court in Kunming."

"No doubt," he repeated after me. "All right, let me see your official document."

"Sorry, I put it in a little bag and it was stolen in a hotel room in Kunming. But we were divorced, a hundred reallies." I lifted my right hand and pointed first up, to Heaven, and then down, to Earth, then to the west, to our ancestors, and finally added, "Let the tiger eat me up within three days if I am not telling you the truth."

The old man didn't reply for a long time.

It was I who spoke first. "I feel awfully sorry. I have no face to see you here.[2] Please forgive me. Goodbye, Uncle."

"No, wait a minute." He ran after me and pushed me inside.

As I entered their house I was on the point of tears. "A college student. Yes, you knew that. You built great hopes on me. But you didn't know that I would fail to develop my abilities. The English I was taught at college has become a useless accomplishment. I have disappointed all of you. I don't want to spoil your daughter's future. Our divorce was for the best."

"Sit down, sit down." The old man patted my shoulder and showed me a chair. "Frankly speaking, some of the things my daughter said were not at all logical. Once she spoke sadly, telling us you had another college girl student. In a flash she chuckled. Many of us were confused."

"Oh, the thing is you still do not believe me!"

"All right. I take your words to be true. You were divorced. But why has Guihua refused one man after another? Well, some of them earn a big sum of money each month. Some of them have a high position in our county. How do you explain such mysteries?"

"Really?"

"All truth. You may go out and ask yourself. Anyway, for years and years she just said you were very kind."

"But did she tell you secretly at home—I mean, about our divorce?"

"No, I never heard the word 'divorce' from her mouth. All came from outside. That's why I want you to make things clear for me. Now you tell me with your own mouth, a divorce, it's unbelievable. What I'm going to show you is also quite convincing. A letter, written by Guihua on the eve of her departure for Kunming."

With these words, the old man rushed out and came back waving an envelope addressed to me. "She wanted me to hand this to you personally. She was very happy. She had been waiting for you for at least two weeks. She said all her wishes had come true one by one. She wanted me to get things ready and organize a special party to invite our friends and relatives to celebrate your return. I am a blind man; here, you read it."

"Is this her own handwriting?"

"Oh, you college students still look down on village girls today! My daughter Guihua is not walking with her own legs, but flying, flying like an airplane!"

I opened the letter and read:

*Dear Shuyi,*

*First, please recall the past, recall the year we were together in Kunming. We hated each other. We had words all the time. We divorced, but at last, we loved each other. Once again several years have come and gone, but we still have many years ahead. I respect you and love you with a pure heart, exactly the same way as before, but to tell the truth, I was wondering if you can still love me or not? I am dying to know this. The changes in the recent past have been so great. I hope your heart has not changed.*

*We were in a park, under a fir tree, do you remember? You said one day we would remarry if you really failed to use your English. At another time you said we might as well create a special little world of our own in the village. I remember I said, "Do trust me. I will keep your advice in mind and learn more new things at home. Certainly I will wait for you." Can you recall? This is what I want you to answer. I am getting anxious to make this out. It's a pity I cannot wait any longer.*

*Over two weeks ago I heard from your brother that you might be returning. The first week I told our village team head[3] I was feeling unwell. No news of your return. The second week I said my father was ill. Still nothing was heard. I was forced to lie. All because I wanted to see you before I left home. I wanted to talk to you face to face and heart to heart, so that I could make a final decision about my career. The task is different this time. I am going away for at least two years, to learn more. A special training class has been organized by a famous Kunming medical institute, directed by the highest authorities of the whole province. Their level is higher than any other class I have joined. The learners are mostly village doctors, or those who have given outstanding service in their hospitals. A difficult test was organized at which I was the only one who qualified from our Jianchuan County. Now they are hurrying me to go and begin the term.*

*Can I find another good opportunity like this? No. How come I was the only person—a woman, too!—to be selected? There are many reasons, but every success has its root. In this case, my success today goes back to the time we spent together in Kunming. Away from your care, without your help, I would have nothing to talk about. I could have done nothing.*

*When I returned to our village, people called me a funny name—Mrs. College Student. I used to say this: "Oh thank you. Thank the Communist Party." That year our county middle school had only one teacher of Russian. More than half of the pupils had to learn English, but there was no teacher for these boys and girls. Once one of them asked me, "Did he teach you English?"*

I scolded him, *"Oh, you silly boy! I am his wife. Of course he taught me
everything. Show me your textbook, let me teach you which is A and which is B, or
'Good morning.'"*

My reputation spread, and later some more boys and girls came to ask English
questions. Wasn't that funny?

The year before last, there came a working team from our county town.[4] One of
them asked, *"I have heard much about you. I just wonder why you didn't stay with
him but returned home?"*

Without delay I made him speechless: *"How can a government worker ask such
a question? Something must be wrong with your political level."*

*"Nothing wrong."*

*"No, your political level is not a progressive one."*

*"You are not a Party secretary. On what grounds are you teaching me a
political lesson?"*

*"But you must believe that the wife of a college student also knows much, knows
not only when to water and reap but also international issues of the world."*

*"Oh, the way you talk sounds just like our office head!"*

*"Stop joking! What is the slogan? Serve the people. We must contribute our best
according to out ability. I am a farmer. So my duty is to use my hoe and grow rice
to support the city workers in the factories. That's why I must return. To respond to
our nation's call. Is that right?"*

*"Yes, yes, reaping more rice in the countryside is also serving the people."*

*"Good! I hope you'll not forget Chairman Mao's teachings in the future."*

One day by chance at the village team head's home I discovered that their
sewing machine was broken. Not only did I repair the broken sewing machine, but
I also showed his wife how to make good use of her cloth and cut a more beautiful
dress for her little girl. Our team head was most impressed. Every year, after we
got in all the grain, he always came to invite me to help the team accountant add
up many figures. Formerly, the teacher of our village night school was so proud
that he never spoke to me. But when I returned from Kunming, he was all smiles
whenever I met him. He even asked me to deliver a report for his students to learn
from my experiences.

The whole village, old and young, all loved me. But what surprised them most of
all was that I could inject a baby. It often happened suddenly. When they failed to
find the village doctor, they came to me. And they were amazed to watch my swift
operations. *"Guihua's hands are lighter,"* they usually said.

It was very strange. In the city I was a silly country girl and, for that matter,
seemed not to have learned very much at all. Who would have thought that in our
village I'd suddenly become the cleverest, the most outstanding, not only in our
team but in the whole commune? Even the head of the county came to ask me
about my personal history and experiences.

Not too long after I returned, our village health worker got married and
followed her husband away. At a village general meeting, the village team head

*proposed that I take the health worker's place. The whole village readily agreed. A week later the County Health Center phoned and instructed me to attend a four-month training class in town. After that, I returned to our village to be the health worker.*

*It didn't last long, perhaps only a month. Then another girl came to take my job. Her official note said that I was to wait for some time. Nothing else. I thought I must have done something wrong, but soon I was called to join another meeting of medical workers. Then I was instructed to leave home and work in a distant commune's health center. Four months later I was instructed to receive a two-year training course in Dali County. Each time I went, I studied everything wholeheartedly and fulfilled each task to the best of my ability.*

*Well, dear Shuyi, matters in the world often connect together. We are not supposed to take this out and leave that alone. Referring to the foundation I had laid in Kunming, people said, "Truly, a college student's wife is not on the same level as other villagers." I got everything in Kunming. Who else could match my rapid success?*

*Coming back from Dali after almost three years of wide study, I was promoted to work in our commune hospital. People everywhere respect me. And I can buy everything I want in a flash. But in spite of this, I am very sad in my heart. The old man is my father, but he didn't show me a smiling face when I returned home. When I see a schoolchild greet his mother, or a mother play with her children somewhere, my heart hurts, as if a knife were cutting it. Whenever I see a young couple working in a field or having an after-supper walk together, I can only take out my purse and look at the picture we had taken in Kunming.*

*After my return it was too easy a thing to remarry, but I had to keep my promise. I wanted to be faithful and true to our love. You are welcome to ask what I've been saying and doing over the past several years. I never spoke a word against you. I didn't write a single line—I hope you don't mind—but I never forgot you. Each year I asked many people to get some information about you. I knew that for about one year you enjoyed yourself a great deal being a translator. I prayed for you to gain greater success in your work. I kept that quietly in my heart. Later, you were seriously criticized in the office and became a victim of the movement. I kept that bad news quietly as well. Then I learned you were punished and sent to a farm. One piece of bad news ran after the other.*

*I am very, very sorry I didn't tell the real truth. I lied even when my father asked. I knew what "divorce" meant. But although I agreed to sign my name, I never made it known to people at home. Instead, all these years, I have been acting just as if I were on a stage. Why, I really didn't care a bit about the divorce, because ours wasn't a true one. It was a temporary separation, a tactical retreat, with a view, an intention, to love each other more and more. On receiving our divorce document, we entered a department store. We had pictures taken. We went to see a film together. We ate meals at the same table. Did these facts indicate a* divorced couple? No! All I want is that you should not use the word "divorce" at all. If my father insists on asking this you just tell him, "No! It's a trick, a game!"

Let's get busy to piece our broken looking-glass into a beautiful whole again. Is it possible? Is there any hope to fix it once more? Are you still single? About this I am in the dark. Do tell me.

I am sorry I cannot wait for you any longer. I am afraid I shall be too late for my studies. It's a pity that this time the place is very far and the time very long. I'm not going to be able to come back for two or three years. So I ask you to write to me as soon as possible. The world today is turning every minute. Last time, you were in Kunming and I was waiting for you at home. And remember this: I have waited for you twice. The second time was shorter, but it has been more than five years already. Now I ask you to wait for me for three years at most. Then the time will be right for us to cooperate and create a little world of our own.

Now a word about home. Allow me to warn you: Don't trouble your brother to share any home property, no matter what kind. I am convinced you are a wise man. You are neither blind nor lame. You'll have to face a short period of difficulty, but it won't be for long. Don't think too much of the sad past; rather, look forward and plan something new for the future. Happiness belongs to a hardworking man. Whether or not we can remarry is still in the balance. Nevertheless, let me assure you, my father is the only man in the house, and I welcome you to come over. Bring everything of yours and stay with my father. Our home is also your home. You'll have a share of everything. If you are unable to repair the broken looking-glass with me, my father and I will still be happy to have you at our house. We will treat you as a brother of mine. Do believe that. My father and mother brought me up, but it was you who taught me to be a useful girl for the country, for my parents, and for myself.

Finally, never hesitate to let me know if there is anything I can do for you in Kunming. I look forward to hearing from you. Wishing you success in everything. Take care of yourself always.

**Guihua**

After I had read this long letter out loud, Guihua's father showed me a fountain pen kept carefully in a small cardboard box. It was the pen I had given Guihua as a goodbye gift.

The old man said, "She warned me to take good care of it and protect it. Oh," he sighed, "so many years now. What's the use of this pen, when. ..."

"You don't like it?"

"Well, how can I say like or don't like. The thing is, *when* will I see the *owner* of this pen?"

It was clear now. He wanted me to be his son-in-law and then give him a grandchild to be the master of that pen. However, I was in a state of meditation and answered him nothing.

"Go and bring your things over and stay with me right now!"

I still didn't answer him.

"Come on, I'll show you!" He pulled me up. "I don't have a lot, but I do have a little for each. See for yourself. All the containers are full to their necks. A very big pig, lots of hens, a sewing machine, a radio, the windows are all glass. Guihua bought me everything. She has made this house like a real modern house of today. But to tell you the truth, I don't like it. I am longing for a noisy home, not a cold, quiet home. I was born in this house, brought up here, and in the future I'll be buried somewhere near our village. Before I go to the West I want to be sure someone is going to take over my home. You know I have only two daughters. In the old society, people rejoiced when a boy was born but were angry if it was a girl. As a traditional rule, I should have arranged for the bigger one to get married and live in this house. But I didn't do that. She followed her husband away. But I insisted on keeping the second girl at home for you. I wanted Guihua and you to keep our home on and on.

"Time is marching forward. It is getting very late. But I believe God will pity me; generation after generation we have been kind to all. A late sower may become an early reaper. I remember Guihua once mentioned another saying of the English people which she learned from you in Kunming: Whatever we do, do it well in the beginning, and then it means the whole project is half done. As you see, Guihua had a very good beginning in Kunming, so, today, everything at home is half done. You must pay attention to the word 'half.' Now come over to this house and continue the next half."

"No, I can't," I replied firmly.

"Why?"

"Well, when children play, they usually each bring a toy of their own and enjoy together. What do I have?"

"Oh, yes, I forgot to ask you another question of vital importance. Now, after listening to the letter, I find out you suffered seriously in that historical movement. Too common a thing. I don't mind.[5] Any physical harm done to you?"

"I'm all right. Healthy!"

"Wonderful! Tell me, do you still have to put on a hat or a cap?"

"No more cap either, beginning from August 1961."

"If today you were still wearing a cap, then you would have to do their Three Musts and Eight Nos. You can do nothing if you have to obey those rules."

"It sounds interesting. I heard about many rules during the Land Reform Movement, but that movement ended a long time ago. What on earth are the Musts and Nos?"

"The Three Musts are: You must report when a visitor comes to see you; you must ask leave when you want to go out of the village; and you must tell the village team head again when the visitor leaves or when you have come back from somewhere. And the Eight Nos are: No smuggling; no stealing; no turning facts upside down; no rumor-mongering and no production sabotage; no harboring evildoers and covering up their evil deeds; no feudal or superstitious operations; no flattering government workers or the common masses; and, finally, no slacking off at work. They trouble you all the time, but you do not have a cap, so no need to let this worry us. You have grasped a high level of education. You know math, physics, from heaven to earth. A farmer's work in a field is much, much easier than those complicated sciences. You can do everything."

"Shall I dig the earth with my ten fingers? Oh, I'm too poor to buy even a hoe or a spade or a bamboo basket."

"Oh, silly. Over there in the corner, four or five hoes, all in good order. They are yours. Not only the hoes, all the other things in this house are yours. My time is up soon. I am getting on each passing day. I want you to come and be the man of the family. Go and tell your brother what we have been talking about. We two will prepare a big supper this very day, and be sure to invite your brother and ask all your sisters to come and celebrate. I welcome all your other relatives as well," the old man ended kindly.

Although I said I would go over and settle down in his house, in fact I didn't do that. The old man's offer was true and sincere, yet I had lost face to remarry his daughter. I was ashamed of myself, even hated myself. And also, as I thought about things, I considered that neither Guihua nor her father understood the political policies of our country as well as I did. Guihua didn't realize how my rightist past would ruin her career—no promotions, no more study courses, all sorts of roads would be closed to her. I didn't want to spoil her bright future with my landlord seal and rightist cap. So I decided to accept nothing from the old man.

### NOTES

1. Mr. He says, "In my native homeland the man always calls his wife's father 'Father.'"

2. *I have no face:* This phrase means "I am ashamed." But the idea of "face" is a subtle one in China. A person is "given face" when honored or respected. An insult or inappropriate behavior results in the "loss of face." Even circumstances beyond a person's control, as with Mr. He's victimization in the Anti-Rightist Movement, can result in "loss of face."

3. Communes were divided into brigades (*dadui*), and brigades, into teams (*xiaodui*). A team often encompassed a natural village; larger villages were divided into two, three, or even more teams. The size of brigades and communes varied tremendously from area to area; but generally speaking, brigades were made up of several vil-

lages, and communes, several tens of villages. For a peasant family, the most important unit was the team.

4. By "our county town" Guihua means Zhinghuazheng. Whenever Mr. He writes "in town" or "I went to town," he is referring to Zhinghuazheng.

5. Here Guihua's father means that he doesn't mind the loss of "face" and status resulting from Mr. He's victimization in the Anti-Rightist Movement.

# 8

# UNCONQUERABLE PROBLEMS
# LEAD TO MARRIAGE

**E**verything in the village had changed. My change was the worst! How to be a man, a useful man, a good man? How to greet a friend? How to treat a neighbor? How to start a conversation with a relative? How to reply to Guihua's letter? How to go back to square one and create a new life in the countryside? In the evenings, when I was left alone, I read that long letter again and again. "Let me go over to the old man's house," I thought to myself. But when I reached my door I seemed to hear, "What kind of man are you?" "Do you know the word 'shame?'" "Do you have a man's 'face'?" "Where is your personality?"

I told all my sad stories to my brother in full detail. Under his guidance, in order to avoid possible difficulties in the days ahead, I eventually made a firm decision—not to remarry Guihua. My decision would certainly hurt her feelings, but this time I had to let her know. I wrote the following letter:

*Dear Guihua,*

*Although I feel very sad while writing this letter to you, please allow me to extend my heartiest congratulations on your great success in medical work. I hope and believe that you will continue to gain greater achievements in our national reconstruction.*

*I shall never forget you. We were unforgettable playmates during childhood. Looking back on that year in Kunming, I only did what I should have done for you. The most important things, like your great achievements in medical services, are due to your own persistence and diligence. I am not worthy of being mentioned, not even one word.*

*Our year in Kunming remains in my mind as if it were yesterday. It's sweet to remember. I was touched to see the fountain pen at your house. Let me tell you, when I left Kunming for the reform farm most of my things were stolen, but not the box with that meaningful pillowcase you embroidered for me. Again, on my way home in a hotel, a thief stole two of my traveling bags. Fortunately, the pillowcase was in the third. So I still have it. Let's keep and protect these gifts as long as possible. Really, that year in Kunming was indeed a romantic page in my life.*

*A word about making a new home. I want to express my greatest gratitude to you and your father for your kindest care and concern. To piece together our broken looking-glass is a very good thing to want. Well, to say this with our lips is easy, but if we really start I am afraid there will be too many problems to solve. One of the most important and most inescapable problems is social pressure, which we might not be able to overcome in the end. You are an advanced medical worker of our country. Your history is as white as new snow. I am a peasant working at the lowest level. My history is as black as dogs' droppings. I am very sorry to have to tell you that I cannot move over to take care of the old man, share his things, and do the rest as you planned at home.*

*Don't be discouraged, though. Yes, I was once a college student, but I cannot match you now. The true college student is you, not me. The world today belongs to people like you. Pay more attention to your lessons and stop considering me. Both you and the old man are getting on. It is very important to consider your futures. Just remember this: Do it yourself. Do not ask me. Be quick. The sooner the better.*

*I can never forget your father's care and your persistent love. When I hear of your return, I'll certainly come to meet you again.*

*Shuyi*

A month went by. I fell into a melancholy state. I stopped eating or drinking. Soon I fell ill. First came the old man, Uncle Li, and a village doctor. Then my four sisters and my eldest sister's son followed, each carrying several everyday necessities—a bowl, a pail, a hoe. They made a simple wood-burning stove at the foot of my bed. Gathering these broken things together, I eventually succeeded in forming a poor home of my own in my one room.

I was born in the countryside, but I left the village as soon as I was able to learn to read and write. Therefore, I knew nothing about farm work. My middle-school days were spent in Kunming. And I didn't do any farm work even at the reform farm. My relatives had made everything ready so that I could begin an independent life in my village, yet there were so many difficulties to face every day.

Most of my time was spent working in the village communal fields. I was given a booklet in which to record my daily work points. Much of the work assigned by the team head had to be done collectively by a group of villagers. Nine times out of ten I was the last to get through with my share. I earned fewer work points than anyone else, including all the women. I was not a qualified farmer. The way I walked, dug the field, cut a tree, tied grass ... all were different from the other villagers. When we were having a break in the fields, the questions I asked them were funny to their ears. For these reasons, and also because I wore a pair of eyeglasses, wherever I happened to be, working in a field or walking down a lane, children would run after me, laugh at me, and make fun of me.

Besides the village communal fields, there were two types of privately owned land. The first was given formally by the team, according to the number of people in one's family.[1] The team government said it would organize a meeting to give my one-member family a share of formal private land, but I waited in vain for this meeting. The second type consisted of little parcels of land in remote corners that the peasants unofficially, secretly, cultivated. My brother had two plots of unofficial land, one at the back of our family tombs and another little piece carved out of a waste hill slope about seven *li* away. Under the pressure of my four sisters, he was forced to let me use a little portion of these two parcels of land. A neighbor gave me some corn, bean, and pumpkin seeds. After I had finished my work in the public fields, I dug and planted all by myself. But I miscalculated the time to pick, and when I went to harvest I discovered that others had stolen my vegetables away.

My aunt gave me a sheep, but this sheep brought me nothing but trouble. I couldn't tie her up at home all day long, so I took her out into the fields with me. If I dug or cut, the sheep would eat other people's plants. If I watched her, I couldn't work. Once my sheep ate some grass that a little girl had picked and placed on the ground. Her father would not allow me to take my sheep home. Finally, after I promised to let them cut her wool when winter came, he released her. In the end I returned the sheep to my aunt and she gave me a little money instead.

One of my sisters gave me two hens. I expected to get at least one egg a day, but when I returned home each evening I just couldn't find a thing. Each time a hen lays an egg she lets out a special egg-laying cluck which we all recognize in the countryside. As soon as the neighborhood children heard my hens clucking, they ran over to steal my eggs. I was a one-person family—there was no one at home to watch my hens while I was out working. I could do nothing.

Once I went up a hill with another villager to collect firewood. I didn't know how to manage an axe. In less than ten minutes the handle broke, causing the axe head to fly off and seriously hurt my leg. That day I was carried home by my neighbor. And I had more trouble finding another person to call a doctor.

But what upset me most was the unsorted, uncleaned grain that I received from the village production team as part of my annual pay for working on the communal fields. In the countryside the man's jobs are: to chop down trees on the mountainside for firewood, to plough with buffalo in the fields, to dig the land with a long-handled hoe. The woman's jobs are: to cut grass with a short-handled scythe, to patch the clothes, to cook, to plant the young rice seedlings, to separate the chaff from the grains. This last job is done by sweeping the grains up off the ground (and of course a lot of dirt gets swept up, too), then placing them into a round, flat bamboo basket, tossing them up and letting the wind blow away the chaff and dirty bits while the grains fall neatly back into the bamboo basket. The grains I received from the team were these swept-from-the-ground grains. I simply could *not* get the hang of making them jump up into the air to let the wind blow away the unwanted parts. I tossed, but most of the grains fell back not into the basket but onto the ground. I myself was covered in chaff, sand, and grass.

It sounds very funny, but really I couldn't stand it. After about four or five months, I stopped doing anything at all. I fell into a state of deep depression. All my relatives came to see me yet again. A family meeting was held. One of my cousins pitied me very much. He invited me to go over to his village and live with him and his family. Their village cowherd had recently died and, as I had experience tending buffalo, their team head and other villagers agreed to my taking over the job. My practical problems seemed to have been solved.

But shortly after this, preparations for a county-level election got under way. My way of living and working in another village ran against the law. I had to be in my own village. If I remained with my cousin's family, the county government would say, "You are a black person. You have no residential qualifications to vote. The government will not treat you as an ordinary citizen. You may lose other political rights." I was frightened. Therefore, once again, I returned to my native village, to my poor, solitary room.

*     *     *

Meanwhile, all my relatives were trying to find a suitable lady to be my wife. I really couldn't maintain an independent home in that society, as life in the countryside requires a family to be successful. It was a hot potato:[2] All the good ladies had married at eighteen or at least by twenty-two, whereas I was over thirty and my only qualification was that I knew some English. One day in the spring of 1963, the cousin I had stayed with came to see me again. He said, "Just next to our village there is a suitable lady for you to consider. She lives in Shangbaodian (Above the Precious Pasture) village. My wife and I have asked her neighbors many times, and it seems she has agreed to have a look at you. Twenty-eight years of age. No mother, no brother or sister. All she has is a father who is as healthy as a young man. Besides, a big vegetable garden, surrounded by some fruit trees."

"What about her house? Has it a leaky roof, covered with dry straw?" all my other relatives asked.

"Oh, it didn't rain that day. How could I tell?" my cousin replied. "But it isn't a straw-made house. She can read and write a little, too, not like ordinary girls."

"A family of two persons, no siblings, a good house, can read and write a little. ..." I repeated some of his words slowly. "It sounds wonderful, but I still don't believe your story. Something must be wrong with this or that, or a village girl of that age would surely have got married a long time ago. She must be a divorced woman, I guess?"

"Oh, I know all about her," my cousin said. "My wife and the girl used to work together. She has never been married. You're wondering if she's good-looking or not, is that right?"

"A beautiful face matters only a little. She must be what they call a 'strange spinster,' a very old lady, or at least forty years of age?"

"No, no, I have seen her many times. Really, twenty-eight! She and my wife worked as cooks in a county-run factory for three years. Their boss promoted her to storehouse keeper. As the person in charge of the meat, rice, and vegetables, she had to keep a record in black and white.[3] She doubled her efforts and make surprising progress in learning to read, write, and also to add and divide. Do you think my wife would find you a bad lady?"

Neither side wanted to "buy a cat inside a bag," so a brief face-to-face talk was arranged for us beside a bridge near the market. I noticed at once that she was not the most beautiful girl in the world, but she seemed to have a sort of stylishness and good taste about her. Her clothes were plain and simple, but tidy and clean. She was a little shorter than me, neither fat nor thin. Once she started talking, I was struck by her voice, melodious like a young girl's.

Of course I poured out all my personal information for her to consider. She leaned against the bridge and listened attentively. Then she told me a little about herself: Her name was He Cuilian, and she was indeed twenty-eight and unmarried. Many had wanted to marry her, but she would not follow her husband away and leave her father all alone at home. And those who were willing to come and live in her house—she didn't like them. That was why she had remained unmarried year after year. So that I could find out more about her and her house and village, we arranged a second meeting at her home.

My cousin accompanied me on the appointed evening. He chatted to her father, giving me and Cuilian a chance to talk further. Her face didn't become as red as the last time. She told me that she had lost her mother at the age of seven or eight. Her father was something of a black sheep in those days, an opium addict. As he was the only son, there was no need for him to join the army; but in order to make some money he sold himself to a rich family and then entered the army in place of the rich man's son. Cuilian was still a little girl then. She grew up here and there, mostly looked after by an aunt and other relatives. Her father served in the army for some time, and then, when the army passed through Kunming, he seized the chance to escape home. After returning, he remarried and went to live at his new wife's village. He was known as the area's greatest tea drinker, but his wife became so poor that she couldn't let her husband drink tea to his heart's content. Upon hearing this, Cuilian bought a heavy bag of tea. Taking this bag of tea, she brought her father back to his native village and they set up home together.[4] In 1958, during our drive to increase steel production, she had been chosen to be a cook in a county-run iron factory. Now she worked in the village communal fields and on her two little pieces of private land.

In talking to her father, I repeatedly stressed that although I was tall and sturdy I could not do much in a field or carry heavy loads on my back. It would take a long period of time to learn farm work. Nevertheless, I had a strong will to learn. I was determined to be a humble man. Later on I might do something good for the family, but I had to get used to everything in the village first. I also made it clear that I had only two hands and two legs—in my pockets there was no extra money. Did they refuse me? No. What I said pleased both father and daughter.

Perhaps a week after that, as I returned home from working in the fields late one afternoon, I found a bamboo basket hanging on my door. Inside the basket were some potatoes and dried beans. I wondered for a while. Just then my neighbor's daughter ran in and told me, "At noontime a strange lady and a little girl came to see you.[5] She said she was on her way to town. We asked her to wait and rest, but she said no. She wanted to give you the potatoes. Then she said that her father would be waiting for you to eat their supper the day after tomorrow, and that you must go to eat even if it rains."

Later, when I began to cook supper, I found a piece of paper under the potatoes:

*Shuyi,*
   *You are good or not? I am happy give you some potatoes and some dried beans. Come I home eat supper back day.*

                                                              **Cuilian**

It was written with a pencil. I thought, "Oh, so many mistakes, but the central meaning is understandable. It is a very good thing if she can read and write a little." I went as she asked. This time, although I told my cousin, I went alone. When I arrived, her father was out. Cuilian was cooking supper. She received me warmly.

"Hello! Come in, come in. Just make yourself at home. You sit there in front of the stove door and keep on adding wood. Don't let the fire go out. The old man will come back soon." Then she disappeared into her bedroom, coming back a moment later holding a packet of cigarettes. "This is for you. I bought it in town the day I went to invite you in your village."

"No thanks. You keep them to honor outside important guests." I showed her my short pipe and loose tobacco.[6] My cousin had prepared this for me before I went to see Cuilian and her father. "This is cheaper. I am not qualified to smoke machine-made cigarettes. Anything that produces a sort of smoke will do, even dry grass!"

"Really? If the old man agreed to smoke straw we would become rich. They say a little wine is good for the health, but smoking is no good at all. Yet all men have to smoke. Anyway, you put that packet into your pocket. Take it home and offer it to other people."

That day she didn't prepare a big dinner, just four dishes, but I appreciated her kind spirit. They had killed a sheep some time before, in winter, and dried the meat. They ate sheep meat two or three times a month, and her invitation was to let me enjoy some sheep meat with them. Pig's meat was expensive. After supper, her father went to rest in his room and we chatted for a while longer in their kitchen.

I really had nothing special to offer, only a bar of face soap. I had bought it in Kunming. I gave it to her as a gift. She immediately opened her wooden box and showed me another new bar of soap. "I have been keeping this soap for two years. They gave it to me as a prize for doing some outstanding deeds at the county-run iron factory. All right, let our two soaps make friends, keep each other company, make a pair. You know, in our daily lives, it's very good to have a pair of this and a pair of that. One person can do little, but a pair of people can do more and better."

Well, this time I wanted to know about her family property. Standing outside her room I saw a very old and tattered quilt, patch after patch. The bed was a short-legged one. Everything looked poor. "Is that your bed?" I asked.

"Of course! I sleep there and I cover myself with that."

"They say you returned home from a factory. That doesn't look like a factory worker's bed."

"Just showing off something cannot make a person grow fat. You may come in and see what I have with your own eyes."

Taking down a big bundle, she showed me all sorts of new and good-quality things: blankets, sheets, covers, pillows. Pointing at the tattered quilt, she said, "That one has a long, long history. Perhaps it was first made when my grandmother's grandmother got married. It often makes me think of our family's bitter past. I still value it. The day when I really get married, of course, I will use the new one. But I will keep this to let my children understand the hardships of our past."

"On such problems you and I have the same viewpoint. I suffered a lot after I was sent to reform myself through labor. I am reluctant to use the new and throw away the old."

Then I related much of my past, all the sad things.

After that dried-sheep-meat supper we became good friends. I enjoyed her company. She was agreeable, and her viewpoints seemed reasonable. We met at least two or three times a month. Sometimes we weeded together on her private land. Sometimes she came and helped me in my village. Gradually I started spending most of my spare time at her house. Slowly we fell in love.

I was deeply touched by some of her answers to my questions. Once, when I warned her I had no money at all, she replied, "A king or a top official in Beijing can never maintain a kingly or official status over several generations.

Things change all the time. Never mind about the poor situation. You are poor. I am poor, too. But as long as our legs and hands are all right, by and by we can have everything we wish to have. Money comes from our hands."

"My investigations show that many men wanted to marry you, and that most of them were Mr. China's people.[7] Why did you finally choose a poor man like me?"

She replied, "I was told you can read and speak English. Your knowledge must be very rich. Some of the comers enjoyed a regular salary. They wore machine-made leather shoes. They 'ate' pen and paper in a glass-windowed office building. But for all that, I think in their heads they were empty. You look poor, but I think a big-school-educated person must own lots of valuable property in his mind. One day you might have a chance to use your knowledge."

Once I warned her, "I am a complete man, as you see, but as a farmer I am good at nothing. You must consider this for three days and three nights before you make a final decision."

This is what she replied: "Everything depends on a person's heart. I have learned everything of your circumstances. You really *do* do things in a different way, but if you listen to me I can be your good professor. If one hand moves it remains silent, but if two hands clap together they produce a sound. You must cooperate with me to the end."

"All right, all right," I replied. "I do not know how to dig the earth or how to plant something in the field, but I know what sounds reasonable and what the difference between good and evil is. I'll be your husband, but actually I'm coming just to be your servant. I am a machine, you are the operator. If you treat me well, of course I'll turn round and round."

I remember shortly before we went to register our marriage that Cuilian said, "The last thing to make clear is this: You must tell me the truth. Your first wife stayed in Kunming for more than a year, but you had no children. I've wondered and wondered. Tell me whose fault it was. You know I am the only daughter of the family. If having children comes to a stop, the whole village will laugh."

"Really, I am perfectly all right, inside and outside. All my first wife wanted was to bear lots of children. I wanted children too, but I feared we would become miserably poor if she gave birth before getting a permanent job. To avoid that trouble, I always controlled myself. She stayed in Kunming, but I seldom stayed with her. Anyway, I've told the truth. But I can't guarantee God's choice for you to bear a boy or a girl."

"Of course for that it's up to Heaven. A boy will make all happy, but a girl is also okay. What I am afraid of is that I bear nothing, have nothing to show in the village."

Speaking from the future, it is very funny to recall our marriage anxieties. Cuilian feared I might one day turn everything upside-down, so she dictated while I wrote out several conditions onto a piece of paper, covering many things about the division of housework. She insisted that after the wedding, under all circumstances, I had to do everything just as she said. At home, nobody was allowed to compare their strong points to the other's weaknesses. In connection with the village's public work in the fields, always remember: What other people could do, we could do too. Speak less and ignore gossip. I was never, never to mention my college days in Kunming. If anyone asked about English, I was to change the subject immediately. In managing our house, the basic policy was to run our family industriously and thriftily. She said, "The most important thing is to sum up yesterday, do one's best today, and plan only reachable goals for tomorrow."

Gossip is a fearful thing, and as our circumstances were so different, all sorts of remarks were fired at us. We were called "a couple full of strange problems." Because Cuilian was twenty-eight and unmarried, people tended to think she must have done something wrong in her early days. Behind her back, many laughed at her for planning to marry a beggar-like man who knew nothing about farming. And most of her relatives were not pleased. But I also heard people say, "After all, Cuilian isn't a stupid girl. She has her own special way of finding a big-student husband." And in my village they said, "Shuyi is not going to become a poor bachelor after all. His big-lady future wife is a nice girl."

A date was finally fixed for our marriage registration. On that very day, before we went to the commune office to sign the wedding certificate, she forced me to have a talk with several aged people of her village. In the countryside, old people are considered wise and richly experienced. In fact, they have no right to check all the marriages, but Cuilian insisted we consult them as it was I, the man, who was moving from another village into theirs. Our commune's Party secretary happened to be visiting his daughter who had married into Cuilian's village. He was also present and began, "Our hands are full. Time is limited so we must get straight to the point. We have visited many of the relatives and friends concerned, but we want to clear things up once more in this village."

"Well, just out with it plainly," I replied.

"Your first marriage in Kunming was divorced, is this true?" a white-haired old woman asked.

"Certainly, 100 percent!"

"How do you explain that they are still waiting for you to be their son-in-law?"

Before I could answer, another woman, one of Cuilian's important relatives, interrupted: "It was said you were driving her crazy. Why did you refuse a doctor's true love and come to marry our Cuilian?"

"Heaven is heaven, hell is hell. I am not a medical worker."

"You were a college student; that wasn't so low."

"Don't talk about the past. Today I am an ordinary commune member. A farmer can only marry a farmer."

"Are you going to settle down here forever and ever?" This was asked by Cuilian.

"Of course! Forever!" I replied.

"All right, that's all. Everybody has heard his words," the Party secretary concluded. "Now it's time to hurry. May you enjoy a happy life here!"

\*       \*       \*

We agreed to throw away many of our Bai people's local traditional customs and keep the celebrations down to a minimum. We didn't pay a lot of money to a fortune-teller-like old man to select a special lucky day on which to hold the wedding party. We didn't rent a gas lamp. We didn't hire a blind man to blow a trumpet outside the gate. We didn't organize a big and noisy wedding parade in order to show off our new furniture, clothes, beautiful quilts, and sheets. Instead of preparing several basketfuls of "wedding candy," we bought only a small bag of boiled sweets to let the children enjoy a little. We decorated our bridal chamber in the cheapest way—collecting a pile of old newspapers, we pasted them onto the four walls. We even made the two "Flowers of Happiness" ourselves. The bride and groom wear these special flowers on their breasts throughout their wedding day, and afterward protect and keep them for the whole of their lives. To save a little money, Cuilian bought some sheets of colored paper and we made the flowers together.

It is the custom of our Bai people that if a woman marries a man from an outside village who is going to move into her native village, she has to go to the bridegroom's house to escort him back to her own house. Usually the bride's family invites many young unmarried boys to accompany her, making a noisy parade to welcome and receive the new groom. Again we simplified things. Two unmarried boys, nineteen years of age, came over to meet me at my home before noon. These two had been chosen from families with plenty of children—this to ensure that Cuilian and I would have many children. They brought me a new jacket and a pair of new trousers, to be worn that very day. They also brought two bottles of wine, specially prepared for the bride-groom's parents. But as I had lost both father and mother, my older brother was the one to accept this gift. My brother and sisters and their families fol-lowed me to the bride's house. That was our wedding procession.

The wedding ceremony took place in the afternoon, after all the guests had arrived. As a rule, the couple go down on their knees and knock their fore-heads on the floor three times, to Heaven, Earth, and then teachers and an-cestors. After this, they do another three knocks, this time to their parents. We got down on the ground and did only the last set of three knocks with our foreheads, to my father-in-law and elder brother. Then we stood up and a man beside a decorated table said, "Now the bride and groom bow to all the relatives and friends present three times." After this, the man said, "Now the bride and the groom bow to each other three times. Now let's watch them exchange gifts."

The gift she gave me was a little handkerchief and a pencil. In return I gave her a comb and some thread.

Following our exchange of gifts, a good friend of my father-in-law's, an old man called Zhao, gave a brief speech. I was addressed for the first time by my new name, He Liyi. As it was I who followed my wife to her house, I had to drop my father's family name and take on hers. Old Zhao chose a new name, Liyi, to replace my previous given name of Shuyi. *Li* means "to keep on steadily," and *yi* means "the children's children." Taken together they mean "to make the family go on and on"—in other words, "to have lots of children."

Everyone then showed their wedding presents. My brother gave me a new shirt. My sisters gave Cuilian some thread and some new cloth. They all offered something, but in fact we didn't accept all the presents. Most of our relatives were also very poor. Later, after the wedding ceremony was over, we returned their gifts. That was why I used the word "show."

Finally, everyone sat down to our wedding banquet. We hadn't invited the whole village to come and enjoy a fancy dinner; only thirty-two people, close relatives and important friends, at four tables. There weren't the traditional eight dishes, only four or five. We were too poor to buy bottles and bottles of wine. Instead, we placed a big cup of wine in the middle of each table. Eight people had to share that one cup.

Nevertheless, we enjoyed ourselves immensely, and Cuilian and I were married.

## NOTES

1. During the formation of People's Communes in 1958, Mr. He's family (like all peasant families in China) had to give up the little patch of land they had retained after the Land Reform Movement. All land now belonged to the commune. In 1961 this policy was softened somewhat to allow each family member, adults and children alike, to receive a piece of land from the commune for their private use. In Mr. He's village the figure was one-tenth of a *mou* per person.

2. *Hot potato:* This is a colloquial English expression meaning "an awkward situation that no one is keen to handle." Mr. He is fond of using the colloquial English he has learned over the years, much of it from the British Broadcasting Corporation.

3. *A record in black and white:* a written record.

4. Mr. He says, "The year Cuilian and I got married we didn't invite my father-in-law's ex-wife, but she came just the same. Unfortunately, her son from a previous marriage died early and she became even poorer. She herself died in the early seventies, leaving behind a daughter-in-law and a granddaughter. Once every four months her daughter-in-law comes to our house and Cuilian gives her old clothes and grain."

5. In the Jianchuan area, a woman never goes to visit her boyfriend alone before they have become engaged. As a rule, she takes along someone younger than herself to act as a chaperon.

6. Mr. He explains, "In China, loose tobacco is cheaper than machine-made cigarettes. Official-like people would never smoke tobacco in a pipe. But poor farmers always buy loose tobacco. Aged peasant grandparents don't need to work, so they smoke their tobacco in a long pipe, sometimes as long as a walking stick. Middle-aged farmers smoke with a pipe as long as a spoon."

7. *Mr. China's people:* This phrase refers to persons attached to a work unit (as opposed to a commune). Unlike peasants, they receive a regular salary each month, are guaranteed pensions, work only eight hours a day, and have Sundays off. Since 1979 peasants have had the opportunity to greatly increase their standard of living, thus making "Mr. China's people" less envied than they were in the past.

# 9

## A JOYFUL TORCH FESTIVAL

**A**s a rule, the day after the wedding a Bai bride goes back to spend about a week with her parents. Later, the bridegroom follows to meet her and they return to their new home together. In the rare cases where the bridegroom moves to the bride's house after the marriage, then he goes to spend the "honeymoon" in his original home for several days. When the time is up, the bride fetches him back to her village. But since I had no parents, we decided not to bother with this custom. In our case, we didn't even have a day of rest. The following morning my new wife's first order for me was, "You put all the animal droppings together in a bamboo basket. Carry them to our vegetable garden. Smash them. Wait for me. I'll come to show you how to spread them."

"All right!" was my answer.

That morning she followed me rather late. While I was waiting for her I heard all sorts of remarks from a group of men nearby:

"Come and look! He just came yesterday and today he carries animal droppings. What a model husband!"

"What kind of a husband? Mrs. He has found a permanent hand!"

"You don't have a great man's powerful manner. Don't be Mrs. He's tail!"

As soon as they saw my wife coming, they ran away. My wife looked at the animal droppings and then at me. She realized I had been a listener, not a talker, to those men. She patted my shoulder and smiled, "Your 'homework' this morning was well done."

In our Bai villages you can often hear people say, "It's easy to be a good wife," but following this they always add, "It is very, very hard to be a good husband." When the bride goes to the groom's house all she has to do is please her husband and his parents. But if the bridegroom marries into the bride's family, not only does he have to make his wife and her parents happy, but he must also please all the villagers, old and young.[1] He has to be particularly careful when dealing with the "masters" of his new village, because if he carelessly ignores little things he might offend someone, and then the other villagers will get angry and bully him. As I started my new life in Shangbaodian Village, I often found myself worrying about this problem.

In the beginning, I also worried about my wife and her father. I wanted to have a bowl of rice every day. I didn't want to have to find a third wife. For a long, long time I did everything just as Cuilian ordered. Life after I got settled down in my new home couldn't be called the happiest, but it was much, much better than the life I had been leading at my old original home village. I didn't have to sort the grain or look after a sheep or find the eggs. My father-in-law and wife took care of the housework. My wife was responsible for the cooking, all mending and sewing, washing both the clothes and the dishes, buying and selling in the market. She also went out to do collective work in the fields, but as she had to cook the evening meal she usually returned home a little earlier than me. When I got home, dinner was nearly ready. She and her father would say, "Oh, you must be very tired. Take a rest first." At table they would say, "Have some more. Help yourself."

For my part, I got up early, earlier than they did. I busied myself without her ordering this or that. Water was a big problem in my new village. The strange thing was that no well could be found in any of the corners of the village. No matter how deep you dug, the ground didn't produce water. So the first thing I did was to run to the river at the north end of my new village to get several pails of water, enough for a day's use, and carry them back to the house on shoulder poles. Then I'd sweep the floor. If I had time, I went out to cut grass for the pigs.

After breakfast, if Cuilian wanted me to go to market with her, I followed obediently. Sometimes she said, "I was told there's no work for men this morning in the village fields.[2] Prepare a bamboo basket and an axe and wait. They will come to call you. You just follow behind and look for some firewood." The eighty-odd households of my new village were divided into two teams, Production Team One and Production Team Two. We belonged to Production Team One, and most of my days were spent taking part in our team's collective work.

The collective work at that time was divided into two types: The first was called "odd jobs." For this type, you received the same amount of work points no matter how much you produced. You had to stay for a fixed period of time, but people laughed and played while working. One morning, for instance, the leader might say, "See that pile of firewood? Just move it over there. It's an odd job." Many people worked slowly and carried a light load. Some honest people carried a heavy load, but their work points were just the same as the others—ten points for the day. In the beginning I often did odd jobs.

The second type was quite different. This time the leader would say, "Today we are going to move that pile of firewood. The point recorder will wait for you at the gate to weigh your loads. Remember, forty kilograms is ten work points." Then people hurried to pick up the firewood and pile it into the baskets on their backs. When the load was heavy, they'd stand on the scales. At the end of the day, the point recorder would add up everybody's weights and give each a total. This figure was converted into work points and written down in their work-point booklet. Some got more, some got fewer.

After a few months in my wife's village, our team lenders started assigning me this second type of collective work. I still did everything in a slow way. I earned the fewest work points in my group every day in every kind of farm work. Most villagers struggled for the second type of work because it offered the opportunity of gaining more work points, but I earned fewer for this type of work than for odd jobs! Sometimes I received only six or seven points. Soon I was known as "Mr. Slowpoke."

From time to time Cuilian's father would ask, "How many points did you get today?"

Before I could answer, my wife told him in a loud voice, "Mind your own business. You just drink tea, smoke, and then come to the table. I don't want you to ask that. He is okay."

After the old man left the room, she whispered, "No need to tell him the truth. Pretend to be deaf whenever he speaks to you."

But since both my wife and I went out to participate in collective work every day, our final total was not so low. For this my wife and father-in-law were pleased. All in all, things went by smoothly.

*          *          *

The year after we got married, the villagers suddenly stopped making fun of me. In fact, they started treating me warmly. Those relatives who for a long time had looked down on my wife for marrying a beggar also changed their attitude. Did we bow to them every day? Did we invite them to come into our kitchen to eat and drink? No. All because my wife showed them—a baby boy!

People usually feel proud if they can give birth to a child in the tenth month after their wedding day. If a woman gets married but fails to bear a child for many years, people will say something like, "Why, not even a straw-made baby! It serves her right. All because her ancestors were thieves and robbers." In our case, we got married in June of the lunar calendar, and my son was born in the following April—exactly ten months later. Our marriage had caused all sorts of gossip. The birth of a boy ten months after our wedding silenced everything. Now I really felt I was part of the family, and a perfect man of the village.

We have different names for babies. If a woman tells you that her first baby is a "runner up and down all mountains," she means her baby is a boy. But if you hear someone say, "I have got another 'runner around a pot,'" that means she has given birth to a girl. One sunny April day, my wife got a mountain runner. It added a lot of joy to my home. Proudly I went outside to hang up the *zeng di,* a round bamboo-made basket used on the bottom of a rice-steamer to hold the rice. A *zeng di* is a sign telling everybody that a woman inside the house has given birth. Pregnant women in particular must pay careful attention before entering someone's gate, because in our Bai villages pregnant women are believed to stop the new mother's breast milk. If the baby is a girl, the *zeng di* is an ordinary one, nothing special. If the baby happens to be a boy, the *zeng di* is wrapped in red paper. So I had to wrap our *zeng di* in bright red paper and also add a pair of red-paper-wrapped chopsticks and a little wine bottle.

On the second day after our boy was born, I was instructed to run back to my home village and report the news. As my parents had died, I ran first to my elder brother's house, then to all my other relatives, and finally to our close friends. I took a bottle of "happy wine" from house to house and village to village, offering a cup to each. Happy wine isn't ordinary wine we get from a shop. In our countryside, all pregnant women prepare this wine at home before the child is born. It is distilled from rice and carefully kept in pottery jars. It is white, sweet, and fragrant.

Offering happy wine is in fact equivalent to giving an invitation card. After emptying my cup the drinker would say, "Thank you! A thousand congratulations!" and then add, "When are you going to hold your baby's one-month-old party?" My wife had taught me many times how to reply: "This is a party to receive, not to give. We prepare a little, but we shall receive a great deal. After they empty your cup don't talk nonsense. Just say, 'Please come to see the baby a month from today. We will drink and eat and have a good time.' If you make a mistake in reporting the news they will laugh at me, not you. You must protect our face. I don't know if I can produce enough milk at the present time, but anyway this is an unavoidable question. If they don't mention it, you keep quiet. If they ask, you must say, 'She has plenty of milk.'"

That year each of my three married sisters had given birth, but their children were all girls. I showed them a boy. In a way it seemed very special. My brother said, "Wonderful! We are so glad to hear you have fulfilled your first mission. For a man going to stay in his wife's house, this is above all. Now people in their village will treat you with respect and honor."

One of my aunts said, "Thank God! This great news demonstrates that you have been a good man all these years. Our God in Heaven keeps an eye on you."

One of the twins said, "God has arranged everything for you. Only kindhearted people have boys first."

The other twin said, "A boy is worth 1,000 *jin* of gold. You must celebrate in a big way."

On the third or fourth day after my son's birth, we did do something very special. We invited forty households, almost half of all the households in our village, to eat sweet dumplings. In our village the largest family was the Liu clan. The Zhao clan came in second. These two big clans made up about 85 percent of all the villagers. Our He clan was not so big, only eight households.

There were a few other very small one- or two-family clans as well, such as the Zhangs and the Mas. Now the Lius and the Hes were very close to each other. But the Lius and the Zhaos often quarreled, even fought. We therefore gave sweet dumplings to the Liu households and none to the Zhaos. The rest we gave to friends and important officials of our village.

These sweet dumplings are made of glutinous rice flour stuffed with a sweet mixture and served in thin syrup. They look simple but are actually a lot of trouble to make. Four women got busy around our cooking stove while I ran from house to house to deliver a bowlful. Each bowl contained four dumplings, symbolizing the four seasons of the year. I had to obey my wife and take and offer those dumplings, but after a while I complained to the ladies who had come to help: "Too much trouble for me! I am tired of running here and there. Can I ask my nieces and nephews to help?"

My wife overheard and got angry. "Of course anybody can do it, but you still have a lot to learn about things in the countryside. Many men long for this but God doesn't honor them with a boy. They own sackfuls of glutinous rice flour but have only girls to show; they can't celebrate in this way. It is just a bowl of dumplings, but it brings you great honor. Understand that!"

*　　*　　*

Soon after my boy was born, my wife became eager to find a person who was very wise at predicting future business. I thought it too absurd to believe a fortune-teller's false stories. Many times I advised her not to trouble herself, but she insisted. What was more, she warned that if I didn't go soon I would have to bear all the bad consequences connected with my boy's future. Dear me, how could I dare to oppose that order? Finally she heard of a wise one who was said to be a "fairy fortune-teller." She prepared a picnic lunch for me to eat on the long walk there. I said, "All right, let me say, 'My master-wife is granting me a holiday.'" She returned me a humorous reply: "If you bring me a bad report, I'm not going to let you eat my supper."

Smoothly I found that so-called prophet. The wise fortune-teller turned out to be a blind woman! As soon as I told her the date and exact time of my boy's birth, she began to deliver her "report." Oh, she talked about many, many things, but now I can recall only a few of her words: "He was born in the fourth month of the year, the most prosperous month. Every plant, tree, crop under the sun grows faster in April. So the boy will grow fast and be prosperous like everything else that grows in April.

"Unfortunately, the boy forgot to bring his gold and water.[3] In order to obtain gold, he has to drink enough water. So if you, the parents, give the boy plenty of water to drink, he will bring a lot of gold home in the future.

"Don't worry. I'll give you some special medicine to solve the above problem: Try your best to find him another father and mother. With the blessings of his new parents, the son's health will improve. The second medicine is to give him a good name. A good name will make him become a well-educated man. In the future, his name will shake the earth, the rivers, and many mountains.

"Congratulations! God has given you a most promising boy. All of you will become rich. You must not forget to come and see me when he becomes a top official. As for other comers, their babies are ordinary babies. Nothing special. It is not fair to ask them for more money. But yours is the best boy I have met within the past three years. So you must pay me 3 *yuan*."

I repeated many good words to thank her and paid the 3 *yuan*.

My master-wife listened to my report with all ears. She was overjoyed, but had some "gold and water" worries, too. She made sure he drank plenty of water.

Only after the very important one-month-old party can the mother carry the newborn out of the gate. Regardless of whether the baby is a boy or a girl, all parents arrange this party for the child. Actually, the main purpose is to honor the new mother's parents. In my own case, as it was I who followed my wife to her house, my parents were the very people to be honored. Once again my elder brother and his wife acted as my parents.

We invited about fifty guests to the party. More than half were little boys, girls, and babies. All the relatives on both sides came. Seated eight to a table, everyone exchanged the latest family information and local gossip while enjoying my wife's banquet. We again served a bowl of four big stuffed dumplings, followed by rice and eight dishes of meat and good vegetables.

After eating, all the grown-up guests had to carry our baby for a while, talk to him, and kiss him many times. Everybody said something like this to my wife: "You must eat well. Have more rest. I hope you have plenty of milk so your baby will grow fat."

To me they said, "Don't worry about work points in the village production team. Your son is more important. You must wholeheartedly serve your wife and the baby. You must wait on her at her bedside. Babies grow very fast. You'll often find yourself tired out at the present stage, but never mind, it won't last long, and when he grows bigger he will bring you all that you need."

Everything turned out exactly as my wife had said. After the guests went home we saw that we had received many baby clothes, thirty Chinese writing brushes, twenty pencils, thirty bottles of ink, a pile of children's books, two large bags of ordinary rice flour and two of glutinous rice flour, seven hundred eggs, eleven cocks, four hens, and thirty loaves of brown sugar. Bai people like to give new mothers brown-sugar loaves because we believe that brown sugar helps produce plenty of milk for the baby. Since the child was a boy, we didn't receive any needles or colored thread.

\*        \*        \*

After our one-month-old party, another "research project" started. Following our Bai custom, we sought and finally found a broken bridge somewhere near our village. Then we chose an everything-is-lucky day from an almanac. The evening before that lucky day, my father-in-law and I went up into the mountains and chopped down several young pine trees.We measured and cut them to size. We also collected some large stones. Next morning we got up before dawn and within an hour had that tumble-down bridge repaired in good order. This bridge is often used by the villagers when going to the hills to collect firewood, and also when the time comes to cut our rice and wheat. Heavy buffalo cross it too, and they often damage it. Each year, people have to repair it many times, especially after the rainy season. Our repair of the bridge was called "A good deed for the people." As soon as the villagers saw the newly repaired bridge, they would say, "Oh, well done! May God bless whoever repaired the bridge!"

Our second job was to burn some incense at one end of the newly repaired bridge and then decorate it all over with dozens of paper flags. Having completed these tasks, we hid somewhere nearby and waited to meet the first person to cross over that special bridge. Before long, we saw a man appear on the far bank and walk toward us. When he got halfway over the bridge I suddenly ran out and greeted him: "Congratulations! You are just the good gentleman to accept a son!" Immediately I pressed my four-colored presents upon him—namely, tea, tobacco, wine, and brown sugar. He was very pleased. That man was Uncle Wang, the newly elected forest-protector of our village.

In Jianchuan County we all greatly admire parents who have exactly five sons and two daughters. Now, Uncle Wang had four sons and two daughters. Our baby would give him the fifth son he lacked.

The next day, as soon as day broke, we went to pay our first formal visit on his new parents, carrying the baby boy and some more presents. As we entered their courtyard we lit string after string of firecrackers and pasted several pairs of red-paper posters onto their doors. The man's wife carried our baby boy for a while, kissing him many times. She did this to bestow happiness and blessings on him. Each one of their family had to kiss my little baby. We had a simple party-like breakfast at his new parents' home. More neighborhood children and guests were invited to eat and drink. This was meant to show that when my son grew bigger he would do something great and have lots of good friends.

Later that day, everyone from my son's second family came over to our house for a formal lunch. They brought several baby's clothes arranged neatly on a tray, as well as a piece of red paper on which the name they had chosen for my son was written in black ink. We said "Thank you" many, many times and pasted that important piece of red paper onto the wall. The name his new forest-protector father had given him was He Lujiang. In Chinese, the character *Lu* is composed of two parts. One part is pronounced *jin*, which means "gold." The character *jiang* means "river." And a river means a lot of water. So my son's name contained both the gold and the water he was lacking in his soul.

We had now fulfilled that "fairy fortune-teller's" order to find the baby some second parents. Each year after they became his second father and mother, we went to visit them at the Spring Festival. Whenever Lujiang met them, of course, he called them "Baba" and "Mama." When the boy grew old enough to walk, he sometimes went to visit them all by himself, clutching a few presents.[4]

What a lot to do now that we had a baby boy! Another festivity I had to participate in after Lujiang's birth was the Torch Festival. Different minority peoples hold this festival at different times of the year. The Bais celebrate it on the twenty-fifth of the sixth month of the lunar year. We organize our Torch Festival in a more spectacular way than do the Yi minority people, many of whom also live in Yunnan Province. For us it is quite a big thing. In Bai areas, the Torch Festival is arranged and prepared by all the parents with new baby sons born since the last Torch Festival.

That year, our Lujiang's Torch Festival was a great one to remember. No birth-control policies were yet in force, and among the eighty-odd households of our village, twenty babies had been born, nine of them boys. Before the Torch Festival, we nine families gathered together some money and ordered a special paper lantern and a funny paper-made boy. These things were made by an old man who lived in another village. He was recognized throughout the whole county as a special expert in making feudalistic decorations for festivals and temples. When these paper objects were ready, two boys were sent to carry them back to our village. It is said that if girls carry that paper lantern and boy back, then the following year all the pregnant women will give birth to girls.

After breakfast on the twenty-fifth, important men of our nine families hurried out with bundles of dry firewood. We arranged and tied them together to form a large torch. Usually this torch is divided into twelve sections, but as our year was a leap year we added a thirteenth. In all it was a little taller than an ordinary electricity pole beside a road. On top of the torch we tied the upper section of a young pine tree and, on top of this, two square paper containers. With these containers we expressed the hope that all the farmers would harvest plenty of grain in the coming year. On the very top, the paper boy was placed for all to see.

We nine masters then got busy decorating the whole torch beautifully. We dressed it from top to bottom with all sorts of fruit and thousands of little colored flags. In a way it looked like a huge Christmas tree. Before sunset, this big project was complete. Up to now, our torch had been lying on its side. As soon as the decorating was finished, more than thirty strong men were ceremoniously invited to help put one end straight into a deep hole. Amidst a roar of gongs, drums, firecrackers, shouts, and cheers, the torch slowly stood up.

Right after that, a big tray of steamed buns, carefully prepared by the nine households, was placed on a table at the foot of the torch, together with incense burning fragrantly in an iron incense holder. The parents of the nine new baby boys, as well as other members of their families, got down on the ground three times to bow to the torch, thanking it for giving them boys. Immediately after this part of the ceremony, the torch masters threw the steamed buns up into the sky. This created a lot of pleasure and excitement. Many struggled to collect the buns as they fell. It is said that if a woman can eat a big piece of one of those buns, she will probably give birth to a boy in the coming year. So those who desire a boy never miss this chance.

After the excitement was over, people began to point at the paper-made boy perched on the top of the torch. Someone shouted, "Look, the boy's face is turning to the north!"

"Ladies of the north, get ready to bear more boys!"

"Let's go and eat a big meal at your table. Can you see, the boy is looking straight at your house!"

At the same time you could also hear something like, "What evil have I done? The boy always looks to the north!"

"Too bad, we southerners will have to wait for another 365 days."

In addition to this public torch, both largest and tallest, many teenagers had prepared their own small portable torches. They had also collected together lots of yellow powder-like resin found at the foot of young pine trees. If you throw this yellow resin into a fire, it suddenly leaps up and burns brighter. When the main torch is finally set ablaze, the teenagers run around waving their little torches and throwing the resin into the fire. This play has two serious meanings: to burn away all the flies and mosquitoes of the coming year, and to congratulate the fathers of the newborn baby boys. The little torch bearers also like to make a resin flame on the legs of the new fathers.

We nine fathers feared our trousers would be set on fire, so it was very hard to decide who was to light the torch. We argued for a long time about this. Unfortunately, I was elected to perform this "honor" because my house stood closest to the torch. I couldn't refuse. To avoid damaging a good pair of trousers, my wife prepared a heavily patched and dampened pair for me. As I was lighting the top of the torch with a long bamboo pole, more than twenty boys, all brandishing little torches, made a ring around me. All at once I heard a series of "*pi li pi la!*" I had put a string of firecrackers into my jacket pocket and one end had caught a spark. That evening, there was no damage to my tattered, watery trousers, but the blackened pocket on my jacket left us a happy memory.

The big torch took three hours to burn out. While it was burning, people of all ages gathered in the little square. The nine fathers went around from group to group offering cigarettes, wine, candy, sunflower seeds, and fried broad beans. Folk-singing competitions were organized. Young girls gave dancing performances. Everybody laughed and had a very good time. The final excitement of the Torch Festival was the collecting up of charred sticks or pieces of half-burned wood to hang outside pigpens or other domestic animal sheds. These charred remains were meant to bring good luck and success in raising pigs, hens, cows, and sheep.

*      *      *

When Lujiang was one year old, we arranged another special party for him: Occupation Choice Day. That day, all our closer relatives and bosom friends were invited to enjoy a big dinner at our house. Lujiang's forest-protector father and mother were also invited. Again, most of our guests were children under five, each bearing a gift as they entered our gate.

The funny game began at noontime. My wife carried our one-year-old boy upstairs to help him bow three times before our ancestors' altar.[5] Meanwhile, in a big, round bamboo container we placed a spade, three or four books, pencils, a fountain pen, an axe, a kill-the-pig knife, a hoe, a blacksmith's hammer, a carpenter's hammer, a bamboo weaver's knife, a toy car, a toy plane, a tailor's piece of chalk, and a cobbler's shoe model.

Mother and child stepped down. People started clapping their hands and repeating, "Happy Birthday!" "Enjoy health all the year round!" "Be a top official!" "Be a big general!" "May you enjoy a hundred years!" "Find money during all the four seasons!" "Be a famous master!"

Following local tradition, my wife handed the boy to a man who was older than I was. The older the better. That afternoon, a sixty-two-year old man carried him for a while, showing him everything we had prepared in the bamboo basket. The old man talked to Lujiang: "Be a good son of the He family. Tell me what you are going to be when you grow up? Oh, of course you can't talk now, but you are welcome to select anything you like. Don't be afraid. We all hope you will grow faster and stronger. You must work hard and bring honor to your parents. And honor to all our relatives. You must work for mankind."

We all hoped Lujiang would become a well-educated man, so my wife deliberately put some school supplies near him. As we also feared he would become a lazy drinker or a big eater of everything, we placed the cakes and candy a little distance away. The old man tried to coax our son into taking something, but he wouldn't stretch out his hand. He looked scared.

One old woman said, "No good! When I was young they covered the baby's eyes and let him feel. Shall we do it like our ancestors did?"

Everybody replied, "No!"

Finally the old man let the boy sit in the middle of the container and pushed everything in front of him. The child smiled and seemed to be singing a song.

His two hands pushed everything away and then mixed them together again. We all watched with great interest. Some laughed. This time the old lady yelled, "Shut up, everybody! You must not bother him. This moment is too important! It will decide his future."

In the end, we were dismayed to see him grasp a little green plastic hoe. Someone cried out, "No, no! Throw it away!" But he would not listen to anyone.

Well, after all, the boy wanted to become a farmer. This troubled my wife very much, but it couldn't be helped. As for me, I wasn't bothered a bit as I really didn't believe in the custom. Such superstitious games were just amusements for people in the distant villages to enjoy for a moment's pleasure. To our relatives I said, "Nowadays everybody has to learn to read and write. You are absolutely wrong if you think that someone who works in the fields doesn't need to read books. I'm going to make him read anyway."

When my wife and I were alone, I said, "Don't worry about this. As a mother, your job is to feed him carefully, keep him healthy. You are good, but only at planting something in the field, cutting grass, preparing a delicious meal. I know more about the importance of a good education. I can make him read and write quickly."

## NOTES

1. Mr. He elaborates on this situation: "We all know that it is difficult to appraise a cook's suitability for the job. Mr. A may say that this cook's dishes taste wonderful. Another Mr. B may say they taste too salty. Still another Mr. C may say everything he cooks is terrible. Anyway, to please one or two persons is easy and simple, but it is too hard to make many people happy."

2. "In a commune, the formal policy was, 'We have work every day of the year,'" Mr. He explains. "After breakfast and again after lunch, we went to 'receive an order or job from the officials.' However, there were days, especially the rainy ones, when not a single soul could be found in front of our team's public grain storehouse. That meant there was no collective work that morning or afternoon. If a villager insisted on finding something to do, he or she went to the team head's house and he would reply, 'Well, you go to get a basket and collect all the animal droppings from all the corners of the world. When you have finished, let me know and I'll send someone to weigh your animal droppings.' The total amount could only win fewer than ten work points."

3. Mr. He explains, "The superstitious countryside dwellers believe that whether a person's life is long or short, rich or poor, all depends on the gold, wood, water, fire, and earth the person's soul contains. They say that if a person possesses all of these five elements in a harmonious mixture, he or she will live a happy, peaceful life."

4. In late 1979 Lujiang's second father and mother both died. Mr. He writes, "Just like their own four sons and two daughters, Lujiang went to serve and do everything at their funeral ceremonies. For this, the reaction of the villagers, especially the aged people, was very good. In finding a second set of parents, some people forget the past. As the child grows bigger, they stop using the name given by their foster parents. As for

our son, my wife and I like the name Lujiang and so up to now, Lujiang is still Lujiang."

5. In Bai houses, the family "altar" is usually cut into the west facing wall of the middle upstairs room. It is rectangular in shape, about as long as a bed, and half a meter wide. On festival days, the family places out fruit, food, and drink to receive and honor their ancestors. Before preparing breakfast every day, the wife of the house places fresh incense there.

國常光月民七人海

*In 1961, after they formally took off my rightist "hat," I was allowed some free time on my own. I went to Kunming for three days and had this picture taken. It is the earliest picture I have of myself.* (Top, left)

*My wife and Lujiang, then ten months old, in 1965.* (Bottom, left)

*In 1967, while I was building highways as a nation's worker, I went home for a two-week vacation and we had this photograph taken. My wife and I are standing at the back; in front of us my father-in-law is holding Lujiang.* (Below)

With two fellow highway builders from a nearby village in 1967.

My wife and I digging in one of our fields in 1977.

Luzhong and I in April 1979. At the time I was working as a substitute teacher.

*After I became a permanent teacher in 1979, I worked very hard in the evenings in my room. This photograph was taken in 1980.*

*My two sons and I in 1982. The dictionary I am holding was sent to me from London by Sara Lim.*

*A family portrait taken in 1982 or early 1983.*

*Holding my prize radio from West Germany, I posed for this photograph in 1983.*

*When my father-in-law died in 1986, we hired a worker to take pictures of the funeral. This one shows all the mourners wearing white headbands or hats. My wife is standing in the middle of the group of women on the highway. I am kneeling down on the right. Because my role was that of the dead man's son, the bamboo "walking stick" I am holding is the shortest one in the procession. In front of me is a paper statue of a local god.*

This is the photograph Lujiang took of my wife, Luzhong, and I at the main bus stop in Kunming just after we arrived for our vacation in the spring of 1988. (Left)

In the summer of 1988, both Claire Chik and I traveled to London. Claire's husband, Warren Gee, took this photograph of us outside Westminster Abbey. (Right)

At my retirement party in 1989 we entertained many special guests with eight bowls of meat and good vegetables in our courtyard. I am sitting in the center at right.

*A family photograph taken in 1989.*

*My wife and two sons seated around a fire in one of our upstairs rooms in the winter of 1990. My wife is mending some old clothes. My two boys are singing a pop song along with the radio.*

*My wife and I visiting a local temple in September 1991.*

*In August 1992 Luzhong and I took a trip to visit my unforgettable host at the Qinghua Reservoir. From left to right are Luzhong, my old host and his grandson, and myself.*

*The pillowcase Guihua embroidered for me in Kunming.*

*Three of my sisters and members of their families gathered together. The two women in front, dressed in traditional Bai clothing, are my twin sisters. The woman on the left, also dressed in traditional Bai clothing, is my youngest sister. Her youngest daughter is standing to the right of my twin sisters.*

# 10

# I BECOME A
# NATION'S WORKER

One day early in 1965, when my son was one year old, the postman brought me a parcel. It was an unexpected present. A very strange thing it was. The sender didn't give a name; all we could see was that it had been sent from a military organization in Kunming. Yet I had no friends or relatives serving in the People's Liberation Army. We wondered and wondered. At first we thought it was a wrong delivery, but my name and the address were correct. Upon opening it we found that all the contents were for a child. It contained a doll, a plastic gun, colored cotton and silk thread, picture storybooks, and new children's clothes of different sizes. We were just mystified as to who could have sent it.

That very night, after everybody had gone to bed, I opened the parcel again and examined each item carefully. Finally, on the cover of one of the books, I found Guihua's name and another two words: "Keep secret." Well, I still wondered about the sender's address. Guihua was studying in a medical institute. What had she to do with a military organization?

A little while later, while I was spending a festival day at my brother's house, Guihua's father gave me something wrapped up in a piece of red cloth. He told me to open it when I got home and added, "Congratulations, young man! So glad to hear a boy was born to you. We still welcome you here. Do drop in at any time you are free. Never forget us."

As soon as I got home I opened the old man's red cloth. First I found a fountain pen, the one I had given Guihua in Kunming, and then a letter:

*Dear Shuyi,*

*News reached my ears as soon as you got remarried. Immediately I started a letter, but failed to finish it. For me it was a heavy blow. It made me sick in bed for many days. It showed that you did not believe my true and persistent love. Why didn't you write a word or two to me before you made a final decision? Why didn't you carefully read the long letter I left at home for you? My true heart was clearly placed there for you to see and examine. I suppose you knew what my words actually meant, but you purposely ignored my desire.*

*Things changed too fast and too suddenly. The way was too long. Away in Kunming I was really helpless. I vowed to stop writing to you forever, but conscience didn't allow me to do that after all. How could I cast you away out of my mind? It was impossible. The situation made everybody change. Considering things from all sides, and combining your particular situation with the present-day society, I eventually came to realize that what you did was not wrong. Therefore, today I am determined to write this letter to its final end. I hope this time we can understand each other better and deeper. I want you to believe that hereafter you and I are still good neighbors, good comrades, and close friends.*

*I must tell you, perhaps you have heard already, I also got married in Kunming not long after I heard the news about your marriage. You might be surprised to hear that he is neither from our home county nor a medical worker. At the moment I am working in an army hospital and married to an army officer, a Han Chinese. The other day I asked him to buy and send at the post office. I didn't tell him much about our special friendship or give him many details, so he enclosed some things for a girl to play with. No good. I hope you didn't mind. In order to correct or to make up for this mistake, I am asking my father to redirect a boy's gift—the fountain pen you gave me in Kunming. A boy must learn to read and write, so please let your boy use that pen first.*

*When I was young, I was like a frog at the bottom of a deep well. I thought Jianchuan was the entire world. After I got married in Kunming I slowly began to understand that there were hundreds of other places on earth, but alas, it was a pity! At that time I was too stubborn to accept new ideas of the world as well. We would have been the happiest couple if I had listened to each word of yours. Too late!*

*We are not so young now. It pains us to think deeply about things. But you must not be too sad. I think we can build another new hope on our coming generation. You learned to use a weapon with which to conquer the wonderful world, but you failed. Do you know I was offered a golden chance to see the big world? But I also failed, simply because I didn't know much English, or any other foreign language. Not so long ago I was given the opportunity to go abroad, to Japan. All agreed, but I failed at the last stage. I hadn't mastered a basic knowledge of any other country's language. We should learn a lesson from this example. It's very hard to say whether you can use your English again or not, but for the benefit of our new generation, I ask you to take special care of the child from the very beginning. You fell down once into the mud, but you must not let your child fall down.*

*I have become the wife of a Han Chinese, but my heart is not Han. I love our homeland. We are not going to stay in Kunming permanently. It seems very hard to return and work in our home county, but we will try again and again until we succeed. Each has his and her family burden now, but special love and special friendship between us will keep on going and improving. Do believe I'll come back*

*sooner or later. Do believe I'll try my level best to see what I can do for you and for*
*each one of your family.*

*Lastly, I guess you'll be happy to hear that my baby is already two months old. A*
*girl, about a year younger than your boy. Oh, I have more to tell you, but not*
*now—next time. I beg you to write to me and tell me if I can do anything for you.*
*May all of you enjoy a happy life.*

*With best wishes,*
**Guihua**

I didn't reply to her letter. I felt very bad, always ashamed of myself, a col-
lege-educated person unable to do anything for society. But, as ever, her letter
moved me very much. I rewrapped it in the red cloth and put it away safely.

\*       \*       \*

Lujiang brought us great joy and happiness. But here I must add this: The
boy's birth made our family change. There appeared many problems in our
daily lives. You know people in the city live on a regular salary given by the
government. Every month when the time comes, they get the same pay, regardless of the weather. But in the countryside, up until the beginning of the
eighties, we lived on work points. A group work-point recorder would follow
us around in the fields, noting down names and numbers of points.[1] Later the
group recorder would pass his notebook to the team's general work-point recorder. In the evenings, people went to see him at his home in order to jot
down their day's points in their own family work-point booklet, keeping a
careful record. If it rained or you were ill or had private matters to attend to,
you earned no work points. (Our important officials received ten work points
every day even if they slept in bed from dawn to dusk, and if they joined the
field work they earned extra points on top of their original ten.)

At the end of the lunar year, just before the Spring Festival, our work points
were added up by the team accountant, and money and grain were given out
according to how many points we had earned during that whole year. Seventy
to 80 percent of the grain we received from the team was apportioned according to our yearly work-point totals. The remaining 20 to 30 percent was distributed according to family size. For this share, nobody looked at your work
points, just the number in your family. A one-day-old baby received the same
share of village grain as an adult.

All through the year, however, it was very hard to tell exactly how much
money and grain we would receive at the end. If the Water God sent us proper
rain, we could reap more grain. If it happened to be a dry year, our crop was a
poor one. I remember one year everybody said we would bring in a lot. However, a thirteen-day rain began as soon as we had cut down most of the rice. At
the end of the rain, 70 percent of the rice had sprouted in the field. By the
time the sunlight appeared again, another 20 percent of the rice ears had fallen

onto the ground. We harvested mostly damp straw. In addition to grain, the second main source of our team income came from several hundred pear trees around the village. Again, our pear crop depended on Heaven. Most years, our team received about 100 *yuan* from our pears. Forty households had to share that money.

In my own village production team the cash value of a ten-point workday varied from 20 to 30 *fen,* depending on our harvest. If I went out to work every day for a month, my total monthly income was around 7 *yuan* and 50 *fen.* Everything seemed all right during our first year. Both my wife and I went out to work. We both earned work points. But when expecting a child she had to spend most of her time at home, leaving me the only person gaining work points to support a family of three, and then four, mouths. I went out to work every day, never enjoying a day of rest. No matter how early I got up or how hard I worked, I often fell behind the others. At the year-end sum-up, my income from the team was poor. After deducting for the grain issued to us, I took home maybe 40 *yuan,* some years as little as 10.

Indeed, we peasants could do many things to improve our living standard, but the country had all sorts of policies to stop us. For instance, I could sell a big pig and use the money I received to buy the necessary equipment to make wine at home. Then I could sell wine in a street. But according to the policy at that time, wine was produced *only* by the country, in a state-owned factory. Or again, during the slack season I could have packed my bags and gone away to a distant county to find a job. But the government ordered all police stations to control giving out travel permits to let people go around. I had no choice but to stay at home and miss this opportunity of earning a little extra money to maintain my family. Nevertheless, I wanted to try something.

In my family, although my father-in-law was the oldest man, all our grain, eggs, dried meat, and money were controlled by my wife. So, one day, I stretched out my hand and said, "My dear finance minister, you know, when you want to catch a rat you have to put something into the trap. Do you think I can do anything if you are not willing to give me something first?"

"What's the matter with you today?" my wife asked. "Didn't I give you the same meal as I had?"

I sat down and told her slowly, "It's like this. You know I have given up the idea of ever reusing my English. Nevertheless, please believe me, with my basic knowledge of Mandarin I have the confidence to try something new, something special. I cannot promise that I will bring you a big bag of money, but I think we can try. As you see, our family population is increasing. You must consider things from all sides and provide me with relief funds. If I am to read scientific reports, I have to buy newspapers and magazines. If I am to visit friends to get their advice and experience, I must offer cigarettes. Can money fly into your purse if you just sit and do nothing at home?"

"It sounds very nice. Of course I want to eat well and wear something pretty, but at present I really cannot give you a penny for your extra use." Then she added gently, "I know you will not use the money to gamble or to buy yourself things to eat. Your aim is to improve our living conditions. Well, to say, think, or plan is easy; but when you actually begin to *do,* you will have to face so many problems. If you don't believe me, just go and feel my purse to see if it is a heavy one or a light one. Really, we are very poor. But our baby boy means we have got a booklet from the bank. Our next generation is ensured. That is also money. Don't be too anxious and sad. If we enjoy good health we won't go hungry. Anyway, you'll have to bear it for some time."

So, my wife didn't give me the economic support I needed. However, her attitude was a kind one. Listening to what she said, I believed her to be a persuadable wife.

*        *        *

My main problem at that time was my father-in-law. Upon learning that I didn't earn many points from our team, he began to grumble and look down on me. When he saw we received only a small share of village grain at the year's end, he gave me an ugly look. Later, he became so angry that he cursed me and even refused to speak to me. I had a hundred reasonable things to say, but I feared he might lose his temper. I had to hold my tongue and bear it.

Behind my back, he went around to visit my wife's friends, pestering them to turn against me. His only aim was to get his daughter to ask for a divorce. When I thought of the father, I wanted to get a divorce myself. After all, a wide gap still existed between the second wife and me; but on the whole, the true relationship between husband and wife was all right. And then there was our Lujiang. Had it not been for him, I might really have had a second divorce. But with a newborn son to think of, I had to consider everything more carefully.

In my spare time I just wandered about here and there, exchanging my thoughts with some of the aged people in the village. I went to visit the local Buddhist temples, because sometimes I planned on becoming a monk and making a living for myself in a remote temple. Each time my father-in-law quarreled with me, I went to stay with one of my sisters or my elder brother. But even the best fish smell after three days. Because of the eating problem, I had to return to my own home in the end and bear everything.

Fortunately, in our house it was my wife who acted as the man of the family. Even the father had to obey the daughter. She was the president of our little country. The father and the husband were her ordinary office workers. If a war broke out between us, she immediately appeared on the scene to make peace. In fact, it was my wife who got my father-in-law to listen to reason from time to time. She often ordered me to have my meals earlier or to let him eat first.

When the old man went out, she said, "Well, our father is this one. You cannot sell a father in the street or drive him away. You cannot exchange him for a better father with other people. Next time, just keep quiet."

Once I got so angry that I began to wrap up my quilt, having decided to leave for a temple. My wife sobbed at the gate. The little son was weeping in her arms. She knelt down and painfully pleaded, "Please stay. If you go you will spoil everything in our family. Change, change, everything in the world changes. Bad things won't stay long. I understand you didn't gain a lot of work points, but it wasn't your fault. I do not blame you for that. From the very first day after we got married, in my eyes, you have been a good husband. Look at the boy, he is a thousand times more precious than a million work points. We must bear it for some time and put the emphasis on the boy."

As we were saying this sad goodbye Mr. Liu, our team head, suddenly dropped in. He took my quilt back to my room. My secret plan stopped.

Like my kind-hearted wife, this Mr. Liu was a good man. In fact, in our eighty-household village, he was perhaps the only true friend I had. When he was young he had served in an army unit for several years. Maybe because he had traveled to many provinces he seemed to understand where my shoe pinched. He didn't have a college-level education, only three years in a middle school, but we understood each other well. When we discussed village affairs, our viewpoints didn't contradict each other.

It was Mr. Liu who often assigned me suitable jobs in the village fields. Once, facing a crowd at a meeting, he said, "When I am arranging various jobs for our group, my principle is to let each person have a chance to do his best. I hate those who put a square peg in a round hole. Our team will never become rich if we do this." He always tried to apply this policy to me. But because I was a man coming from another village and in my past history had been punished, some of his colleagues, those who belonged to the Team Committee, didn't always agree to his suggestions. Mr. Liu wanted me to dig or weed. That job was easier. I could do more. But the other leaders assigned me to join a group of women, to cut various crops, or to plant rice seedlings in water. How can a man catch a woman's speed in the field? I was so slow at planting that the women, laughing, suggested I supply them with rice seedlings or hand them buckets of water. At the end of the day, I received only ten work points, while they received at least sixteen or even twenty!

Once when Mr. Liu and I were alone together, he said, "Lao He, really I am very sorry for you. Too bad I am not the only master of this village. Our local team policies are made by many. I am only one among them. You are a fish, but unfortunately this village is a dry pond. I tried to bring some water for you to swim in and grow, but other leading members of the committee feared that if we stored too much water, the fish might grow too big and one day this fish might make huge dangerous waves. Here I bring water for you to swim in, over there they are making holes to let the water run out. Nearsighted people! You have received a higher education, but I failed to make them believe you could perform something good for our team."

When I told him some of my personal affairs at home, he said, "Not strange. Everybody has their own family problems. We can never enjoy a peaceful day. Your father-in-law, don't hate me when I tell you the truth ... Had it not been for Liberation he would have died a long time ago. He was most notorious. Talking to him is like talking to a buffalo. Leave him alone and cooperate with your wife. She is not the strongest woman, but everybody says that from her doings and sayings it seems as though she had been trained for some time in a school. Anyway, a village production team is not for you. You are a round peg, our village is a square hole. This village is not your permanent home. If there is a chance, you must leave Shangbaodian and do something else somewhere."

Not long after Mr. Liu stopped my departure, something new did happen in our county. The Yunnan Department of Forestry in Kunming came to Jianchuan to recruit forestry workers. A short-term contract, three to four years, was signed between this department and our county authorities. Mr. Liu took me to meet the man in charge of the agreement. He told me that each month they would pay a worker 39 *yuan*. Now, if I worked in our village production team I could earn only 7 *yuan* and 50 *fen* a month. And that money wouldn't reach my hand until the year-end came around. On top of this, although of course I couldn't use my knowledge of English, I would have a chance to make good use of my Mandarin.

My wife agreed to let me go. My elder brother and all my sisters were pleased to hear the news. A few leading members of our Team Committee, however, insisted on letting another young man, of poor peasant origin, take up the post. But it happened that at a higher-level meeting the officials supported Mr. Liu's proposal: to let me leave the village and become a "nation's worker."

\*  \*  \*

On March 25th, 1965, about 150 workers selected from Jianchuan County were gathered together. It took two days for our four trucks to get to a county called Yongren, to the north of Kunming. After that, we had to go on foot. Each carried his own luggage. We didn't reach our final destination until the last day of the month. A couple of days later another 150 men selected from Eryuan County arrived. That year, almost 1,000 young peasants were recruited from many counties throughout western Yunnan and organized into groups, called "work areas." We were called the Tenth Work Area, and our main job was to build a highway so that trucks could come and haul the logs away to the cities.

It was in a valley that we built our grass-roofed dormitories. Everything had to be moved over several mountains. As a rule, we spent two months building dormitories and then began to build several miles of highway. As soon as the highway had been checked and accepted by the technicians from headquarters, we moved on to build more dormitories and another stretch of highway. During the first year, we moved here and there four times. In 1967 we spent half a year in a newly industrialized city next to the Yangtze River, called Dukou, in Sichuan Province. The road we built there was for the use of the local coal mines.

That first year, since I was older, the leaders assigned me to work as a cook. I liked this job very much. My responsibility was to wash the rice and then heap it into a huge steamer. Sometimes I also helped the other cooks wash and cut the vegetables. I worked quietly, but when we moved to Dukou the leaders somehow discovered that I was a college student. Before long, I was asked to be the chief assistant of our work area's technician. This Master Geng, as we called him, taught me something from his surveyor's course book. In the daytime, I carried a three-meter-long cylindrical ruler and followed my Master Geng. Sometimes I acted as a secretary, copying work reports for the headquarters office. When the officials at headquarters were too busy, they asked me to attend planning meetings in other work areas for them.

I enjoyed my job. I worked hard and listened to Master Geng carefully. We became good friends. He told other leaders, "Lao He does everything well, no mistakes. He is just the helper I need." Some of our daily necessities, such as sugar, soap, and meat, were hard to get hold of. But often my Master Geng made special arrangements for me to buy a little more than the rations allowed. When the rainy season came, my fellow workers wore handmade hats and shoes. For me, the head of the work area issued a machine-made raincoat and a pair of rubber boots. Each time I was sent out on public business I was given more than enough money to spend on transport and food. In this way, for a long time, I earned a little more than the ordinary workers.

The cultural level of the workers was not so high. Only about 10 percent of them had studied in middle schools. Many couldn't write even a simple letter to their parents. But before they had become forestry workers they had learned to do many things in their native villages. In English maybe you'd call them jacks-of-all-trades. There were folk singers and dancers, musicians, dressmakers, bakers, painters. It was an enjoyable thing to learn something of everything, but most of my time was spent among the bamboo weavers and carpenters in our work area woodwork group. When I had a special chance to buy extra rationed goods, I bought as much as I could and gave most to my carpenter and bamboo weaver friends. When the postman brought us letters from home they made a circle around me, kindly and cheerfully asking me to read news from their relatives or friends. Often it was I who wrote the reply as well. In return, they were only too pleased to teach me everything they knew. By 1967 I could weave a bamboo basket or a long-handled bamboo spoon. I could make a square wooden box, a small chair, a short-legged table.

Each month, right after I received my monthly salary, I kept 15 or 20 *yuan* in my pocket and mailed the remainder to my wife to help her maintain the family. Sometimes I asked our work area purchasing agent to buy and send a parcel home for Lujiang to play with or eat. Of course I missed my wife and son very much, but when I thought of my father-in-law's bad attitude, I remembered how much I hated him. And, frankly, I liked doing this work much more than being a peasant.

As we were about to leave Dukou, in the spring of 1968, a big reorganization took place. My happy days at the Tenth Work Area came to an end. Only two of the work areas continued building highways in Yongren's mountain corners. A few work areas remained in Dukou, but they entered into different kinds of industrial enterprises. Our Tenth Work Area became the Sixth Work Area, and our 300 workers were transferred to Ningna County in Yunnan, also to build highways. Starting in July 1968, we were called "Contracted workers of Ningna County's Forestry Bureau." The former leading officials, the office workers, the secretary, the accountant, and the technicians all went away to other organizations. I said goodbye to Master Geng.

A week after we got settled in Ningna County, I showed my official document, written by the Tenth Work Area secretary, to my new leaders. They received me warmly. I was welcome, they said, to share the same dormitory as the administrative staff. Within a few days the new technician, a Master Zhan, had become my good friend. I very much enjoyed being his assistant, too.

\*     \*     \*

But alas! The morning sun never lasts a day. Various troubles began to appear when the flame of the Great Proletarian Cultural Revolution spread to Ningna County.[2] The movement went around on a grand scale. Each worker was handed a most powerful weapon—a red-covered book containing Chairman Mao's quotations. At the end of a day, instead of asking each other, "How many cubic meters of earth did you move today?" the workers asked, "How many of Chairman Mao's quotations have you learned by heart today?" Highway building became a less important thing. If you had no inclination to go to work, you could sleep in bed for the whole day. Or if you did go, it didn't matter at all if you forgot to shoulder your spade or hoe. But if you forgot to take that red-covered book, you would be seriously criticized.

In the mornings, before we set out for work, everybody had to line up and shout revolutionary slogans together. Big-character posters were pasted onto the walls. Several quotations had to be read in chorus before a meeting could begin. When you wrote a personal letter to your friends or parents you had to include some of Chairman Mao's teachings at the top of the paper. We had to learn the Chairman's story by heart, and we were all required to recite his Old Three Articles—"The Foolish Old Man Who Moved Away a Mountain," "Serve the People," and "In Commemoration of Dr. Bethune"—from the very beginning to the very end. It was said that as soon as we were able to recite "The Foolish Old Man Who Moved Away a Mountain" we would be able to build the road faster.

In August, a Cultural Revolution Work Team arrived in Ningna. The members wore military uniforms and most were middle-aged. All they told us was "Our Cultural Revolution Work Team comes from a high-level military organization. Only soldiers of the People's Liberation Army are true followers and supporters of Chairman Mao." They organized a series of important meetings. One day, at a big rally, all our leaders were ordered to line up on a platform. Many were forced to wear white pointed paper hats one meter tall and to hang big wooden placards, saying something like "Running dog of Liu Shaochi," around their necks. They were accused of being double-dealers who outwardly supported Chairman Mao's proletarian cause but secretly planned to turn the people's New China into a capitalist country.

Mr. Zhan, my master technician, was a middle-aged man, a graduate from a university in north China. One day while we were chatting about the Cultural Revolution, he said, "I began to love Chairman Mao soon after I entered the university. His proletarian revolutionary line is the greatest line in the world. I am for all his policies. I haven't any problems at all. Nobody dares to touch a hair of my head." During the first meetings he always sat among the ordinary workers. Before long, however, his past was revealed in several big-character posters. They said his family history was an ugly one. His grandfather had failed to fight against the Japanese invaders in northeast China. In fact, this grandfather had followed the Japanese to harm our countrymen. The posters also accused him of having a wrong revolutionary line: Instead of learning from the workers, peasants, and soldiers, he relied on a handful of people who could read and write a little. After being struggled several times, he was forced to carry water for use in the kitchen and to clean out the public lavatory.

Late in August, several members of the Cultural Revolution Work Team left our leaders and came to inspect things among us ordinary workers. On the third day after they began, I was told to join a regular workers' group. Thus my job as a technician's assistant ended, and all my dreams of perhaps one day arranging a "sitting in an office job" disappeared into thin air. I was nevertheless happy, because nothing serious had befallen me. During the Anti-Rightist Movement I was a bachelor, but now I had a family. I had a child at home. No wisdom like silence. Keep my mouth shut and my eyes and ears open. All kinds of diseases come in through the mouth and all kinds of troubles go out from the mouth.

I didn't join any of the revolutionary groups that had sprung up, nor did I do anything unusual in public. I just followed suit. If my group members shouted, "Safeguard and defend our revolutionary headquarters headed by Chairman Mao and his bosom leader-friend Comrade Lin Biao!" I copied them. When they shouted, "Workers rise up wholeheartedly to join the unprecedented Cultural Revolution!" of course I repeated after them right away. I had learned how to weave a bamboo basket and how to make a chair. I had gained a general knowledge of surveying. I had saved enough money to buy a set of carpenter's tools. It wouldn't be too long before I went home.

But as I was silently planning this new future, the fires of the Cultural Revolution flamed on me. One morning in September someone in my group ran up to me and said, "I'm afraid ... maybe ... well ... Have you seen their big-character poster?" I rushed out and saw the poster. The title was written in red ink: ANOTHER VICTORY! The second line read: WE MUST STRIP AWAY HE LIYI'S "BEAUTIFUL COAT!" Under the headlines was written:

> Thirty-eight-year-old He Liyi, our former stinking technician's false assistant, was born into one of Jianchuan's biggest landlord families. His reactionary father sucked the blood of millions of people. He Liyi himself grew up exploiting thousands of poor peasants. The Party sent him to study at a college but he turned out to be an anti-Party element. He is a rightist, a reactionary stinking intellectual.
>
> In 1965, He Liyi disguised himself as a commune member and joined the ranks of the workers. The wolf secretly crept into the office and seized power, becoming a wholehearted follower of the capitalist "roaders."
>
> Soon after the arrival of the Cultural Revolution Work Team he escaped. Can a wolf in lamb's skin run away? No! Workers, soldiers and peasants are the main forces of our motherland. We are the masters of our country! Can we build the road if we keep a wolf in our work area?
>
> Comrades, open your eyes wider, and watch this wolf twenty-four hours a day. Let us come together and skin, wash, and sweep him out of our workers' ranks!

That evening I became the target of our group meeting. Once again I was forced to make a report of my past history. The second evening they asked me to confess how I had secretly "seized a chair" and become the helper of our technician. What had I been planning to do with the capitalist "roaders"? On the third evening, to avoid further trouble, I was forced to confess my "wrongdoings": "Please forgive me, give me a chance to turn over a new leaf. All your criticisms are kind and correct. It was the Party who made me a college student, but I didn't do anything good in return. I came here to build a road, but actually I was a running dog of the people in authority. I am very sorry. Please let me stay. Hereafter I shall follow all of you. I'll open fire at the enemy and protect our Party Central Committee."

I thought very soon they would make me wear a paper hat and give me a "big cleaning"—make a public show of me and then send me home. I prepared for this nearly every day; but, very strange, nothing happened to me after I criticized myself.

Several months later, a new work team arrived to conduct another, more up-to-date investigation. Some of the people in authority previously criticized were now set free and returned to their original posts. Master Zhan was one of these. But after his public humiliation he had become "cold" and, in a way, looked like a madman. Although he was now reinstated, the workers no longer trusted or respected him.

At the same time, those who had been very active in organizing workers to rebel were seriously criticized. On seeing these sudden changes in the movement we were all puzzled. No one could make head nor tail of it. I was able to read many articles in the newspapers and magazines, but even I was confused. One morning this man stood up and fired at that man. The next day another man appeared. The previous two were *both* criticized. Who was the true supporter and faithful follower of Chairman Mao? I really didn't know. I was too tired to draw a clear line between them. Every bird likes its own nest. No matter how the old man cursed me, his words were not so cruel as a political struggle movement. I was looking forward to returning to my home county.

In July 1969, the Ningna County Forestry Bureau finally announced that our contracts were over. On my way home I bought some clothes for the whole family, along with several books on raising rabbits and bees. I had wanted to keep rabbits and bees before, but I was too poor to buy a book then. With a view to trying my skill, I also bought a set of carpenter's tools.

My wife had borrowed 20 *yuan* for me the day I left home. When I returned, I placed 170 *yuan* into her hand. The day we had said goodbye, my son was only a baby, about a year old. Now she showed me a five-year-old boy. It was very easy to recognize my wife when the bus stopped, but I could hardly believe the boy standing beside her was my son.

"Hello, Cuilian," I said first. "How are you? You must be very tired?"

"Well, Lujiang's father." She looked as though she was going to weep. Gazing down in front of her, she let out a sigh and then smiled a little. "Xiao Jiang[3] was seriously ill many times, but he's all right now. Not so bad, all in all."

"Is he our Xiao Jiang?" I turned to the boy and stretched out my arms. But he was moving closer to his mother's legs.

"Come on, your baba, here he is!" My wife lifted him up. "Don't be afraid."

I took him in my arms and asked, "How old are you? Can you tell me?"

"Let me see. ..." My son showed his hand and began to count: "One, two, three, four, five, six, I am almost six now. Is that right, Mama?"

"Yes, you were only one when your baba left. I had to carry you on my back all the time; otherwise you picked up the chicks' droppings from the ground."

"Really?" my son asked his mother.

"Yes, you even *ate* some of the chicks' droppings!"

"Now I can run faster than Mama. I can run to our village school, too!"

"You can?"

"Their teacher scolded me. They didn't let me in. But I learned how they sing songs. Mama says the more I run, the bigger I grow. The faster I grow, the sooner I will be able to read a book and sing songs."

"You are a good boy." I put him down. "As soon as we get home I will give you something special. Now, you run up the hill and see if I can catch you."

As we watched the boy run ahead of us, we both smiled and smiled.

## NOTES

1. Mr. He writes, "Our team was divided into several groups. Each group was formed by ten or more families, ranging across many different ages. Sometimes the middle-aged women went to weed over there and the teen-aged boys and girls stayed here to dig. As for the group leaders, we had strong men, weak ladies, old and young."

2. The Cultural Revolution had its roots in Chinese Communist Party (CCP) in-fighting between members of the Maoist faction and those they accused of "taking the capitalist road." At the height of the Cultural Revolution, Red Guards rampaged through cities and countryside, attacking the Four Olds: old ideas, culture, customs, and habits. In the anarchy that followed, destruction and persecution occurred on a massive scale.

3. Xiao Jiang is Lujiang's nickname. *Xiao* means "little." When speaking directly to their children, parents in China always use a nickname rather than the child's full name.

# A TWO-MEMBER
# FAMILY MEETING

The final outcome of my being a contracted nation's worker was a good one. After my return from Ningna County, many things in my family began to change and improve. The Cultural Revolution was still raging on, but as I didn't join any special groups or take part in any "It's right to rebel!" activities, nothing serious happened to me. My wife was particularly happy about this. Political safety, she said, was a priceless gift for the whole family. In addition, with the money I turned in she bought a big mother pig for my father-in-law to look after. That mother pig cost 100 *yuan*. With the remaining 70 my wife purchased several bags of grain. As a result, our empty containers were filled up to their necks. We would not go hungry.

Before I had gone away, my father-in-law troubled me all the time. Actually I had become his enemy. Now his manner was changed, and not only because I brought back 170 *yuan*. A movement called the Socialist Education Movement had begun in the cities in 1963. It reached remote areas like my home village late in 1964. Before this movement ended, the Cultural Revolution had started. The two movements mixed together. Originally the Socialist Education Movement was aimed at weeding out corrupt and self-seeking village cadres, but for a time it was also called the "Four Clean-Ups Movement" and its targets were landlords, rich peasants, all types of counterrevolutionaries, and all kinds of wrongdoers such as smugglers, pickpockets, and those who stole public money or the country's public property.

Well, as a young man, my father-in-law had sold himself into the reactionary Kuomintang army. Liberation found him heavily addicted to opium. Originally his class position was perfect: poor peasant. But because of his two sins, when the Land Reform Movement started back in the early fifties he was given two bad names: "army riffraff" and "village loafer." In the late fifties and early sixties the villagers forgot about him. Year after year, he lived a plain life like many of the ordinary people. The Cultural Revolution had nothing to do with him. He was an aged old man in the countryside. Strictly speaking, he should have had no problems.

But people at the rural level, in the process of carrying out a political movement, always behaved as if they were following a traditional custom. As soon as the villagers were instructed to implement a new movement, those with "history" problems naturally came to mind as targets to be struggled with. In my small Shangbaodian village there were not many outstanding or serious problems among the village cadres, so the target of the movement was redirected to the village bad elements. It was a simple and easy thing to pick on them yet again.

Moreover, my father-in-law had an enemy. His name was He Dachen, and he shared the same gate and yard as our family.[1] His hatred toward us began a long time ago. As I mentioned before, my father-in-law was an opium addict. And he only had one daughter. He Dachen hoped this two-person family would disappear. In this way, he could eat up my father-in-law's house and other private property. Whenever he had an opportunity, he was a chief instigator against my father-in-law.

Thus, during the course of the Socialist Education Movement, my father-in-law was dragged out in public for a second time. They renewed his former caps: Kuomintang army riffraff and village loafer.

At every evening meeting the team leaders forced all the village's four kinds of bad elements to kneel down on the platform. Not only grown-ups but even three-year-old kids had a good time struggling them. Sometimes a "helicopter ride" was arranged. If the villagers were too busy to organize a big meeting, the bad elements were made to clean the roads about the village and all the public conveniences. If any kind of celebration or big mass rally was going to take place, it was always the four kinds of elements who were ordered to do all the preparations. Public property found to be in disrepair had to be restored by them. One evening a heavy storm damaged a telephone pole. The village head immediately ordered the bad elements to go into a distant mountain valley and cut down a new tree. Every season of the year they came under the village's careful and powerful control.

For a time, when our county was building a huge modern bridge over a river twelve *li* away from our village, all the county's bad elements were ordered to go and work there for short periods. After I returned from Ningna, our county authorities ordered my father-in-law to join them four times. Each time he was instructed to go he had to work for at least two or three months, carrying big, heavy rocks. All of them were required to make their daily meals themselves. Every other Sunday my wife asked me to take rice, vegetables, cooking oil, and salt to him. Every time I went I found him feeling very sad and terribly sorry for himself. Formerly he cursed me, but because he now had his own problems he no longer behaved as before. Each time I took him his provisions, he said, "I was wrong in the past. I am very, very sorry. Thank you." With the change in the old man's attitude, peace returned to our family.

\*       \*       \*

As for my special sister, my first divorced wife Guihua, truly I often thought of her. I was upset to discover that the meaningful pillowcase she had embroidered for me in Kunming had somehow got lost while I was away. By the time I returned from Ningna County, she and her family had been transferred back to our Jianchuan. However, I consciously kept a certain distance between us. I always reminded myself of this: "She is not an ordinary village girl any longer. She has joined Mr. China's Big Family. Our political and social status are not on the same level." During and after my time at Ningna, we exchanged only a few letters. Occasionally some friends or relatives told me they had seen her, but I pretended to hear nothing.

\*       \*       \*

On the whole, the national situation seemed to be changing a little. Our provincial radio station had begun to broadcast English lessons for the first time in years. Every now and then, usually on Saturdays, some boys and girls came to my house to ask English questions. Before long, I was told that our county's middle school in town was desperately short of English teachers. Our team head, still the same Mr. Liu, put in a good word for me to become an English teacher. The school authorities eagerly agreed, saying, "We would give you a big welcome if you could come and teach." But when the proposal was being studied at a higher level, they turned it down with an emphatic "NO!"

Once again I was taught the importance of a person's past history. The government had taken away my dirty rightist cap, but that cap had left a mark on my forehead. I could jump into the Pacific Ocean or the longest river in my country, but I could never wash that mark away. "I have no more ambition to struggle for anything higher," I said to myself. "Let the water run under the bridge." But although I had given up on my first love, English, I began to think and plan for life in the countryside. I had started collecting carpenter's tools, useful books on domestic animals, relevant agricultural articles. As long as Cuilian and I loved and cooperated we could maintain the family, and, maybe, become more successful as peasants.

One evening during our Spring Festival holiday of 1970, after all the other members of the family had gone to bed, we held a two-member Family Meeting in our kitchen. The aim of this important meeting was to decide how best to use our resources and time in order to raise our standard of living. We sat close to the stove and talked. Although a small power station had been built in our village in 1965, we were too poor to use electricity. The flickers from the smoldering wood in our stove were our only light.

First, we had a general look at our country's various national policies. Being poor farmers, how could we find the time or information to make a detailed research into Beijing's programs? All we could do was to guess at their general direction. My wife said, "In town today, I saw no more big-character wall posters. And on my way home I overheard something about a struggle meeting organized in another village to struggle a bad element."

I said, "That means the Great Proletarian Cultural Revolution may be coming to an end but another movement is about to begin. Our old man is known as one of the village's bad elements. We must all use our eyes and ears, watch and listen to others attentively, and be particularly careful when we use our lips."

The second item on our agenda was to make a careful study of the whole commune, all thirty-five villages, with special emphasis on the four bigger villages and two smaller ones that formed our brigade, and finally on our own village. What were the main characteristics of our Production Team One? In examining this problem we spent much time discussing the Team Committee members who controlled power: the team head, the vice-team head, our production team's grain storeman and general accountant, one or two richly experienced old farm hands, and one or two villagers who had become members of the Communist Party. We had to have a thorough understanding of the personality and working style of each one. Among them we could see two types. Some were "active"; they liked to flatter when they contacted higher-level officials. Maybe you could call them "yes-men." Ordinary villagers hated them but dared not oppose them openly, because if someone offended them in the morning, late in the afternoon they would think of a way to retaliate. They always liked to show their power.

Other team officials were reasonable and fair. When an important document was received from a higher level, instead of saying, "No problem; let's just do as the document says," they'd reply, "Wait a moment. Have you considered our actual local conditions and the practical effects on the villagers?" They decided things through reason and not according to a shadow. The broad village masses supported them, but they weren't always the most powerful. They couldn't prevent the unfair things, one after another, that happened all the time.

Each winter a special sum of money was sent from the provincial level to help the poorest farmers buy cotton-made coats or blankets. Year after year it was the same people who remained poor, and some officials envied them this money. Once or twice they secretly shared it out among themselves and their closer relatives. After our fair officials found out, they criticized the others seriously; but it was too late to get the money back.

When it came to dividing up the team's public produce, such as pears, straw, pumpkins, or, for the occasional festival, a little fresh meat from a village pig, our officials did it carelessly. They divided according to the total number of us team members, placing things in heaps on the ground of a courtyard. Then they ordered someone to go from house to house, calling people to

come and take their pile home. Each team member, old and young, was entitled to one pile, and we paid the low, low state price for this produce. But
some piles were good quality and some of them were bad. Those people who
were close friends or relatives of the leaders got the good ones—because they
were told first. Once I overheard a villager saying, "Isn't that funny! Too
strange! All our piles were small and rotten. We got only one piece of meat.
What about the powerful people? Most of theirs were beautiful, fresh, and
very large."

We came to the conclusion that the most important things in our daily lives
were "relationships," person-to-person connections. Only those who were
particularly skillful at staying on good terms with the leading circle of the village got on. My wife said, "I know sometimes at the year-end you doubt the
cash figure they fix for ten work points in our team. But you must never dare
to ask to see their books. Always remember: Bear everything, and never, never
offend people, especially the important ones. If they hate you they will give
you trouble in a hundred different ways."

Next we discussed our team members. Production Team One was situated
in the southern part of our village and also known as "Liu People's Team,"
because most of the members belonged to the Lius and the Hes. Production
Team Two, a little larger than ours and situated in the northern part of the village, was known as "Zhao People's Team."[2] Two-thirds of its members belonged to the Zhao clan. Sometimes the two teams planned and did everything on their own, sometimes they came together; sometimes they respected
and helped each other, sometimes they became angry and shouted at each
other in the village square. After the Land Reform Movement, the government forgot to solve the problem of ownership of the nearby mountains. This
was the main reason the two teams quarreled.[3]

The Zhao clan said, "It was the Zhao people who first arrived here and settled down first. Therefore, the mountains belong to the Zhaos."

The Liu people shouted, "No! You Zhaos were robbers and thieves. All the
mountains are our Lius."

Regarding this problem, I said to my wife, "We mustn't offend the people
in Production Team Two. Our attitude must look like Switzerland's attitude
in international affairs."

We went on to discuss our work-group members, our nearest neighbors, all
those we had to contact in our daily lives. Who always supported the team
head? Who were friendly? Who might give us a hand? What had we to say in
front of this person and what not to mention in front of that person? All these
questions were answered and agreed upon. Cuilian concluded, "In organizing a happier family, unity at home and particularly between husband and wife
is most important. If you unconsciously tell others about your husband or
wife, you create a chance for them to gossip. Our family is like that pumpkin
over there. The old man, you, and I are three seeds inside that pumpkin. If

one day one of these seeds gets rotten, it will spread its disease. But if we show outside people a love-each-and-united family, nobody is able to break our united tie."

The third thing we discussed was our own family economy. In connection with this big topic a heated debate arose over the issue of where we could best earn money and grain: from our village production team or from outside the team? We argued for almost an hour. Finally we both agreed to put the stress on developing household sideline productions *outside* the team. We came to the conclusion that only by performing a successful job at selling home-produced goods in the market could we have a chance to earn a little desperately needed cash to buy clothes, medicine, oil, salt, and baking soda.[4]

Through collective work in the team we could get the bulk of our grain. But it was already quite clear that the total grain we earned through collective labor could not feed our hungry mouths the whole year round. The trouble was that in recent years no one had the will to plant well and weed carefully in the village communal fields. Old and young, all looked at one another and performed their collective duty in a perfunctory manner. As a result, the fields returned us a poor crop. We concluded that it didn't matter if the grain we got through collective labor was insufficient to feed our household population. We could use the extra earnings from our own sideline productions to buy grain in the market and make up the difference.

The fourth item on the agenda was to sum up our past failures, analyze existing family problems, check the farming tools, weigh her purse and my wallet, determine what had to be bought right away, what could be put off for some time, how to stay on good terms with the troublesome old man, and, of course, how to bring up a good boy. Each of us made a self-criticism and expressed our true thoughts clearly.

The last thing was to draw up a concrete agreement about the division of labor, the important problem of how to share our housework and cooperate with one another. The principle was that each member, old and young, had to do everything to the best of his or her ability. The following was our family's division of labor:

> **Old Mr. He,** my father-in-law, was responsible for all the pigs. Every day, right after breakfast, he had to drive the mother pig outside so she could forage for food. He must take special care of all the baby pigs. He must observe and tell us the exact time for our mother pig to meet a father pig.

> **Mrs. He** was to act as the top official of the family. Her main duty was to take care of money and grain. Everybody had to get her permission if they wanted to buy something. Of course she was responsible for all buying and selling in the market. Her second job was to deal with

outsiders. Her third job was to produce beancurd to sell in the market. She also had to make three meals a day for four people and all the pigs.

**Mr. He** was to give up the idea of being the important man of the family. His position was to appear not as the husband but as a long-term hand. His main job was to go out and join the collective work as a permanent representative of our family. His second, more important job was to help Mrs. He with the daily task of grinding soya beans for her beancurd making. Every day, after supper, he had to carry twelve pails of water to our house for the following morning's use. Beancurd making requires plenty of water. He was also responsible for cutting a load of firewood in the mountains before dawn. In the evenings he had to practice his carpentry, help our son to recognize a few characters and those twenty-six English letters, and have a look at our vegetable garden, bees, and rabbits.

**He Lujiang,** *our son,* was to sweep the floor and count the hens and chicks three times a day. If a chick was found to be missing, he had to report to his mother and then bring it back at once. He was also responsible for cutting wild grass to feed our rabbits.

*       *       *

Our Family Meeting turned out to be a successful one. The results in 1971 and 1972 made us all happy. Of course it was hard work. Beancurd making is a heavy job. Both my wife and I had to get up very early every morning, around four o'clock. The first thing we did was to pour our soya beans, already softened by soaking, one spoonful after another into the center of a round stone. My wife and I then took turns pushing this stone-grinding machine around and around by hand. One person can do this only for a little time, as it is very tiring. When there was no moon, our only light came from a pinewood fire. No sooner was this job finished than I had to take up my axe and bamboo basket and walk and climb for at least an hour. Day broke and I began to dig roots and chop branches in the mountains. I returned at about ten o'clock, had a hurried breakfast, and then went out to join the collective work in our village communal fields.

Everybody knew I wasn't a good, experienced farmhand. In the villagers' own words, I was "Mr. Scholar" or "Mr. Pen." During the first years they looked down on me, often saying things like, "In our Farmers' University we are your good professors. You just copy us." But now, unexpectedly, whatever I did in the village turned out to be successful. My results were attractive and very convincing. I didn't dig and plant more than the others, nor did I carry heavier loads on my back. But I secretly rejoiced at the limited knowledge gained during my student days in Kunming, which I now put to good use. I bought some more relevant books, combined my bookish knowledge with the local specific conditions, and then began to think and try repeatedly on my two vegetable gardens—the smaller one linked with my house and the bigger one outside the village.

Time and time again the villagers planted wheat or corn only to find the seeds either eaten by a kind of worm or gone rotten. They had to plant and re-plant. Then one day I read an article on how to keep away the enemy under ground: "The best way to prevent worms damaging our seeds is to mix them with 'prickly bush' leaves. Many types of worms are afraid of this leaf because it produces a strange smell. Before planting the seeds, place them into a con-tainer with vegetable-seed oil and soak them for a while. Sprinkle on a little 666 powder.[5] In this way, the seeds will germinate earlier and nothing will come to attack them." I tried this several times, and it really worked.

In my village, people did nothing after a pumpkin began to grow. Once a book told me: "When the pumpkin grows up to two meters long, you cut off the head branch. Then, later, it will grow more and more branches. In this way, it will grow more pumpkins." I found that if I let my pumpkin plants grow in a natural way the branches would grow longer, but in the end the total number of pumpkins I got was smaller than by using this new method.

I planted my pumpkins in a big bamboo basket inside my courtyard, and let the branches crawl and climb up onto my warm roof. I took all possible mea-sures to keep away the frost. Once another article told me that the best way to grow vegetables was to build a glass house. I could see the reason why, but how could I afford to buy glass? (Even the wooden windows in our house were filled with paper, not glass.) However, I still tried an idea of my own. My "glass house" was made of straw. Besides this, in early spring, when the weather was still chilly, I always prepared a pile of half-dried grass or leaves around my vegetable garden. Very late, at about two or three o'clock in the morning, I'd get up and set fire to this pile, making a circle of smoke. This is the method I used to make my young vegetables feel warm and germinate at an earlier date.

Every early spring, people in my county town ran short of fresh vegetables. By this time of the year they were nearly all relying on dried vegetables. Using my new methods I found I could harvest in March or April. I was the earliest villager to sell fresh vegetables in the market, and all my bargains were gone in a flash. I sold local cabbage, spinach, pea-greens, and pumpkins. Once I went to Heqing County, about seventy *li* away, on foot. I hurried back with some young tomato plants. Soon I was selling tomatoes as well at an early date.

Of course, in the beginning I occasionally wasted money and entirely failed in some of my personal experiments. Once I bought several young apple-tree plants. Peaches and pears were too common in our district, too cheap, of no economic value. So I went to another county and, with great difficulty, bought the young apple trees. I planted them near our public pear orchard at the back of our village. I made a stick fence for each sapling as protection. But it was no use. Not only did children graze their sheep, goats, and pigs in the orchard, but the team cowherds also drove the teams' collective cattle and buffalo to graze there. When the second spring came, my apple trees were all damaged by the animals. Later I planted three expensive chestnut trees right next to my private land. My neighbors pulled them up, saying, "People can plant whatever they like on their private land. But as for fruit trees, you must build a wall around them; otherwise others will come to pick your fruit and destroy our crops under their feet."

We have a saying: "When no light can be found in the east, then go to find it in the west." With the help of a friend who lived in another county, I obtained a new type of wheat seeds. I planted them just as my friend had instructed me to. When our villagers plant wheat they usually carry animal manure and spread it all over the field. Then they drive two buffalo back and forth, ploughing and turning it up. After this, they use a hoe to smash all the bigger earth clods. Then they go up and down throwing seeds around. My experiment was quite different. I didn't throw down my limited seeds irregularly. Instead, first I found a ruler and a piece of string. I dug the ground neatly. All the lines must look straight, following the string. Then, at regular marks on my ruler, I placed my wheat seeds one by one into the ground, covering them up carefully. Later, when I wanted to add more fertilizer, I dug slowly until the roots appeared, and then placed the manure carefully onto the roots. In this way, I made full use of both seeds and fertilizer.

That summer of 1972, my private share of wheat surprised the whole village. Even some young men from the commune's Experimental Group came to visit me! Too bad my private land was so tiny. Even after all my careful efforts we still couldn't get much out of it.

In autumn, it is strange to tell, fruit such as peaches and pears from my hand seemed sweeter than those of my fellow-sellers. Actually, I had no special growing secret this time. It was all because I was very good at making contacts with customers from out of town. My fluent Mandarin surprised my buyers. I mostly sold to truck drivers, and soon had many "yellow-fish-monger" friends. My fruit was transported to Kunming, together with my name and address. Other villagers had to carry their fruit on their backs to market and spend the whole day selling. Many times, my fruit was sold in my village, sometimes under the very fruit tree from which it was picked.

Once a driver friend took me to visit his son who was engaged in taking care of rabbits on a state-owned farm. Previously I had kept only two or three smaller rabbits. They lived on grass and, therefore, were much cheaper than grain-fed chickens. If we had no money to buy pork, we occasionally killed a rabbit. But my driver friend's son advised me to raise another kind of rabbit— a bigger kind, with long hair used for making a type of expensive wool. I bought five or six, and in less than a year I had between thirty and forty. I began selling rabbits, rabbit hair and rabbit skins in the market.

The day I was visiting rabbits on the state-owned farm, I made another good friend who was responsible for bees. He taught me his scientific method of building houses for the bees and explained how to keep them clean. In 1973, I started selling honey in town. It happened once, due to transportation problems, that sugar was hard to buy in our area. On that occasion my honey sold at the speed of electricity. I made a good profit.

Sometimes I looked like an idler of the village, but actually my mind never took a rest. I always had three things about me: a pencil, a notebook, and a packet of cigarettes. After striking up a conversation with people, I would "steal" their skill away while chatting and offering cigarettes. They never objected, just smiled and said, "You are an interesting fellow. Come again." By constantly watching an old master carpenter and also an expert who was hired by our team to direct everything at our tilery,[6] I secretly learned more knowledge of making chairs, benches, and producing bricks and tiles.

Although we weren't one of the powerful families in the village, Mr. Liu was still my good friend. He often thought of ways to help and protect my family. He secretly told me, in advance, when our team was going to share out some produce. Sometimes, if the village received an important directive from the county government, Mr. Liu came to my house and told me about that newly received document. For a time the policies were often changed, and if you weren't warned it was easy to get into trouble. Mr. Liu would say something like, "The coming rally is very important. We all have to go under all circumstances. You will be criticized in public if you refuse."

*   *   *

If someone wanted me to compare one period in my life with another I would tell them, "The period from 1969 to 1972 was not so bad." I couldn't say I was very rich or free from care, but even today I still remember this: Before my employment as a contracted nation's worker in 1965, we often had to sell our two daily eggs in order to buy a little salt. My wife's purse was filled with air. If one of us fell ill, we had to run several *li* to many other villages, borrowing a *fen* here and a *fen* there from our relatives to buy medicine. Now such problems disappeared. Whenever my wife went to sell our products, our neighbors envied us. They didn't remember what a big sum of money we had to use to buy a bag of grain on the black market. Rice was most expensive. Our income was on the increase, but we were certainly not rich enough to eat pure rice three times a day. We still had to cut corners.

I have forgotten exactly how much we earned and spent during this period, but I can remember our total income for 1972 because it was higher than that for all other years. That year, our four-member family received only about 1,200 *jin* of grain from our production team. Just half of this was uncleaned rice. The remaining half included wheat, barley, broad beans, corn, and peas. We had to use some of this to feed our chickens and pigs. After the price of the grain had been deducted from our yearly work points, we received nearly 50 *yuan* in cash from the village.

That year, 1 *jin* of rice cost about 70 *fen*, at the black market price. (The state price was a mere 14 *fen*.) So, with that 50 *yuan*, we could buy only about 70 *jin* of rice. Well, a grown-up usually eats at least 50 *jin* of rice each month. Hundreds of thousands of peasants were in the same boat—we all had to think of ways to buy more grain to maintain our families.

What about the income from our household sideline production? In 1972 we sold five big pigs, earning us altogether 350 *yuan* cash. This was the old man's economic contribution. My wife was a bad finance minister. She didn't write down everything she sold. What remains in my memory is that we sold beancurd, eggs, hens, goats, rabbits, honey, fruit, and vegetables. After we paid out money for soap, salt, baking soda, cooking oil, chemical fertilizer, farming tools, and medicine, we were left with a profit of 200 *yuan*. The total reached 550 *yuan*.

Looking back, I think our success during this period was due to the following five points:

1. I had saved 170 *yuan* while working as a contracted nation's worker. That economic foundation was the mother of every little subsequent success.
2. We put the stress on the correct position. Rather than relying entirely on our collective village production team, we gathered our main strength from developing household sideline productions.
3. The four members of our family enjoyed good health. Having strong bodies, we accomplished all the housework smoothly. The domestic animals were also in good condition. Not a pig or a chick died.
4. Good cooperation, correct management, and mutual understanding were maintained from the beginning to the end. No angry faces, no rude manners, no complaints, and no big quarrels.
5. With the exception of my father-in-law's unavoidable problems, my wife and I, the main force of the family, had no political troubles in the village. We maintained a very good relationship with Mr. Liu. With his friendly support in all respects, both openly and secretly, we were able to solve many problems.

**NOTES**

1. Bai houses are built on the basis of two typical layouts. One is called *si he wu tianjing,* which means "one big courtyard with four smaller courtyards at each corner of the main one." Four rectangular houses are built around a central public courtyard;

the long sides of the houses face the main courtyard, and the smaller private courtyards are located at the short ends. The second layout is called *san fan yi zhaobi,* meaning "three houses facing opposite directions and one reflecting wall." Again there is a central courtyard, but it is formed by three houses and, along the fourth side, a wall. All the houses have two stories.

2. Mr. He explains, "Many Liu families live in the southern part of our village and the Zhao families in the northern part. Our He family lives in the middle. There is a wider lane in front of our gate. To the north of this lane, the Zhaos live."

3. "For a farmer," Mr. He writes, "a mountain with crowded trees and all sorts of plants means a pile of money. You gather not only firewood to cook daily meals but also pine-tree needles and other green leaves for fertilizer. One person was elected by both teams to be the forest-protector. If the person belonged to Team One, he purposely gave trouble to firewood collectors from Team Two. He confiscated their axes, knives, and bamboo baskets. The thing was just the same the other way around. In recent years there have been no more quarrels, because the nearby hills have become bare. Nowadays, it is difficult even to cut a little stick to drive a buffalo."

4. Baking soda is used whenever buns are made from wheat or barley flour. A spoonful of soda is mixed with water, and then flour is added. The buns are baked or steamed in a wooden steamer.

5. *666 powder:* benzene hexachloride.

6. *Tilery:* a factory or kiln for making tiles.

# 12

# STEALING OTHER PEOPLE'S SHIT

One evening in March 1973, my wife-boss of the family suddenly said to me, "Time is up. I cannot wait. This evening I am going to declare something top important."

"Is this the second session of our Family Meeting?" I asked.

"It's a Secret Emergency Meeting."

It was very late. Lujiang had fallen asleep on a bench. His mother hurried him to bed. As she came out of the bedroom, she asked, "Did you hear what I told him just now?"

"No. I was thinking about how to teach him a little English."

"At the moment there is something much, much more important, much, much greater than teaching English."

"Eat and drink, rice and money?"

"Yes, yes." She smiled, but immediately went on: "Although they are not exactly the reason why I want to hold this Emergency Meeting. Just now I said to Xiao Jiang, 'Sleep well. Very soon you won't be lonely. Just wait!' Understand now?"

She was all smiles; but to tell the truth, I really had no interest in smiling back. "It's getting late. Please deliver your opening speech."

"All right. You are a silly husband. You did everything, but now you are trying to run away."

"What do you mean? Is this the way to hold an Emergency Meeting?"

"I shall start the meeting now. Do you remember the Englishmen's proverb you taught me in the past?

"You give me too much trouble! How can I repeat all the things I taught you? Hurry up with your report."

"Oh, this is part of my opening speech. You and I must be 'In for a penny, in for a pound.'"

"Well, when did I neglect something? Is this your so-called Emergency Meeting, Mrs. Chairman?"

"Yes. Wait a minute. I have one more saying: 'In every beginning, think of the end.'"

"Oh, be careful. In this house, the wife rules the husband. But don't forget I am your teacher in many matters. It's too funny! You are using what I taught you to give me a new lecture."

"No, no, no! You are my secret director behind the curtain. I am in fact an ordinary actor. Let's continue with our meeting. I give you a week to make a five-year plan."

"What plan?"

"Yes, everything must be planned. Our country has several five-year plans. You and I must have a five-year plan for our four- or five-member family. You must use those sayings as the main principle of our plan."

"Say it clearly."

"To build a new house at the northern part of our yard, within five years."[1]

"Build a house! Our population is only four! To repair the old house is okay, but it's wasting money for four people to add another new house."

"Four people? You forget, 'In every beginning, think of the end.'"

"No, let me ask you, if I want to break wind, do I have to take down my trousers first to let the terrible air fly away?"

"Oh, you must not pour cold water onto my boiling heart! You are a big-school student, you still look down on me. You know, I lost Mother early in my childhood. Father became an opium smoker. He stole Mother's things. He sold the stairs. He ruined the house. After he escaped from the army he dropped me away again and remarried another woman. He cared nothing for me. All those years I was forced to be a slave girl for my aunt. The whole village looked down on me. They said my family was going to come to an end. My house would become a temple of ghosts and weeds. ..." As she said this she wept painfully.

"Oh, come on, I'm sorry, I apologize. I'll make a five-year plan tomorrow morning."

"After the nation's liberation, Chairman Mao, the Communists, saved me. That year all my relatives wanted me to marry a rich government worker. But I always had a thought of my own. You were worse than a beggar; but I loved you, so I finally married you. God pitied me. He gave me a boy. In 1967, while you were in Ningna, he fell seriously ill. For days and nights I didn't sleep. Now he has become a schoolboy. For years and years the aged people kept on saying a woman could only bear children. Not a single woman in this village's history has ever built a house. I don't believe it. I'm determined to break this record. I'll tell them to inform the world that I can build a house one day."

"You talk like a great gentleman. I support your idea with both hands up, but let me tell you another proverb: 'More haste, less speed.' Have you never heard people say that if we want to build a new house we must own three

heaps? One heap of stones and earth, one heap of money, and one heap of labor force. We have 550 *yuan* this year. We need *six* times 550 *yuan* to build a
simple house!"

"I am not forcing you to build a new house for me tomorrow morning.
What I want you to do is make a plan, not a one-day plan, but prepare for five
years to realize a plan. Money we can make gradually. A hen produces an egg a
day. In a week's time we collect seven eggs. Anyway, you know many small
things make a great thing. It's just because building a house is not an easy task;
that's why I want you to make some preparations to pave the way, to do a little
bit for the future. You will see with your own eyes what's going to happen in
our family. If God gives me a girl, it's simple; but if another boy is coming, we
must prepare another house."

"Oh, my great Chairman Wife, why were you talking in a zigzag way? Now
I begin to see the light. All your sayings meant the same thing: We must prepare something for the coming baby!"

My wife was deep in thought for a while. Then she asked, "I hope the next
one is a runner around the pot. And you?"

"Well, maybe a runner around the pot would make perfection still more
perfect."

"Yes, in our family, a girl means adding a flower to our most beautiful brocade, but too bad. ..."

"Why do you say 'too bad'? I think it's good, a happy event."

"It's not a needle-bearer that's coming, it's another book-bearer."

"You mean a boy? Which doctor says so?"

"I didn't go to a hospital doctor, but that same fortune-teller told me yesterday. She said the forthcoming child will be a brother, not a sister. If it's a
girl, one day she will leave the house and marry another man somewhere, but
a boy means he will bring a girl to live with us. That was why I had to hold an
Emergency Meeting this evening."

"You still believe that blind woman? For myself, I believe only half. I believe
science; a doctor's machine in Kunming will show you the truth."

"My fortune-teller is very famous, as good as a medical doctor. If the coming creature was to be a girl, I wouldn't let you behave like the silly man who
takes off his trousers before he breaks wind. It's a boy. We must prepare
enough rooms. If we as parents just stand by, later when the two boys grow
bigger they will fight each other."

"Yes, quite true! When I think of the problem further, I am sorry. It is my
fault. You know, over the past years, people said the only reason we remained
poor was because both you and I were the stupidest couple in the world.They
said a lot of women were trying their level best to bear children, as many as
their wombs could contain. As soon as a new baby is born to the ground, the
parents enjoy another share of the team's cheap public grain and produce.
How can a baby eat a big man's share? So they advised me to copy the example

of other couples: Bear more children and receive more from the commune. They are uneducated people. Shortsighted. I smiled and nodded, but had no intention of copying that foolish example. Well, now the same trouble comes to me. A father's burden is all right, but you, as a mother, you'll have to bear a heavier load."

"Well, well, can't be helped. What's done cannot be undone. We must not let our 550 *yuan* sleep in the box. You make a five-year plan tomorrow or the day after tomorrow. In my opinion, if everything ahead goes smoothly, we will have another 500 or 550 *yuan* next year and in the third year. Do a little each year. You go and buy some logs first."

"All right. It's going to be a big thing, really not easy; but, anyway, let's try it."

Two months later, I bought several bags of grain and sixteen logs. That afternoon, many villagers were astonished to learn that the logs were ours. The two horse-cart drivers helped us remove them down onto the ground. Our team head Mr. Liu and many other men also came to help with the unloading.

Some villagers congratulated us: "Great, great! Mr. and Mrs. He are a perfectly new type of couple in our village. In my memory, our Mrs. He is the first woman who can lead her husband to build a new house for their children's children." Others were skeptical: "Mr. He's new house will appear in our village on Lijiang's market day." Lijiang does not *have* a fixed market day—you go to buy and sell any day of the year in that county.

My second son—indeed, it was a boy!—was born in July of 1973. Of course we were happy, but it was not such a big thing as the birth of our first child. We did celebrate when the baby was one month old, but in a smaller way than with Lujiang, and there was no Occupation Day party. Again that fortune-teller told my wife, "If you want your second son to grow peacefully, you must use the power of nine buffalo and two tigers to find a foster father for him, a hunter; otherwise misfortune will befall him one day."

This time, an old friend introduced us to a hunter who belonged to the Yi nationality. He lived in the valley of a distant mountain. Our friend took us to see him. I carried the baby and my wife carried our gifts—two bottles of wine, some brown sugar, and several packets of best-quality cigarettes. We started out before dawn and arrived around two o'clock in the afternoon. The hunter's family received us warmly and invited us to share their lunch of potatoes.

After lunch, the hunter asked about our new baby's elder brother's name. He thought for a moment and then said, "Let him be called He Luzhong." The *Lu* is the same as in Lujiang. *Zhong* means "clock."

As we said goodbye, the hunter added, "You know that the left part of the word *zhong* is "gold." That means your second son will make more money than his older brother."

My wife was very pleased.

Four months before the child's birth, the mother had stopped doing her regular housework, including our household sidelines, of which the most important was beancurd making. Ordinarily, much of the housework was the lady's job, but at a time when she was expecting another baby, naturally I became the only person in the house to shoulder everything. We had no mother-in-law to help. It was a great strain. And then right after the boy's birth, she had to rest for several months.

Of course, the mother couldn't go up the mountain in the mornings. So, besides my own job of cutting firewood, I had to take her place by cutting grass and collecting dry pine needles on the mountain slopes. We used these things to make beds for our domestic animals. A little while after sunrise I returned home with my mountain produce. Then I had to hurry with all the other household chores. When these were completed I usually went out to buy or sell in the market, normally my wife's job. I found this a most troublesome problem. In a village market square the buyer and seller negotiate the price for a long, long time. My wife often scolded me or showed anger for giving the seller too much money, or for taking too little from the buyer. The other job I found most tiresome was getting our wheat or barley ground into flour, traditionally the wife's job in our area. This had to be done every time we ran out of rice. The nearest water-mill was seven *li* away from our village, but it was usually so crowded that I had to go from mill to mill and wait for hours and hours. During the second and third months, I occasionally found time to go out to work in the village fields.

Both my wife and I were exhausted all the time. But when we looked at our new little son, or saw Lujiang kiss his brother, we felt our brocade was perfect.

\*         \*         \*

Our second son's birth seriously weakened our family economy. Income from the village team, and especially from our household sideline productions, dropped steeply. How could I work at our sidelines or join in the field work every day with so many chores to do at home? Two or three months after the birth, my wife started preparing the daily meals, feeding the pigs, and seeing to other odd jobs around the house. She began doing part-time jobs outside the home during the fourth month. When my second son was about six months old, my wife started making beancurd again, but only for friends and neighbors. In return they gave us firewood. Not until Luzhong was over a year old did we start making beancurd for the market once more.

No sooner was my wife strong enough to shoulder some of our daily burdens than a kind of swine fever, hog cholera, spread from village to village. Instead of selling fat pigs at the market for a good profit, we often found ourselves burying them at the back of the village. For a time we kept as many as eighteen pigs—at least twelve anyway, including the baby pigs. But when this acute disease spread over the countryside, they died group after group, quickly. In our village about 30 percent of the pigs died. It was said that in some villages all the pigs died. Everybody suffered hardships and fell into a state of sadness and low spirits. By 1976 we had only one pig left. And then this pig, which we had carefully kept for our own use, also died. In 1977 the whole family was so poor that we didn't know the taste of meat.

Our hens and cocks also suffered a series of troubles. Like the pigs, they too were attacked by a kind of disease and died pitifully. Even eggs were hard to come by in our family. In the past, when we ran short of cash, we used to sell two eggs and with the money buy daily essentials. Now, month after month, we had not a penny in the house. When summertime came around, we had to make a smoking fire at the foot of our beds every night, as we had no extra money to buy coils of drive-away-mosquito incense. Our clothes grew shabby, and little by little it became my wife's evening job to mend and repair. Shirts, trousers, and jackets became heavy, patch after patch, and stinking.

The food we ate, too, became rough and coarse. Rice was available about half the year. The only solution for the other half was to eat rough grains such as barley, corn, and beans.[2] When the new crop was in the blade and the old one all consumed, you were considered lucky to have even rough grain. The year 1975 was a year of serious drought. People's hands, shoulders, and backs could never get rid of the dry weather. The young rice plants couldn't be planted in time. A large number of the dry crops on the hillsides died from lack of water.[3] The following year the problem of feeding our mouths became even worse.

For breakfast, typically everybody ate wheat-flour buns. For lunch, we ate several potatoes and drank two bowls of thin soup. We thought supper was the most important meal of the day so, when it was available, a little portion of rice was added to our vegetables, but never enough to divide the total amount into five bowlfuls. Most of the rice went into the mouths of the old and the young. My wife and I ate just several spoonfuls, not to stave off hunger but as a kind of medicine to maintain our lives.

Because our food was bad, I often suffered stomach trouble. Every month I had to stay in bed for several days. It was the same trouble with my second son. He got sick nearly every month of the year. This was one of the most painful things in my life. Much money was spent in the hospital buying medicine for the younger boy. These health problems meant that even after Luzhong was a little older, neither my wife nor I could join the collective farm work in the fields every day. My father-in-law did odd jobs only now and then. Our two boys depended on us. In my five-member family we had no well-experienced, strong farmer to gain work points every day. Our year-end income was too poor to speak of. The poorest year was perhaps 1976. Based on the family's work-point booklet, we received 900 *jin* of grain, which included rice, wheat, broad beans, and so on, and about 15 *yuan* cash for the whole year.

The Cultural Revolution was still raging on, but down in our villages it began to take a different direction. Political disasters added to the natural ones. Sometime in the mid-seventies, our local leaders began putting the emphasis on participation in collective work. This was stressed above all else. Previously, year after year, in our village production team the policy for working days looked like "do it as you please." It didn't matter whether you worked in the village fields for the whole month or only for several days within a month. Now such choices disappeared. Women had perhaps three or four days holiday in a month during menstruation. But at a big meeting our team head said, "Now listen to my words: This month all the men have to come out to work in the fields for twenty-nine days. At the month-end, if your work-point booklet shows you have come out for the whole month, then the work-point recorder will add another twenty points as a reward. But if you worked only twenty-eight days, he will deduct twenty points from your booklet as a punishment."

Pressing family problems or person-to-person business could be conducted only in the early mornings or late afternoons. The team head even grumbled when I took a day off for being ill. Time for household sideline production became limited, although we were desperate to supplement our team income. Everybody felt that this new policy was too strict, but we were powerless. When we went to check our work points at the end of a month, we could hear the man say something like, "You are very good. You love our village. You are not a lazybones. You worked throughout the entire month. Therefore, the team will give you some extra points as a reward."

In the market, the so-called Market Control Committee was growing more powerful than the county government! To make a long story short, people who wanted to do business in the market were said to be those who had capitalist ideas. And if they had capitalist thoughts, they had no desire to build a rich, strong, socialist country. Sometimes you were allowed to sell certain homemade products, but only a little. If you placed out a big heap of goods onto a sidewalk, people would say, "You want to get rich. You are a money maker." As a result, a seller couldn't meet his buyer openly. All kinds of bargains were conducted secretly at street corners. Consequently, everything became expensive.

*       *       *

After our last pig died in 1976, not only were we without a piece of home-produced meat the entire following year, but when we cooked, all sorts of vegetable oils had to take the place of lard. We render down the fat from our yearly pig, usually killed, dried, and salted during the winter season, to make lard for all our cooking needs in the coming year. That year we had to search for other oils.

One day I ran into a mountain-corner poor farmer as I was trying secretly to buy cooking oil. I noticed he had several bottles of oil covered in his basket. The price he demanded was cheaper than for other vegetable oils. I bought one bottle from him. He told me, "Mine is peach-pit oil. Don't worry. Exactly as good as other oils. I collect all the peach pits I see in my spare time. I break each pit, take out the little heart. Finally I put them all into an oil-press machine, then oil drops down."

I tried this experiment right after I learned his method. Pit-collecting work began on my way home that very afternoon. Exactly one year after I bought that bottle from the poor farmer, I succeeded in producing eight bottles of peach-pit oil. Part of my meat problem was solved. I sold four bottles and kept the remaining four for home use. However, this job was really not easy. The whole family had to help me. Half of the peach pits were collected by me, 20 percent by my father-in-law. My wife and older son picked up the other 30 percent. The trouble was that we were not peach-orchard owners. The pits had to be collected one by one, from all corners. If you wanted to produce a bottle, you had to collect hundreds and hundreds of peach pits.

In order to collect more, wherever we went, we never stopped roving our eyes over the roads, roadsides, fields. If I saw someone eating a peach, I waited until the eater threw away the pit. After I finished my field work in the afternoons, I used to run for about fifteen minutes until I got to our commune market.[4] I went there several times a week. When the weekly market day came round in Jinghuazheng, I sometimes pretended my stomach ached and asked for a day off. In fact, I told my group a lie. I didn't go to a hospital. I walked the nine *li* to town in order to be a peach-pit collector. Sometimes I said to a group of peach-eating people, "Ladies and gentlemen, I use the pits to make medicine. Please put them here in this cardboard box. If you throw them down, the pigs will eat them up." On market days there were always many pigs wandering around the streets. Very often I had to struggle with a pig in the gutter before I could pick up a pit. Once I had a quarrel with the pig's master as well!

In my remaining spare time I made and sold my self-produced furniture. Every day, as soon as I got home, I took up my saw or hammer and set to work for a little while. Even when I was having lunch I looked at my unfinished chair. Right after I put down my chopsticks, I took up my hammer. If it was early, I went on sawing or hammering. If it was late, I shouldered my hoe and ran after the others. After supper, I lit a lamp and began to work. If there was nothing special in the house, I used to do carpentry work for at least three hours. Nine out of ten days I went to bed between twelve and one.

Where did I get my raw materials? I selected half from my firewood allotment. Fortunately, the "mountain's master," the forest-protector, was Lujiang's foster father Uncle Wang. He secretly allowed me to cut whatever I wanted. From 1973 to 1979, I made all designs of wooden rakes and harrows, bedsteads, small short-legged round tables, stools, benches, and chairs. From an aged famous master-carpenter of our area I learned to paint my furniture beautifully. Once I made forty sets of ping-pong bats and painted them brightly. There is a time for everything, as the saying goes. I went out to sell them on June 1st, International Children's Day, a big celebration in our country. (Lujiang asked me to give him a pair to play with, but I couldn't spare even a single pair. The question of feeding our bellies was above all.) After the autumn harvest, I made a kind of little rake for people to use once they have ground their glutinous rice into dry powder. These also sold well.

In 1973 and 1974, there was no serious difficulty in selling my homemade furniture openly in the market. But as the market policy tightened in the mid-seventies, selling became a dangerous business. Sometimes the Market Control Committee caught you, confiscated your products, fined you, even arrested you. Sometimes they didn't discover you. It was always a risk.

In 1976, again using a health excuse to fool my team, I took a dangerous trip to Xiaguan. I went to sell thirty little benches, two round tables, and five long-legged chairs. I carried them on my back and left before dawn, taking care that no one in my village should see me. A truck driver charged me a big sum of money in return for transporting me and my small furniture to Xiaguan. All the way I had to pay for his meals. That afternoon, I hung the thirty benches on the two ends of a pole. For safety, I traveled from lane to lane, moving all the time. In less than two hours I had sold everything. In fact, two-thirds of those benches I exchanged for grain coupons, not money.

The following day, I left my hotel room early and went out to sell the chairs and tables. I was just untying the rope when all at once I was surrounded by a group of young strangers. They were dressed in plain clothes, but after a few minutes they showed me their identification as market inspectors. Listening to their questions and seeing their attitude, I realized I was in trouble. I pretended nothing was wrong and replied carefully. Each minute the circle around my chairs grew larger and larger. Several people shouted at the tops of their lungs. Some criticized, some wanted to buy, some took a chair and quietly went away without paying me. Luckily, I caught sight of a good friend of mine. There were crowds of people, animals, and all sorts of noises, but this seemed like nothing to me. My attention was focused on using my eyes to make contact with my friend.

One of the market inspectors pushed me in the back: "You haven't sold any, I know. The punishment won't be too serious. Be good and just follow us to the Market Control Office. They will pay you."

"No, that's too easy for him! Arrest him right away!"

They marched me to their Market Control Office then and there. My heart was in my mouth. My friend also followed the crowd. At the Market Control Office he spoke up for me: "I can vouch for this man. He comes from a nearby village. ..."

"Confiscate his goods at once!"

"Really, he is not a smuggler but an ordinary peasant. All homemade products. ..."

Finally they paid me for my self-made things, but on the basis of the state price, about half the price I could have received in the market.

\*     \*     \*

Our China is a very big country, but I must say, everything in China is slow and backward. Many of the farmers in my Jianchuan County today still have to drive a buffalo, our "tractor," about the fields. A large portion of the fertilizer we use on our vegetables is produced not in a factory but in our own private lavatories. This nightsoil has to be collected from all the lavatories and then spread on our fields. It's a dirty job, but if you are a farmer it's a must.

At the beginning, many of my friends, including some close relatives, advised me not to do this dirtiest job. However, I didn't agree with their viewpoint. My theory was: My college education is a thing of the past. My name is not written down in Mr. China's book. I am only an ordinary peasant, and a peasant's job is to grow more grain. In the course of increasing production, a farmer should use more manure; otherwise he will fail to get in a bumper crop. Machine-made chemical fertilizer is wonderful, but I am too poor to buy that very often, and human excrement is considered many times more effective than animal droppings. Anyway, I had no time to consider the difference between a college student and a peasant in the countryside. I didn't care whether it was a clean job or a terrible-smelling job.

I needed nightsoil—not only to spread on my private land but also to offer to our work team. Our team welcomed human excrement with open arms. It had been set as a rule that if you offered two pails of nightsoil, the team would give you 18 work points as a reward. And 18 work points meant almost two whole days' worth of work points. If everything went by smoothly, I could steal several pails of nightsoil within three or four hours before day broke. If I went out to work in the field from breakfast to supper for thirty days, I gained 300 work points. Now, if I offered two pails of nightsoil for thirty days, I would get 540 work points. So, as you can see, it was well worth my while.

In order to accumulate more nightsoil, I dug a sort of den in my private vegetable garden. I carried many stones and lined the den with lime and cement. This shit-container was perhaps the largest one in our village. I bought several wooden pails and several flashlights. In addition, I ordered three big iron spoons of different sizes. These I nailed to the ends of three long poles. Where did I go with all my equipment? This was a very, very important question. Every household took extremely good care of their own private lavatory. A person would get into serious trouble and be punished if caught stealing private shit. So all the public conveniences became my evening offices. None of the villagers cared if public shit was stolen. And as for the village officials, they welcomed the extra excrement—more fertilizer would make our village fields grow better crops. So they turned a blind eye to my stealing activities.

It was a two-*li* walk around to the local bus station, commune office buildings, our schools, and the hospital. There were some state-owned hotels and restaurants in the marketplace, but I avoided their public lavatories because someone was engaged to watch the valuable nightsoil. Later they sold it to our local communes. Even after a late night doing carpentry I still woke early, as soon as I heard our cock crow; or, if we had no cock, the position of some stars in the sky told me it was time to get up. Immediately I picked up my two pails. I left the village quietly. As I approached my "office" I had to be more careful, making sure there was nothing unusual. The moment I entered, I hurried with my long-handled iron spoon. If I couldn't fill up two pails, I had to steal more nightsoil from a second or third lavatory. If I found there was plenty, I ran back for more. Returning to our village, I emptied the pails into my private manure pit.

Well, some nightsoil is thick and some is thin. When our team head said, "Today every household must carry their shit out," I secretly added some water into my pit. In this way, four pails of thick shit became six or seven pails of thin shit. I had to spend one whole day, sometimes several days, emptying my pit. The villagers called my den of nightsoil "Mr. He's private human-excrement factory." Some said, "Mr. He is not only a manager of an underground furniture factory but a manager of shit as well." At the end of a year, the total nightsoil I offered was Number One in our village.

Let me give you a concrete figure. A neighbor of mine was as old as I was. In 1975 his personal work points totaled 3,000. My personal work points totaled 5,200. Why? He slept and slept until daybreak, while I ran out to steal shit. When it rained heavily, or when people were celebrating a festival, they usually enjoyed themselves or relaxed in bed. But on these occasions I was the busiest man in the village. Rain and festivals were golden opportunities for me to steal from all the public lavatories. Year after year, I spent the five or six days of my Spring Festival holiday in all the public conveniences. Once during this festival I managed to steal eight pails at the local bus station.

My total work points for 1975, my best shit-stealing year, surprised everyone. I even heard things like "Two hands working in the field can never achieve that number!" A big help it was, but even those 5,200 work points were not enough for our five-member family. When my wife and father-in-law's work points were added to mine, our total family figure that year was 8,000 work points. It was considered "almost okay" for a five-member family to earn 15,000 work points annually; on average, each person in the family should have 3,000 work points. So from these figures you can see how poor we still were.

Well, friends, sometimes I dropped my flashlight down. Sometimes a pail broke and nightsoil splashed out. Once I was caught at our bus station by one

*Stealing shit. (An artists' rendition by Li Zhao and Pan Qing)*

of the workers there. My pails were smashed, and I was further punished by being made to sweep the floor in the bus station, around all the dirty corners. The second time I was caught I had to write a self-criticism report. But on the whole, I was a good stealer of shit.

## NOTES

1. Mr. He says, "Ours is a *san fan yi zhaobi* courtyard. We own half of the west house and also the northern side of the courtyard. But this northern house was a very simple one—year after year we just built a shed for hens or pigs. He Dachen and his family own the rest. Our 'reflecting wall' is very simple and low. It is built of earth and has no special decorations on it, according to our local traditional customs."

2. Rice and wheat, known as *xiliang,* are considered the best grains; grains such as barley, corn, and beans, known as *culiang,* are considered coarse and inferior.

3. *Dry crops:* Rice has to be grown in a flooded field under a few inches of water. In contrast, all other crops are known as "dry crops."

4. The center of Mr. He's commune, which includes a middle school, hospital, and market, is located about 2 *li* away from Shangbaodian. Jinghuazheng, the center of the county government, is a larger and more important town located about 9 *li* away.

# 13

# TWO MISFORTUNES AND A "PUBLIC PARADE"

Life in the village became harder with each passing year. I was a farmer, but, funny, although I worked in the fields all the year round I had to buy more and more grain from the market to maintain the family. By the time Lujiang's younger brother was three or four, my wife and I had doubled our efforts many times. I really made good use of each minute of each twenty-four-hour day, yet we still could barely feed our family. In order to earn a little essential cash, we were forced to risk the market week after week. I knew I had to be very careful, but it had also been reported openly at a village general meeting that the main purpose of the market clampdown was to stop illegal operations by smugglers. A smuggler bought things cheaply here, then sold them at a higher price there. He secretly bought grain coupons, oil coupons, cloth coupons, and meat coupons, then resold them for a profit. This was illegal. But anything produced at home by ourselves was supposed to be within the market law.

After the birth of her second son, my fourth sister managed to give me 200 eggs and a cock. I had been to attend her baby's one-month-old party, and after all the relatives went home, she asked her mother-in-law to sit next to me. Then she related my sad story to the old woman. Before my sister opened her mouth to speak more, the woman found a big basket and said, "As brother and sister of the same mother you should help each other. Take these 100 eggs and go sell them." These were given openly, but a few days later a good friend of my fourth sister came to see me. She said in a whisper, "Just now I came from our county town. This is top secret among brother and sister. This morning your fourth sister asked me to sell their cocks and eggs. Oh, they received a lot. She told me to save 100 eggs and a cock and on my way back to give them to you."[1]

The following Sunday was rainy and there was no team work. Therefore, my wife and I arranged between us that I was to sell the 200 hundred eggs and the fat cock, and also two hens and two jars of honey at the big market in

Jinghuazheng. She and Lujiang were to sell homemade beancurd at our local commune market. My second son was still a toddler, so my father-in-law was to stay home and look after the house and the little boy.

Well, I was an ordinary commune member. All my things were home-produced. So I openly placed my eggs and honey on the pavement, then stood next to them holding the chickens in my arms. Soon I was circled by a crowd of buyers. All of a sudden my hands were struck by a heavy blow. The cock flew away, and the two hens jumped up and disappeared. I ran after and managed to catch the cock and one of the hens. I returned only to find a big mother pig eating my broken eggs. The two jars of honey were broken into pieces, and some children were licking their fingers.

"Look, a typical capitalist." A man with a red cloth badge on his sleeve pointed at my forehead. "Haven't you studied the market policies?"

"I am a peasant," was my reply.

"Shut up!" another man roared at me. "Which commune are you from?"

"You pay me money for the damage!" I protested.

"Over there, go and kill the pig!" Then a roar of laughter followed.

"It's your fault. Who invited you here to sell these things?"

"Let's arrest him!"

"No, wait a minute!" Suddenly there appeared two armymen. "Well, what's up?" said the first. "It isn't an international big question. Buying something to feed our mouths. ..."

The second armyman gave me 10 *yuan* and took the cock and hen.

"No, only one, not two at one time!" The man with the red badge snatched half of the money and returned the hen to my hand. Finally he turned to the crowd. "That's the policy today. Very good policy. Free, everybody can sell. Everybody can buy. But not too much. A little. Everybody is allowed to buy a little and sell a little."

"A little, a little," the armyman repeated, tucking the cock under his arm. "All right, all right. A little is better than buying absolutely nothing!"

Carrying the crowing cock, he walked away, followed by the first armyman.

I continued standing there, trying to sell the hen. A while later the armyman who had bought the cock returned. He patted me and pushed me a little, saying, "Young man, it's too late now to do anything about your honey and eggs. Everything is in a state of confusion lately. The best policy is to go home right now."

A short time before sunset, as I was nearing to our village, I saw Lujiang running down from our commune market square. "Give me money, be quick!" he said, tears running down his cheeks. "Mother is going to die if we do not place the money on their table."

He explained that while they were selling beancurd, a group of market officials had kicked down our beancurd stall and Mother was seriously injured.

"How was that?"

"My mother couldn't forgive the kicker. She ran after them. Suddenly they turned back and my mother was knocked down to the ground. Just then a three-wheeled tractor passed by and ran over her left leg."

"Where is she now?"

"Outside our commune hospital's main gate. Those doctors wouldn't take her inside unless 50 *yuan* was paid in advance. I just cried; my mother wept most painfully. We began to fill out a hospital form, but we didn't know if they would accept or reject it. Then suddenly there came a white ambulance. Four well-dressed people climbed out and one of them, a lady, examined my mother's leg first, asking her some questions. A nurse said to leave my mother alone unless she paid the money. Another said her leg couldn't be operated on at this little local hospital. On hearing these words, my mother said to me, 'If you love Mother, ask somebody to carry me home right now. You must know, if I die outside our house the God in Hell will not allow me to see you again in the other world. My soul will never be able to return home! Hurry up and call your father or grandfather.'

"Their gatekeeper watched all this. He came forward and volunteered to carry Mother, but a young doctor shouted at the old man, 'Don't you know whose wife this woman is?'

"Before the old gatekeeper could reply, the lady from the ambulance shouted back, 'Whose leg is injured, this lady's or her husband's? One thing is very clear—I know a doctor means a person who heals another person. This woman's leg is in danger. We must do something; we cannot just stand and look!'

" 'Yes, yes.' The head of the hospital passed her our half-filled out form, and said in a lower voice, 'Please look at this form, here, the woman's name, her husband's name, occupation, a rightist. ...'

"The ambulance-lady gave our form a swift glance and said, 'I am not a member of your hospital. I am just a traveler who chanced to pass by. But I am also a medical worker. Regulations are our working law, a system we must all obey. Fifty *yuan* first is our regulation, but who always has 50 *yuan* about him? Money is less important at this moment. This woman will earn a lot of 50 *yuans* if her leg is all right.'

"The gatekeeper nudged me and said, 'Life is above all. Hurry up, my boy.'

"I started to run home, but that lady ran after me. She comforted me in a low voice: 'Don't cry. Run slowly or you'll fall. Don't worry about that sum of money. Tell your father not to worry a bit.'

"She spoke like a mother, very kind, but I was still afraid, because as I ran on I still heard, 'NO! Don't admit her!' "

\*       \*       \*

In the distance we could see the hospital. Nobody around. As we came up to the main gate the old gatekeeper clutched his two palms together and said,

"Thank Heaven and Earth! Thank Chairman Mao! Your wife must have done a lot of good deeds for the poor in her life."

"Is she all right?"

"Don't worry, don't worry," the old man said. "If she had not done good for the poor, Heaven would not have created such a good opportunity for her!"

The old man went on to tell us that a high-level doctors' car had come along. On seeing that the accident was unusual, they had taken my wife to Jinghuazheng, to a bigger hospital, without delay.

"Who paid the money?" I asked, putting my hand into my pocket. "I earned only a little today."

"No need for you to worry about that," the old man explained. "That lady from the ambulance gave the orders, and we carried your wife into the car. Just go to the county hospital in town and see her."

The sun had gone down. We went home and had supper in a hurry. Carrying some quilts and a set of cooking implements for my wife's use in the hospital, my son and I set out for Jinghuazheng. It was getting late. We couldn't hitch a ride as all the vehicles on the road seemed to have come to a stop. Not even a bicycle or a horse-cart came along. And then, to top it all, down came a heavy rain. I hurried my son; he slipped in the mud. Both of us were completely drenched. All along the way I thought, "If my wife is crippled, we will become poorer and poorer. If they won't operate without the money. ..."

We slowly dragged ourselves forward in the dark. At perhaps ten o'clock, when we had walked half the distance, a jeep slowed down and stopped behind us. The driver leaned out of the window and shouted, "Are you going to the hospital? Are you from the Haihong Brigade of Diannan Commune?"

"Yes! How did you know all that?"

The driver urged us to get in at once. From the back seat, a cock gave a sudden crow the moment my son sat down. I felt even more puzzled, because I immediately recognized the cock as the one I had sold that very afternoon. The buyer must have something to do with this jeep, I thought to myself. The jeep belonged to the Department of Jianchuan People's Armed Forces. But a hospital has no contact with an army organization. Who had sent this jeep to meet us on the way? Upon inquiry, all I learned was that an officer had bought the cock that afternoon. A sudden instruction had ordered the driver to meet a father and a son in a village.

It was just eleven o'clock when we got to the county hospital. The rain had stopped. The place seemed deserted. We rushed to the operating room, but there wasn't a single soul there either. We wandered up and down, examining each room of each building. Suddenly a little girl about my son's age appeared and, in Mandarin, asked, "Oh, excuse me, are you from Diannan Commune?"

Lujiang answered, "Yes. We want to see my mother. She was sent here to have a leg operation."

"Oh, Uncle He, sorry to have kept you waiting," the girl addressed me. "Come on, just follow me."

We followed closely. Her hands were fully occupied with a thermos, a basin, two glasses, several boxes of cookies, and a coat or two. The little girl opened Room 49, but no one was inside. My son was bitterly disappointed not to see his mother. He was about to get angry, but I stopped him and asked the little girl, "Are you the daughter of a Doctor Li? You came from Kunming some years ago, right?"

"Yes. Perfectly right."

The little girl started pouring tea and making the beds for us. She said, "Wash, change your wet clothes, eat these cookies, and then say goodnight. Everything is ours, not the hospital's, so it's all free; make yourselves at home. Aunt He had to be taken to another, bigger hospital 120 *li* away. The ambulance will not be back before ten-thirty tomorrow morning. The driver is going to give us some information about the operation. Don't worry, my mother says that Mrs. He will be all right."

"It's really very kind of you to have everything prepared here," I said to her. "I wonder if you have learned to speak our Bai dialect?"

"Oh, not much, only a little. Everybody is too busy to teach me."

"Your mother can teach you every day."

"Every day? Oh, how can that be?" the girl replied sadly. "I should have become a Bai girl by now if my mother could teach me every day. Her 'every day' links with 'hospital,' not me. In a 365-day year, she hardly has a 10-day stay at home. Early this morning she rang us to say that she was coming home, to stay for a whole week. My father bought a fat cock in Jinghuazheng market this afternoon, planning to prepare a big dinner. But then the doctor responsible for the operating room here was away. My mother had to accompany Aunt He to the bigger hospital. Before they started, she first phoned my father, hurrying him to send a car to meet you at your home. She just ran up and down; didn't even drink a cup of water, much less have supper with us!"

At last we said goodnight. All the day's mysteries had been explained. The good deeds done for me by Guihua, her daughter, and her armyman husband disproved a local saying of ours: "Only my father and mother are good and kind. All other people under the sun are bad and cruel."

*       *       *

A little after sunrise the next morning, we were awakened suddenly by the repeated callings of a child. My father-in-law, carrying my second son on his back, had come to knock at our door. He had somehow managed to borrow 50 *yuan*, which he handed to me. Later, a nurse showed me to the office where you pay for hospital services. The accountant seemed very kind, for he made me a cup of tea the moment I sat down.

"They have taken her to another hospital," I began. "Probably 50 *yuan* is not enough now?"

The man began to smile. "We are not making a bargain in a street. This is a hospital."

"Yes, I know we are talking in a hospital. But I was informed you have a special regulation, paying 50 *yuan* in advance for a minor operation."

"Oh, I understand your problem now. Please take care of your 50 *yuan* and wait for a minute." He rifled through some papers and then said, "Here's your receipt. No mistake at all."

"But I haven't paid yet!"

"The 50 *yuan* was paid last night. All written down in black and white. Everybody was very busy yesterday."

Coming out from the man's office and into the corridor, an old lady hurried toward me. "Excuse me, I guess you are Mr. He?"

"Yes. What can I do for you?"

"I have brought you good news. Our car just arrived back a moment ago. The operation was successful. At midnight yesterday evening Doctor Li asked me to hand this letter to you. Take care of that letter. There is something important inside it."

I read the letter then and there:

*Dear Liyi,*

    *In helping my sister He recover at an early date, I was really too busy to write yesterday. The danger is over now. Go home and get busy as usual. Don't worry a bit. She will be back after a week or so.*

    *I want to tell you a thing of the long past, almost ten years ago now. You were away working as a highway laborer at the time. I was in a mobile medical team that year. There was a whooping-cough epidemic in many villages around here; therefore, we worked in this area for several months. Your son also caught the disease, and I was called to your home to inject him. That afternoon I didn't know the son's father happened to be you. The next day in the hospital, at midnight, I was called out by an old man. It was a very cold and windy night. The same boy. I injected him again in my doctor's room. When day broke, as I was going out, I found a pillowcase lying on the floor beside my chair. It was I myself who had embroidered that pillowcase. Immediately I knew how it had fallen down there. Your father-in-law had dropped it as he was leaving. I still have it today. I was very happy. Because of this, I went to your house many times to take special care of your son. But I didn't tell your father and your wife who I was. Before long, I left your commune. You didn't tell me the name of your village. I found your house myself.*

*Late this afternoon, on my way back to our county town, I chanced to meet the
mother and her son at the gate of your commune hospital once again. She was
familiar to me at first sight; however, I didn't let on to my colleagues. As for the
50 yuan, that is an unreasonable system. Everybody has to comply with it. I paid it
for you before I left. It's a secret. Don't let the children know.*

*I am playing a football game. No, I should say, I am like the football myself!
After my name and personal history were transferred to our Jianchuan County
Hospital, everybody admired and praised. In reality, it has just been a trouble. I
work one month here and two months there, rolling here and there all the time,
wherever I am sent and needed. I am sorry I'll be unable to take care of Mrs. He
all the time, but you can be sure I'll let her go home as soon as possible.*

*Very, very late now. No more time to tell you more. With unbreakable friendship
and special sisterly love,*

**Guihua**

*P.S.: Do please accept the enclosed 40 yuan and 50 jin grain coupons. The 40 yuan
is for family use. Don't buy or sell openly. Burn this sheet and be silent.*

I tore up the P.S. Holding the money and grain coupons, I stood there for a
long time. As I recalled my past, tears ran down.

Once again, when it was time for breakfast, Guihua's daughter, Xiao Ying,
brought us everything. With the money and the grain coupons we immediately went out and bought a big bag of rice. Xiao Ying accompanied us back to
our village. To express a little of our gratitude I gave her a hen and a bag of
apples and pears. I also sent a letter to Guihua, thanking her warmly.

Ten days after that, the same jeep brought my wife right back to our gate.
The whole village rushed out to watch. Most had seen a jeep, but only one or
two had ever had a chance to ride in one, or even get a close look at one. Many
villagers asked me this and that. However, I didn't want to spoil Guihua's
good reputation, so I replied in a confused way. Finally I said, "Tribute must
be paid to the Communist Party. It wasn't a single Mr. So or a Mrs. So, but
our country as a whole."

Approximately a month after that, the county hospital staff notified me to
see them on business. I had to fill out another form concerning my wife's operation. While I was there, that same old lady handed me another letter from
Guihua:

**Dear Liyi,**

*Last month I was happy to have done a little for my sister He. Is she getting on
well? I hope she is.*

*Many thanks for your letter, the hen, and so many apples, too. We enjoyed them
very much. In fact, I was not showing off or acting for other purposes. I was only
performing a doctor's duty, and a little, little bit in returning your love and
special care. Still the same thing: It was you who paved a wide way for me to jump*

*onto and run a long distance within a short period of time. Anyway, don't mention it from now on.*

*Allow me to tell you something more. Do you really know what I like and what I don't like? I always like to put on a new dress, buy a new purse, and eat fresh vegetables. All these are material. What about a person? An entirely different matter. In my day-to-day dealings with people I'm not fond of making new acquaintances. I prefer to contact and improve old friendships. That is why I want to be a good friend, a good sister of yours. No matter where or whatever might happen, I'm always ready to help you. I'll stick to this as long as I have breath.*

*Some more about my work. I love my line—not "like" but "love." Being a doctor is indeed very good, but I hate to be a "doctor of so many hospitals." The problem is this: Nowadays I cannot express this complaint openly and bravely, especially in the presence of a group of people. We have to watch what we say. It is best just to repeat the same popular things that everybody else is repeating. Whatever we do, we must not hide ourselves in a corner. We must read the daily newspapers, listen to the radio, pay attention at meetings, watch how the society goes. It's not so interesting to me. Nevertheless, everybody has to learn and get used to it.*

*This time I meant to have a heart-to-heart talk with you at our hospital. It seemed quite easy, but I still failed to meet you in person. However, it doesn't mean I am proud or look down on you. On the contrary, I still think of you with respect. In the past, whenever I had a chance, I inquired after you, tried my best to get some new information. I did see you two or three times, but I couldn't acknowledge you in front of others. Sometimes I think, "Let's arrange a special day, bring everybody together, and have a good time." But a day for that kind of enjoyment has not yet come. We are not in the same line. This society has created a barrier between us. That we understand the practical situation in our hearts is quite enough.*

*As I see the world, our society is like this: Some do serve the people heart and soul. They do everything for the interests of the broad common masses. But at the same time there are some, at all levels, who are lazy, corrupt, and self-seeking. There are too many unreasonable regulations as well. You are fully qualified to contribute a lot of service to our people, but actually you can do nothing at all. You are what they call "A hero who has no place to show his ability." It's wrong! It's a pity!*

*The bearer of this letter is a reliable friend, so I will tell you a little more. According to a recent report, the Cultural Revolution has brought little benefit to the broad masses of our country. And I think that there might be a new policy, new reforms, in the near future. This is a very important national question. You and I are as little as two drops of water in a big sea. We can only wish and hope, wait and see. I want you to understand the present situation in your heart, not to speak out. Be very careful at the present stage of transition, or you might offend someone and get into trouble. You were once a college student; now you live and work in a*

*village. Be more careful. Don't sell or buy unless you have to. Speak less wherever*
*you go. Lift your hoe higher and dig the earth deeper.*

　　*If you have time, try to refresh your English. I doubt that you have any English*
*materials. Mail me a list of English books and I'll see what I can do for you.*

*Guihua*

Guihua gave me money and grain coupons. A great help they were—yet, there are 365 days in each year. Before long, all the money and grain went into our mouths. Guihua had warned me not to sell or buy in the market, but practical problems forced me to take the risk. I had another frightening close call in town. Be careful, be careful, I said to myself over and over again. For a time my mind misgave me over many matters. I seemed to have lost my self-respect. If I saw an acquaintance coming toward me, I would run to another corner then and there. I seldom went to town or joined village meetings. Once again I began thinking of going away to settle myself in a desolate temple surrounded by huge mountains. Sometimes I thought of committing suicide; but, looking at my two boys playing happily or sleeping quietly, I pitied them very much. If I should die, how could they make a living?

Really, every day I grew very angry as I saw how the top officials ran things in the village. In particular, I hated our vice-team head, a Mr. Zhao, very much. He belonged to the minority of Zhao families in our Production Team One; most of his closer relatives belonged to Production Team Two. Many of my team members also hated him. Most supported the team head, my friend Mr. Liu. Politically speaking, Mr. Liu and Mr. Zhao were on the same level. They shared and swapped the tasks involved in arranging team affairs between them. Sometimes Mr. Liu went around the fields to inspect the work being done there. Then Mr. Zhao stayed in the village to supervise those who worked on our team's threshing ground or in the grain storehouses. Sometimes one seemed more important, sometimes the other. For a time, Mr. Liu was the more powerful and was called team head. Mr. Zhao was called vice-team head.

Culturally speaking, Mr. Liu could read and write. Having served in the army for several years he had gained a rich general knowledge through wide travel. Mr. Zhao was older, an ordinary peasant. Some said his agricultural knowledge was very rich. However, he couldn't use a pen, nor could he read a newspaper or a directive or a written note from a higher level. He just used his mouth and waved his hands to give orders. Since Liberation he had been very politically active, especially during the Land Reform Movement and other political campaigns. Gradually he had become an important member of the Team Committee.

Because Mr. Liu was literate, he was liked and trusted by the officials at a higher level. He frequently went to attend important meetings in town. Once our team was instructed to send a leader to take part in a planning meeting. Mr. Zhao volunteered to go, but he returned sadly after a few days. They didn't want Mr. Zhao, only Mr. Liu. Later Mr. Liu went to join that meeting. The villagers could see the situation clearly: "Our county officials are clever. They know which village leaders are capable. Zhao is a king, but only in our own village. Away from our village he is a good-for-nothing. Probably one day Mr. Liu will leave us to work elsewhere, at a higher level. ..."

In fact Mr. Zhao did succeed in replacing Mr. Liu as team head, but not because Mr. Liu was promoted. In 1976 Mr. Liu was suddenly dismissed from office by force. He was given a cap—as "productive forces element."[2] My friend Mr. Liu became head of our team's brick and tile factory. The post of formal team head was given to Mr. Zhao. Most of the team members disliked Mr. Zhao's production arrangements, but we could do nothing. Like a dumb person tasting bitter herbs, we were unable to express our discomfort.

Mr. Zhao and I had always been on bad terms. Mr. Liu had protected and helped me as far as he was able. Mr. Zhao did the opposite. He inflicted all kinds of hardships and insults on me. I couldn't move forward an inch. I made up my mind to keep as quiet as possible for some time. Allowing my "underground factory" to fall idle, I stopped making furniture. I also stopped doing business on market days. But it was no good. Some people, headed by Mr. Zhao, always tried their power to find fault with me.

One day, my older son overheard that a group was coming to search our house. In the big cities, such people were called "red guards." In the countryside we called them "activists of the new type." They wanted to sweep away anything that went against socialism. "Sweep" meant going into people's houses to search for "reactionary" books or "capitalist" production. They didn't search all the houses in the village, just those that had "problems."

A quick family decision was made to tackle this new situation. Selling our products in the market was out of the question. The best way was to put them into our mouths. So we ate all our remaining rabbits, about forty total, within three weeks. And we placed most of our beehives at our relatives' homes, keeping only four ourselves. Altogether we had five jars of honey. One evening, my wife carried four in a basket and secretly buried them in our private land. The next day my eldest boy took out the smallest last jar and invited many children to eat. As for the small chairs, we hid them in our pigsty. A few carpenter's tools we covered with rice flour.

One afternoon, such a group did indeed burst into our house and search all the corners. They seemed very disappointed to find hardly anything at all. Only one thing made me sad. They didn't miss the English books, saved for me by Qiyan, which I kept under my bed. I never thought they would destroy my books.

\*　　　\*　　　\*

Like the grown-ups, my two boys suffered. In my house, we had a grandpa, not a grandma. As a tradition, we couldn't force an old man to look after the children. Besides, he had to watch the pigs while they foraged in the fields all day. And the mother had to work. In our case, Lujiang was the only person to look after his younger brother Luzhong. When my second boy was one year old, Lujiang started taking him to school with him. Besides the school bag hanging from his shoulder, he had to carry his brother on his back. Sometimes the little one shouted or cried while a class was in progress. Then the teacher made Lujiang stand straight in the corner or sweep the schoolyard. Sometimes both returned happily, because, as Lujiang explained, his little brother had learned to sing a few words of a popular song.

Once Lujiang refused to go to school. No matter how we persuaded, again and again he strongly refused. Later his mother told me the inside story of his refusal. On the previous day, his younger brother had had an attack of sickness and diarrhea on a bench. All the classmates shouted at him, and the teacher gave him a stern scolding: "I give you two roads. One road is to wholeheartedly study at school. The other is to be a babysitter at home and let that rightist-father be your teacher. For now, you will sweep three classrooms out."

Frankly speaking, what the two boys suffered at school was an understandable matter. However, my two boys were also wronged away from school. One Sunday, after breakfast, both my wife and I had to work in the fields. As there was no school that day, I told Lujiang to carry his younger brother out to play in the village. At the gate I said, "Have fun for a while, but on your way home don't forget to bring back a pumpkin from our vegetable garden for supper."

We returned from work a little before sunset. As a rule, the two boys should have returned earlier than us grown-ups, but they were nowhere to be seen. After sunset we began to worry about their safety. Just as we were about to go out into the lanes to look for them, the two brothers came weeping painfully in, carrying a broken part of a dusty pumpkin and several pears. The mother immediately picked up the younger one.

"What happened to you this afternoon?" I asked.

After sobbing a while, the older one related: "My brother wanted to eat a pear, so I took him to the pear orchard at the back of the village. The man in charge gave us one each. While we were playing under a pear tree the man asked me to weed the vegetable garden next to his hut. I did as he asked. Next the man wanted me to look after his two sheep. Again I did as he asked. He made us watch those sheep for a long, long time, but it was easier than weeding with my hands. Finally, he was so pleased that he gave us twenty pears as a reward. Half were picked straight from the tree, very big and beautiful. The other half were collected from the ground, not so good but they were okay. We said goodbye and went on to our private land to collect the pumpkin.

"On the way home, at the village corner, a group of my schoolmates saw the beautiful pears and ran after me. I gave them one each—of course, not the bigger ones. But they forced me to give the beautiful ones. I was reluctant to give them away, so we began to quarrel. Just then that damned Mr. Zhao appeared.

"'Hurry up, Team Head Zhao!' one of my schoolmates said.

"'Shall we open a struggle meeting against He Lujiang?'

"'Why? To struggle his father He Liyi is okay, but as to his children, we must not struggle them unless they run against our policy.'

"'Well, he stole our village's public fruit,' another shouted.

"'Look, do they own a private fruit tree outside the village?'

"'He always steals from our team!'

"'Really?' Mr. Zhao asked, looking serious.

"'Yes, not only did he steal our public pears but he also stole a pumpkin from our public land. Look, what's this?'

"One of them took my pumpkin away and smashed it on the ground then and there. The other boys victoriously took away all the pears. Mr. Zhao pointed at my head and said angrily, 'Oh, oh, I never thought you little ghosts wanted to follow in your rightist-father's footsteps!'

"My brother let out a cry. He was frightened, but I hated Mr. Zhao and I was not afraid of him. 'I didn't steal!' I said. 'It was Uncle Dun who gave them to me! I got the pumpkin from our private land. Let's go, I can show you where I cut my pumpkin and you may ask Mr. Dun in person!'

"'No, didn't you hear the voice of the masses? No need to investigate. The eyes of the broad masses are very bright and clear. Your father carried stones in a labor-reform farm. Now it seems you, too, want to go to a labor-reform camp! Maybe I should hold a struggle meeting and give you a 'helicopter ride' like we gave your grandfather at our village meeting?'

"'Do as you please! I want my things back. They are mine.'

"My brother wept louder and louder, but I still wanted Mr. Zhao to pay me. I threw the remaining pears at him. Then he slapped my face several times.'You will die this evening!' I cursed him. He was furious and kicked me down onto the ground. Then he went away. Mrs. Zhang passed by and helped us home. But father, I really didn't steal. You may ask Mr. Dun tomorrow."

I believed my son's report. Mr. Zhao really wasn't a good man. His nickname, "Dry-grass-ball," meaning a useless, good-for-nothing person, fit him perfectly. He bullied little children. He openly insulted and injured our whole family. I couldn't bear it. However, I knew he was a leader, one of the controlling powers in the village. And I? I was born into a landlord family. I could never get the better of him. But my wife was born into a poor peasant family, and she herself was a "glorious peasant." She was most furious. So troubled, in fact, that she immediately put the weeping child into my arms and stood up.

"I'm going to teach Dry-grass-ball a lesson this evening. If I retreat today, he will advance tomorrow!" And with these words she seized a long-handled axe.

"No, no!" I calmed her down. "When something important happens you must consider it from all sides. Think of the children, think of the poor old man, think of me, your husband. Look before you leap. Is this so-called team head a human being? No, he isn't! He is worse than a dog."

"Well, a village woman I am. I cannot write and read, but I believe I understand Chairman Mao's policy better than all the other women in this village. I know what is evil and what is good. I'm not afraid of this kind of leader."

"All right, all right!" I made her sit down. "You mentioned Mr. Mao Zedong. Yes, Chairman Mao is a great leader, but he is in Beijing, thousands and thousands of miles away. Here in our village Mr. Zhao is greater than Mr. Mao. Anyway, you must know that in a war, we sometimes retreat; but that doesn't mean we fail. When the correct time comes, we can go forward again. It will not be too long. It's not worthwhile talking to an utterly unreasonable person like this Dry-grass-ball leader."

She sat down and cradled Luzhong quietly. She seemed to understand my words. That evening, only the old man ate a little. The younger son cried many times. We were all sleepless.

On my way home the following afternoon, a little before the sun went down, I saw that damned despotic Mr. Zhao in the distance. He gave me a proud look. His appearance immediately reminded me of the previous day's saddest story. As a local custom, when an ordinary peasant sees a team head or other leading member of the village, he or she has to bow and say something like "Comrade Leader, have you eaten?" But this time I went on my way, pretending I hadn't seen him there.

Who'd have thought that he would speak first? "Hi, wait a minute! Is He Lujiang your good little rightist son? Always walks off with the village's public things on the sly. A three-handed kid. I suppose you know that he steals from our team, don't you?"

At that moment some villagers passed by. Many stood around us, creating a chance for him to show his power before a crowd of people.

"Do you know what a good deed he did yesterday? I criticized his behavior, but he refused to accept this. What's more, he threw pears at me. Was this what you taught your son? I am protecting Chairman Mao's great revolutionary line. He damaged my socialist village."

"Well, Mr. Zhao, I have gone over the whole story. Last night we questioned him. Today I went around to conduct an on-the-spot investigation, and I learned everything as clear as daylight. My son didn't steal, but he did throw pears at you. That was a mistake. I apologize for that in front of everybody here, in public. But he really didn't steal. May I add this: Let's suppose my son actually did do it. So what? He is a little schoolchild! You are a big senior leader of a forty-household team. Why didn't you go to ask the man in the orchard first, and then judge the situation second? Moreover, he was carrying a baby on his back. Did you think about his young brother?"

"Oh what are you? How dare you answer me like that!"

He looked around at the crowd and was hot with rage. The villagers knew who was right and who was wrong. It is always the onlookers who see most of the game. He looked around again, but it seemed that no one there sided with him.

The crowd was becoming larger and larger. Mr. Zhao uttered not a sound. More people smiled at me. I left him alone. However, before I had walked even five steps, he yelled at my back, trying to rescue his failing situation. "You must be more careful. I order you to give your son a good lesson. Otherwise you will be sorry one day."

Judging from his angry manner and his last few words, it outwardly seemed that I had gotten the worst of it. Yet in my heart I was happy and pleased. Coldly and politely and steadily I replied, "How to teach my son a lesson? Well, that's my own business!"

\*     \*     \*

Arriving home, I pondered for a few minutes, considering how to tell my wife about the meaningful quarrel I had just had with Mr. Zhao. I meant to let her amuse herself at that damned team head's expense. But who would have thought that there'd be no sign of smoke coming from our kitchen? My wife was tightly holding my younger son, looking very worried. Standing next to her was Lujiang. His painful face showed that he had wept many times.

On seeing me home she cried, "Yesterday that should-have-died team head must have frightened our younger child. Now he refuses to suck milk. No wonder he cried many, many times throughout the whole of last night. Early this morning I found something not so normal, but I thought it didn't matter. Now he feels hot and looks worse than before!" Turning to the older son, she questioned, "Who told you to play in the pear orchard? Hadn't I given you enough to eat?"

She shouted and slapped the older boy in the face. I immediately dragged her away. Lujiang started screaming with pain, his cries so heartbreaking that I nearly wept.

Farmwork in our village was still very strict. If you didn't go out to work with the group for one day, they would not only deduct some of your original work points from your booklet but would also make you bear an ugly label: "A person who undermines the foundations of socialism." Therefore, no matter how seriously ill the child had become, all we could do for him was to prepare some homemade herbal medicines. We had no chance to go to market, sell, make a bit of money, and then buy good medicine.

Several days passed. The younger son's temperature came down. However, because he had taken too much of our home-produced medicinal herbs, he also developed diarrhea. Even a strong grown-up man would become skinny in two or three days if he suffered this problem. Our son was very young and sickly. Something had to be done. But what could we do? No one was allowed to leave his or her group.

On the seventh day, Luzhong's diarrhea problem became worse. He was a child of nothing but skin and bone. Only his eyes indicated that he was still living. How sorrowful we were. My wife worked during the day and sat up all night. She wept bitterly. She looked extremely tired out and completely hopeless.

The eighth day happened to be our county market day. I made a firm resolution: No matter how many work points they would deduct, no matter what kind of evil names they would give, we had to go to market. Our younger son was more important than all else. I took out some new chairs and put them into a bamboo basket. My wife carried the child. We planned to sell the chairs, get money, and then go to a doctor.

Everything went by smoothly. We sold some chairs, saw a doctor, and bought a bottle of Western medicine, as well as a little cooking oil and salt. We worried about our absence from the group, but we had obtained the medicine and so were happy.

As we entered the village, all at once we saw a group of village idlers playing a game of bridge in front of Mr. Zhao's house. He sat there grandly, his field-inspecting straw hat beside him. It was too late to hide ourselves. Mr. Zhao threw down his bridge cards. In a leisurely manner he walked toward us, saying, "Have you had a good time in the market? You stroll around here and there on a busy farming day. Having fun hand in hand! What a lovely couple! Really a great couple! So great that you didn't even say a word to me about your departure. Are you or are you not looking at a village master?"

We didn't say anything, just listened to his lecture. At that critical moment I was very angry. So was my wife. Her eyes became bigger and redder. She hadn't slept for several nights. Seeing that a big clash was about to begin, I signaled to her to be quiet. Controlling my rage, I said to him, "Mr. Team Head, we went to town, but it wasn't because we wanted to wander about or have fun. Will you please have a look at my second son? Since that afternoon when he was frightened, he has been ill. It has lasted for eight days now. Our hearts hurt to see his serious health problems. Furthermore, I did go to see you last night, but you were out. This morning we left very early. We didn't want to disturb your sleep before dawn. That was the very reason we didn't come to ask leave at your house. Please forgive us."

As I spoke, I drew back scarf to give him a look at my sick child. I never thought that his gaze would rest on my bamboo basket. The moment he saw my two remaining chairs in the basket, he jumped for joy as if he had discovered a stretch of unknown land. He laughed madly and said, "Fine! My underground-furniture-factory manager, don't you fool me. One person to see a doctor was okay. Two! A couple! This is a living example. Under the banner of seeing a doctor you were realizing capitalism in a big way!"

"Well, Mr. Team Head, really we couldn't help it. No money at home. Money had to be changed from chairs. Without money how could we get medicine? She went to join a line, while I went to sell the chairs. ..."

"You shut up! I don't want to buy your story. Both of you have two faces. For years and years you have been intending to destroy our collective farming system. You purposely undermine our socialism."

"I don't think so, Mr. Team Head."

"What? Was it 'I don't think so'? You two didn't join the group work today! Recently our farmwork in the village has been very busy. That was a big crime. Under the false cover of seeing a doctor you openly went to do capitalism. What's that in your bamboo basket? The proof is as big as a huge mountain. You can never deny it!"

"All right, if you insist on your wrong theory, I'll ask you something! I have proof, too. You were playing a bridge game. Let me count, one, two, three, four. ... Does this mean you are organizing a strong force to support the cause of socialism? What were you doing here just now? Working in the field or playing cards? Was that your way of building a new socialist village?"

I was so angry that I said what I wanted to say in my heart.

Mr. Zhao the despotic team head jumped up and down with anger. "What a big rightist of the landlord class! Look, a class enemy is firing at us poor and middle peasants now! You can never erase your class origin. It looks like this big rightist hasn't had enough fun in the town streets. Shall we let him enjoy some village fun now?"

"Okay!" many shouted with the same voice.

"Hurry up, get a rope!" Mr. Zhao ordered. The other bridge players ran in all directions.

"You bandits and rascals! What right have you to bully us!" my wife shouted. "You bully the weak and fear the strong!"

As she said this she looked around. Obviously she was thinking of a way to help me, with a stick or a stone. I told her, "Don't do that. You must believe me. I am not at all afraid if they want to make a show of me in our village's small streets. Even if they arrest me and send me to Kunming or Beijing, I am not afraid of them. Medicine cannot be easily gained and earned. Remember, give him medicine in time and take special care of him. Hurry. ..."

From the quick speed with which they brought everything out, I realized they had planned all this before I returned. I was tied up and my two little wooden chairs were hung around my neck. Someone brought out several cardboard placards. On them they wrote "Capitalist," "Bad Element,"

"Running Dog," "Rightist," "Landlord Son" and also hung them round my neck. With a shout of "Go!" I was vigorously pushed forward.

At the start, this "public parade" was performed in our own village, from lane to lane. Later they put a tall paper hat onto my head. They also painted my face black and white, exactly like a clown in a circus. Untying the rope, they forced me to take up a broken gong and gong-beater. Finally we left our village. I was ordered to go ahead of everybody, beating the gong, traveling from village to village with lots of curious children following behind. In a way, it looked like a parade on a festival day. If we met some people I was made to stop and deliver a "report," saying, "My name is He Liyi. My father was a landlord. I was a rightist. I am now a 'capitalist roader.' I hate to work in a collective group. I share the same trousers as Liu Shaochi. Please look at me. It serves me right. I am completely wrong. Hereafter I must be good. Please criticize. ..."

I reported this in four or five villages, covering about four *li*. This public-show performance satisfied my captors' desire. Returning to our village, one of them took off my little chairs and, finding a big stone, smashed them up. They walked off singing, proudly and victoriously.

Under the dim light of the stars, I painfully collected up my broken chairs. In order to buy a little salt or a few other household necessities I had spent long evenings making them. I looked at the stars and sighed and sighed. My older son met me at our gate. Bitter tears ran down our cheeks.

### NOTES

1. Mr. He writes, "People often do this in the countryside. Sometimes the woman steals rice, dried meat, or cooking oil from her house and gives it to her poorer relatives. Sometimes the man steals. Sometimes people do it openly. It depends on the relationships among the people in the family."

2. *Productive forces element:* As Mr. He explains, "This means someone who sticks to production and pays no attention to the political affairs of our country. At that time it was widely being criticized as a wrong theory."

# 14

# AN UNFORGETTABLE HOST

That "public parade" happened in the autumn of 1976. In the spring of 1977, when another new year began, no exception, I liked to think of many things, to hope for new changes, and to plan for the future. After a cold and stormy winter came another spring. The many plants broke the frozen ground. Spring decorated the land with a colorful coat. Green leaves gradually appeared, and all the buds began to peep at one another. Little bees swiftly circled among the flowers. All the birds once again reappeared in their former favorite haunts. It was spring that brought life, hope and happiness. But, alas, all these belonged to the land, belonged to the animals, birds, and flowers. As the spring wind blew over my out-of-the-way Jianchuan, people's feelings didn't go along with the natural beauty.

One morning shortly after our Spring Festival holiday, my group leader told me to attend an important general meeting. At team meetings, people didn't work with any farm tools, but they were still given a whole day's work points. If the team didn't offer work points, nobody would go. Personally, I had no interest in such meetings because as soon as they started talking about a certain topic, I knew exactly how they would continue. All I heard were the same old hackneyed, stereotyped expressions. But the changeable situation in our country at that time had become increasingly complicated. It would do me good if I went to listen for a while.

Well, in a meeting, strictly speaking, people should listen quietly or speak in turn. But nobody in my village seemed to have heard about this. That morning, most of our team members attended, and it looked like a day off in a market square. Mothers tended their children and played with them. The rest of the women busied themselves with making shoes, mending their shabby clothes, knitting, or weaving grass ropes. Young men played bridge or chess games. The middle-aged men smoked their tobacco and gossiped. Some fell asleep in the corners. Some whistled or hummed. Some played hide and seek. Some cried and some laughed. Two speakers, our team head Mr. Zhao and the ex–team head Mr. Liu, took turns speaking in the middle of the crowd.

Very, very strange. Every time the ex–team head Mr. Liu spoke, it looked as if a policeman had entered. All sorts of voices stopped. It wasn't at all strange if we thought over the things he was saying. The listeners knew what they wanted and what they didn't want. The common people wanted to eat, to wear, and to live. On the other hand, as soon as the team head Mr. Zhao began to speak, everybody went back to their games. He never mentioned a word about production, about the farmers' practical problems directly affecting their everyday lives. I still clearly remember a passage from his speech:

"We are walking on a most correct, the world's most advanced, road—the socialist road. We have the greatest revolutionary teacher—Chairman Mao. The distance we have covered is a glorious distance. Only under the brilliant leadership of Chairman Mao could we achieve this. We must actively respond to Chairman Mao's great call to learn from the Yan'an spirit and the Dazhai spirit.[1] The peasants of Dazhai have set a good example for us to copy. And we must never forget how our old revolutionary leaders lived and worked in the early thirties in Yan'an. Today we must develop that spirit: hard work and plain living. Recently in our village there are some, not all, who see that we are a bit poor and that our living conditions are not so good, and they begin to grumble. But although we are poor, we Chinese people have backbone. We are people of integrity. We would accept *grass* out of socialism rather than *grain* out of capitalism. Our road is a collective road. We rely on our socialist Big Family. We do everything the village team wants us to do. This is the shortest road allowing more and more people to get rich. Unfortunately, right here, in our own village, there are some people, well, I don't want to mention which Mr. or which Mrs. I guess you all know them. They specialize in underground factories. Their capitalist tails are growing large and long. Let me make it clear, people of this type will destroy themselves one day."

Mr. Liu's speech was completely different. He talked sense. He didn't mention the word "revolution" or the word "socialist." Rather, he talked about certain concrete problems of our team. For example, he pointed out which new measures should be taken before soaking this year's rice seeds. Which stretch of public land should be sown first and which next to follow. Which group must be reorganized with the coming of another spring. ... As Mr. Liu spoke, many nodded in agreement.

When we returned home after the meeting, my wife asked, "Do you know who the man was that Mr. Zhao meant when he spoke?"

"Well, that man isn't far in the sky but right near beside you! Don't worry about that. Singing political terms, quoting slogans, and bullying people are his profession. He is living on that. I am afraid he will become the first hungry ghost of our village if one day he loses his rice bowl. Believe me, you just watch and see; sooner or later this Mr. Zhao will have a fall."

"Maybe, but at the moment it is Mr. Zhao who rules you, not Mr. He who rules Mr. Zhao. You can never say a word against his local-made village policy."

\* \* \*

In July 1977 a directive from our county authorities came to our team: "Appoint one permanent laborer to the Qinghua Reservoir." This is an enormous reservoir located in a valley between several huge mountains, about fifteen *li* away from my home village. More than half of Jianchuan's land needs water from this reservoir. Here the working conditions were hard, the distances long, and, in addition, the daily work points low. The broad masses were not idiots. They had no interest in working there; all refused to accept a job in a valley. Therefore, in the past, all the odds-and-ends jobs at the reservoir were done by the entire county's four kinds of bad elements. They were ordered to take turns working there. But this time, the authorities wanted only one person from each team to go permanently.

As soon as the directive reached our village, the four kinds of bad elements began to worry. Most of them were almost seventy years of age, and the physical labor at Qinghua would have been too much for them. Now, strictly speaking, although I had been punished in Kunming, according to our national policy I didn't belong to those four kinds of bad elements. My cap had been taken off many years before and I was a clean person. But I had repeatedly offended Mr. Zhao. I was clearly in danger of being appointed.

One morning on my way home, carrying two pails of water, I met Mr. Zhao. He usually gave me an angry look whenever we met. That morning, he suddenly smiled and said, "Congratulations! An important directive instructed us to send a permanent worker to Qinghua Reservoir. You were selected by our Team Committee to live and work there. For you really it is a golden opportunity. You must gain a model worker's title and bring honor to our village."

I stopped but didn't say anything.

"This is a good chance. You must celebrate. Hurry back and get things ready. Go, tomorrow morning."

I stood for a long while, as if someone had given me a heavy blow on the head. Maybe I was an evil-doer in a previous life? I walked on a few paces, then stopped. I restarted walking, but again stopped. If a Paradise and a Hell did exist, then perhaps my wife and I had both done too many wicked deeds, and now God had come back to punish us.

I shall never forget how anguished my wife looked when I told her the news. We sat opposite each other. Silence followed. Lujiang sat beside me. His brother had fallen asleep. After a while my wife asked, "Is there any hope left of asking them to let you stay at home?"

"No more hope. Mr. Zhao has seized everything into his hands. He can push anyone he likes. Only by pushing me out of home can he be pleased; otherwise his dog's head will never be satisfied. Well, don't worry about me. I must go! Maybe a little change might bring me something good or better. You know, a reservoir surrounded by mountains and hills, the weather, communications, medical care ... everything is bad there. But if you consider the problem from another corner, a new viewpoint appears. First, it's a reservoir, a sort of nation's organization. Working as a peasant in a village production team is like being a rich man's long-term hand. They say many changes at Qinghua Reservoir have taken place in recent years. They have several regular holidays each month. Something like a worker working in a factory. They have a Sunday for rest. I can come back home each Sunday if I want to. In a village we do not know when we can get a Sunday. Second, mountain corner people are plain and honest. They seldom struggle each other as we often do here. Maybe I can do something peacefully there. At the moment, what I am worrying about is you. Your new leg trouble. ... Maybe something has gone wrong with your former operation. The other problem is that the child is young and the old man is getting on and on, and you will have to join group work in the field every day. Inside and outside, I'm afraid you cannot run our family."

Another silence followed. All at once she picked up the sleeping child and handed him to me. Slowly she said, "I shall make my last effort. Stop considering all sorts of consequences. Let me go to his house and bow to him first. He should understand our actual difficulties. Once in a blue moon, maybe, he will change his heart."

I knew it was no use, but still I held the boy and watched her walk off lamely. Twenty minutes later she sadly returned with these words: "He says you will have to go anyway. You must accept. It's a political mission. It's a re-education reform for your capitalist thoughts, a good chance for you to perform meritorious services to atone for your crimes."

"He is an expert at using those political terms! Talking is an art. People like that tyrant seize this art as a top secret and will never share it with others. All right. Go start preparations for me this evening."

I set out early the next morning. The rain hadn't stopped. I carried my luggage and a set of cooking implements in a bamboo basket. I said goodbye to my father-in-law first and saw my elder son off to school. My wife and younger son followed me for a way. Just outside the village, my wife broke the silence: "You must do everything carefully after you get to the reservoir. Don't overwork. Forget us at home. No matter how stiff things are, I think there will be a way for us to live on. Take care of yourself."

The muddy road was very slippery. We walked slowly, watching each step ahead. Perhaps a *li* had passed when I stopped to hold my second son's little hand. I comforted mother and son: "Go back, please. Turn a deaf ear to Mr. Zhao's tyrannical policies. All you have to do is take good care of the old man and our two boys. They are our future. They are our hope. There must be a way in the world for each person to gain a living. Everything will be all right in the end."

I turned away and continued my fifteen-*li* journey alone. I reached the top of a small slope and turned back to have a last look at my village. There I saw my wife, still standing beside the road, looking at me. The corner of a blue scarf wrapped around my little boy's neck waved in the wind. It was too far to see their faces. As she saw me looking back she turned away, and it seemed as though she was drying her tears. Then she waved and waved, hurrying me to go ahead and wishing me good luck at the reservoir. As I looked into the distance at her weak, skinny hand, tears curtained my eyes.

I turned to the north, toward the flat plain of my homeland, my lovely Jianchuan. Was it a poor and narrow land? No! Everything seemed beautiful. Why could such a land not contain me? It kept on raining. The grey sky seemed to be falling down. I gritted my teeth and gave the mother and child a last wave. Then I firmly turned and walked in the direction of Qinghua valley.

I staggered along the muddy slopes, not resting at all, despite the ceaseless rain. By noontime I reached my destination, a village beside the reservoir called Xinlongcun (New Dragon Village). When I first stepped into this village it was completely deserted. Perhaps people were having their lunch. As I was wandering up and down, trying to decide which household to enter, I met an old man, about sixty, who wore a goatskin coat and was carrying a long-handled hoe. Carefully staring at me for a moment, he said, "Hello, Young Nephew, you look like a reservoir permanent worker. Have you found a host household yet?"

"Not yet, Old Uncle," I replied. "If it's convenient, I was wondering if you could put me up at your house?"

Again he gave me a long, steady look and then smiled. "Okay. No problem, no problem. My older son works in a distant county. There are not so many people in the house at the moment. Come on, this way, just follow me."

"You are very kind, Uncle."

I followed him in. Shooing a chicken out of the room, he began, "Young Nephew, you look unwell. You know we haven't any doctors in this mountain valley. It's a troublesome problem if you get sick. But don't worry, you are very lucky. I am an old-fashioned local doctor. My medical herbs prove to be very effective."

A teenaged boy, his grandson, appeared. "Xiao Ming, let me introduce you to this uncle. He is going to stay with us for some time. You help him clean the room and do the bed." Then he turned to me. "Young Nephew, I suppose you haven't had your lunch. Join us together, just something simple. Come."

I refused again and again, but he insisted. At the table I was given a share of cornmeal cakes and a big bowl of turnip soup. I was deeply touched when I looked at the old man's smiling face.

\*          \*          \*

The next day, after I had finished all the required procedures, I began, as that despotic village head Mr. Zhao had put it, "to perform meritorious services to atone for my crimes." Although only one person came from each team, the total number of laborers reached almost 400. Our main task was to build a long dam in the valley, with high, thick walls. It was a gigantic project. A large number of us were assigned to carry stones, some carried sand, some dug irrigation canals, and half of the 400 were engaged to carry earth in bamboo baskets. Our jobs varied many times each week. Every day people felt tired out, but, as in a city factory, we worked only eight hours a day. As soon as that eight-hour period was over, the remaining hours belonged to us. On weekend days, more than half of the workers returned home.

In my home village I used to work all day long and then late into the night as well. Here in Qinghua valley I suddenly found myself with hours of spare time on my hands. Many of my co-workers played chess games or various musical instruments. I did nothing at all. How could I forget all the tragic circumstances at home? After supper, I just smoked quietly on my little pipe. My father-in-law had given it to me on the eve of my departure, saying, "Mountain-area people smoke tobacco in a long pipe. Learning to smoke with a pipe will bring you some mountain-area friends."

One day, my old host's pigsty door broke. I was what they called a "halfway carpenter," so I immediately repaired it for him. He had a vegetable garden at the back of his house. Without his asking, I volunteered to weed and water. I wasn't expected to pay rent, but I made up my mind to get busy helping the old man as soon as I returned from the dam every day. Over time, my host observed me with great interest and showed particular concern. We began to chat about personal family affairs. After a long time of careful observation, I came to the conclusion that my old host was a venerable man who was always happy to help others. He was an honest and frank farmer, had pure motives, and was sympathetic when I related my past sufferings. Finally he knitted his brows and sighed a long sigh. "Oh, my poor nephew, no wonder you looked very sorrowful and showed me a pale face when I first met you. I thought you were ill."

One evening, after a long period of silence, the old man suddenly asked me, "Do you know how to chop down big trees?"

I told him I wasn't a standard chopper, but I could do everything slowly. He was on top of the world when I said this.

"Poor Liyi, now, come near," the old man moved nearer and spoke softly, in a whisper. "I have a special plan, a secret way for you, but you must not tell anyone else. This is a man-eats-man society, you know that." He paused an instant to look around, and then continued. "On Sunday, you just follow me. I will teach you which to chop, not every day, but once in two or three days. We leave them there and then bring them back slowly. Later we can sell. ..."

As I listened to his special plan, I felt like a thirsty man who had discovered a well of water in an isolated desert. The happiest day of my life was the day I was told I'd become a college student. That day I was sure my future career would be devoted to the great cause of my country's education program. Now, the old man's special plan touched my heart as deeply as on that day almost thirty years before. I was so moved that I held his hands tightly for a long time. Tears ran down. I uttered, "You are my father. I give you too much trouble!"

Thereafter, I got up two hours earlier in the mornings and followed the old man up to a hill at the back of the village. Late in the afternoons after I returned from work, quite regularly, we both hurried back up the hill to chop down some more trees before returning for supper. Within six weeks his yard was filled with several piles of dry firewood. When he had time, he also climbed a distant mountain to collect good local medicinal herbs. One Friday morning, my host borrowed a horse-cart. We loaded our dry firewood into the cart.He said to those who had come to help, "This year, after my grandson succeeded in getting into the county's middle school, he has asked me for money each week. If I do not sell more firewood, I can hardly let him continue his lessons."

That evening, right after he returned from Jinghuazheng market, he straight away produced a roll of cash and put it into my hand, saying, "Take good care of it. Altogether 41 *yuan!* This is the result of your hard work. We will do it again in the future. Tomorrow will be Saturday. Xiao Ming will come back to spend Sunday here. Give him the money and he can take it to your home safely on his way back to school. Besides, I have some special medicine for your wife's leg trouble." Pointing to a bunch of herbs, he said, "This will go with your money. Don't worry, I have a way to heal her legs."

I took the money with both hands. I didn't know how to thank the old man. My hands trembled.

When I left home, I never imagined I would get to know such a father-like old man at the reservoir. The time I spent with him in chopping and moving the logs was not as much as I had spent in making chairs at home. What's more, I got more money! We kept it a top secret. It was very safe. I was free to go home each weekend, but during the first stage I seldom went home. I spent most of my spare time with the old man. My old host helped me three times. The first time, I accepted the whole 41 *yuan*. The second and third times, I returned half of the money he gave me.

One Saturday afternoon, my old host's grandson gave me a letter from home. Judging from the handwriting I guessed it was written by my elder son. He wrote:

*Dear Baba,*

*My mother says she has received your money and medicines three times. She can now go out to work in the field. My younger brother follows me to school again. He can run about, not so troublesome as before when I had to carry him on my back and make him sit with me. Every day mother talks about you and that old grandpa with whom you are now living. Every time she talks, she smiles first and then dries her tears. She says you must thank this old man and try to help him do some housework. Xiao Ying's mother came to our house to see you. My mother told her to see you at the reservoir. We hope you do everything well and give our regards to grandpa's whole family.*

*Lujiang*

My first wife, Dr. Guihua, did indeed come to the reservoir to visit me. That day, Guihua was accompanying a patient to Xiaguan and I was working. So we talked in a hurry. I thought maybe she was bringing me something good to eat. But no. The first thing she asked was, "Have you heard the news?"

"Chairman Mao has passed away?" I replied.

"No, no, no!" Guihua looked unhappy. "Dear me, Lao He, I'm afraid you are still living in a drum. Chairman Mao's passing away is old news now. More and more big news is appearing in the newspapers."

"You are going to become a lady hospital director?"

"Oh God, I've no time to joke with you! It's not about me. It's about your own political problems. Look, I've collected several copies of Beijing's *People's Daily*. I want you to read the articles I've marked with red ink. We heard an important report last month. I'm not sure if you can use your English or not, but at least the government is going to reconsider your problems, maybe offer you a job." Guihua turned to her daughter and said, "Xiao Ying, you hurry to the ambulance and get the English books and the dictionary I bought the other day."

While Xiao Ying ran to the ambulance, Guihua went on: "Recently many people like you have begun to contact their old organizations. Everybody knows something big in our country is going to take place. You must write to your former organization at once."

"It sounds nice, but Guihua, you and I are like two little shrimp in the big Pacific Ocean. Working in this distant valley I am afraid. ..."

"Oh, that's just the reason we must write first! There are thousands and thousands of people with political problems. Do you think they will come to you first if you keep quiet here? As for the dictionary and textbooks, you must brush up before they come to use your English."

Xiao Ying returned with the books. We said a hasty goodbye. They climbed into the ambulance and drove away.

All the articles, editorials, and speeches that Guihua had marked indicated a basic change. It took me ten days to finish reading them. Madam Mao's misrule was criticized. Some criticisms of Chairman Mao also appeared. China's greatest grandfather had been very wise, but his Cultural Revolution policies had brought too much damage and destruction. It was a waste to force so many educated people down into the fields or up into the mountains. Too many unjust caps had been put onto people's heads. Immediate measures had to be taken to solve all these past wrongs.

A week after Guihua's visit, I wrote three letters to Kunming. One was to my former organization. The other two were to friends of mine still living in Kunming, asking them to get some inside information from my former organization. I had stopped writing letters to all my friends many years before, but things were different now. Three months went by, yet I heard nothing from any of them. I was disappointed. I couldn't understand why I didn't get a single reply. I began to see that despite our country's new direction, no one would come to settle my personal problems soon. Like old and weak snails trying to get out from the bottom of a deep well, our officials moved slowly. I would have to continue doing whatever odd jobs I was assigned around the dam for quite some time. So I still did nothing with those English books.

By 1978 we could openly say, "The Gang of Four has fallen down!"[2] Each month saw a series of new policies. Many of the unreasonable regulations and systems were knocked down one by one. In the field of education, for instance, formerly a good-at-every-subject middle-school student had no hope of walking through a university's gate if his family political background was "incorrect." On the other hand, a certain student who might be very poor at his lessons would be warmly offered a place at a college if his "political behavior" was good. Now everybody had to join a competitive nationwide university entrance examination.

The relationship between Guihua and me also entered into a new stage that year. Before 1978 we had to pretend to be cold to each other whenever we met in public. We could not express our hearts openly with our mouths or our actions. After 1978 such difficulties began to disappear. Her job, too, had changed. In 1977, after demanding an improvement in her working conditions, she was allowed to work permanently in our county's hospital in Jinghuazheng. She was all smiles whenever we met, and we could say hello to each other in a natural way.

One Sunday in the spring of 1978, I left the reservoir before dawn and arrived home just as my family was getting up. After breakfast, my wife and I went to sell pears in town. As soon as Guihua spotted us she herself brought out a bench and a mug of hot tea for each. Later her Xiao Ying brought us a big lunch. We joked and our conversations ran from east to west, from foreign countries to our home village, covering many, many subjects.

*         *         *

One day I lost my little pipe while working near the dam. As it was a gift from my father-in-law, I was eager to find it. My host gave me a large piece of paper. I drew the shape of my pipe and wrote my name, and of course offered a reward. I pasted my poster onto the bulletin board where we read newspaper articles or got new information from the authorities every day. Many people stood for a little while to read my poster. By the third day, still nobody had returned the pipe to me. On the fourth day, a work-inspector of the reservoir, a Mr. Ma, read my note. He became mad like a crazy dog. "He Liyi, you are a saboteur! Do you know how much damage your pipe has done to the dam? Everybody stopped to read your note. We have more than 400 workers here. Suppose each spends only one minute to read that note—tell me this, how many minutes are there in an hour? How much did that broken pipe cost anyway?"

He stalked off.

On hearing his sound scolding, I felt as though I had fallen into a mist five miles thick. I couldn't make out north or south, east or west. I sat down on the dam, blankly staring at the wavering waves. Recollections of my long past flashed by, one after the other. I had enjoyed a naughty childhood. I had once proudly pinned on a college badge. I had experienced the sweet happiness of meeting a good friend. I recalled how I had felt when I was given a rightist cap. How I had prayed and hoped that all my troubles would go away for good! But now I thought, "Who knows if this will affect my political rehabilitation?" Suddenly I stood up. I wanted to tear down that note.

As I was stretching out my hand to rip it down, another hand stopped mine.

"Was it you who lost the pipe?" asked Xiao Zhang, the reservoir technician.

"I am sorry. I lost it several days ago, but I am not going to get it back now."

"Was this note written by you yourself, or which Mr. wrote it for you?"

"Yes, I lost the pipe and I wrote the note. I'm very, very sorry. I was wrong." Hopelessly, I closed my eyes.

"No, I enjoyed reading it," Xiao Zhang said, smiling. "You wrote well—brief, but to the point. I don't think anyone else here could have written a note like it."

"Well?" I couldn't believe my ears.

"Judging by the words you wrote, I would say that you have graduated from a middle school. It looks like a college-level note. Maybe you are a 'nameless hero' here?"

"I once studied in a college, but now. ..."

"Really? Which college? Where?"

"In Kunming."

"Oh, I see. No wonder. Not strange at all." Saying this, he handed me a cigarette. "Forget it. It's easy to get another pipe."

While we were smoking I gave him a few more details about myself. He asked if I knew anything about fish breeding or surveying. I told him that for some time I had worked as a highway technician's helper. As for keeping fish, I had seen this done only in a small pond in a village. He listened to me with interest and seemed very pleased.

Nothing happened that evening. I nevertheless started packing in my room. My host was a sensitive man. He asked many questions, but I didn't tell him about the trouble created by my pipe. As nobody came to see me that evening, I went out to work as usual on the following day.

During the morning break the reservoir inspector Mr. Ma came up to me. "He Liyi, the Party secretary of the reservoir headquarters wants to see you in person. Hurry up! You do nothing here, but he is exceedingly busy all the time."

"Everything is over now! I will be punished again," I thought to myself as I staggered along the upward path.

When we arrived at the Party secretary's office, I was rudely pushed in by Mr. Ma. He shouted, "Good morning, Party Secretary Gao! The man you ordered, He Liyi, has arrived."

Two men came in from an adjoining room.

"Lao He, how are you? Take a seat, take a seat," Xiao Zhang said and began making me a cup of tea.

"Oh, Comrade He Liyi. You must be very tired. Sit down, sit down." Party Secretary Gao, about fifty, smiled broadly. Showing me a seat, he placed a cigarette into my hand.

Both of them showed warmth and respect. I couldn't make out what in the world was going on. Mr. Ma also looked puzzled. He wanted the Party secretary to punish me, but instead I was being treated like an honored guest. Mr. Ma saw that the situation had changed. Like an electric flash, he changed his former attitude. "Lao He, make yourself at home."

Now the old man who was addressed as Party Secretary Gao began, "Comrade He Liyi, someone told me that you have graduated from a Kunming college. You have culture and knowledge. And you have seen someone breed fish. I think you are just the person we want. The county authorities have required us to raise fish in our reservoir, but people here are all low-level or no-level workers. They know how to eat fish, but they do not know how to make a fish grow. From today on, you will become Xiao Zhang's teacher, a helper of his technical problems. You have been educated in a high-level college. I think you should contribute more service to our county, work for the welfare of our county."

"Lao He, from now on, it's you who are my master." Xiao Zhang shook hands with me.

Mr. Ma went out silently.

Thereafter, Xiao Zhang and I worked in full cooperation and with unity of purpose. For my part, I did know something about surveying; but to tell the truth, my knowledge of fish breeding was too poor to speak of. In all my life it was only outside our reform farm that I had seen how Lao Wang managed it! In spite of this, I offered all I knew and did everything possible to the best of my ability. In the mornings, we spent most of our time on surveying, walking slowly up and down over the hills or along the long dam. In the afternoons, we usually worked in our office. Many people said "Okay, good!" to my work as a technician's helper.

The Party secretary wanted me to move my bed into the reservoir dormitories, but I feared I'd miss my old host. Not long after this, my old host's grandson brought me a letter from home. It was from Kunming, sent by one of the friends I had written to earlier:

> *Your letter was received a long, long time ago. During that period, the relevant authorities were too busy to consider your problems. I could get nothing good to tell you. I went to see them again last month. Work has begun now. There are too many cases like yours, and many problems are involved in each case. It'll take time to settle them all. You will have to be patient. Anyway, they said all the past problems would be cleared up sooner or later. My suggestion is this: Go to your local authorities. Report your personal information for them to consider.*

On hearing this news, Xiao Zhang was so excited that he lent me his bicycle. He said, "Your job here is not a bad one, and everybody likes you; but another sort of work seems more suitable for you to develop your talent. You may go at any time to contact the relevant people. Here I can take care of everything."

Xiao Zhang's viewpoint was correct. I was no longer doing heavy jobs like carrying stones or removing piles and piles of damp earth. In a way I looked like an important or special man. However, according to our national policies, politically speaking I was still a "worker from the village." All those who were ordered by their village government to work at the reservoir were called *min gong*, and we were quite different from *gong ren*, those national workers who work permanently in factories or other government enterprises. I didn't get any extra pay either, just those same miserable ten work points a day. At the end of the year, I would have to show a letter from the reservoir authorities to our team head. My work points from the reservoir would be added to those my wife had earned in our team, and grain and money would be given to us accordingly. We still received very little.

So I got busy. I wrote a detailed resumé. A man working in my county's Educational Affairs Bureau took my resume and said, "It's a good thing to know you have graduated from a college. This problem involves many policies. We will discuss it at a meeting. Just go back to your reservoir and wait until we tell you."

I walked out of his office and straight away went to see Guihua. We took a stroll outside her hospital.

"Yes, the suggestion from my friend in Kunming was good. I feel relieved now that I've handed in my resumé. On the basis of many editorials, I think that Mr. China is going to offer me a job to suit my qualifications. But in reality, you know the mountain is high and the emperor is far away from us. It's still not easy to get a formal rice bowl."

"Don't be so pessimistic. You must watch out for the big things that are going on now. You see, after Chairman Mao, we have another Chairman Hua. He is going to make more foreign friends. English is needed everywhere."

About two months after this conversation, I was called for an interview by some gentlemen at our county Educational Affairs Bureau. They arranged an examination to test my actual skill in English. The outcome was very good. Now I was formally qualified to become a teacher of English. But the main trouble was that nothing had been heard from my former organization in Kunming. After I was sent to the reform farm in 1958, this old organization had undergone a change. A new Research Institute of Yunnan's History was set up, similar to the previous one, but under the direction of the Yunnan Provincial Committee for Border Area National Minority Peoples' Affairs. When this reorganization took place, my personal file—a large paper bag containing my personal sayings and records concerning my doings, behavior, scores at school, birthplace, and so on—was transferred to the Yunnan Provincial Committee. The staff of this organization were now responsible for my past political problems, and it was from them that I was waiting and waiting impatiently to hear.

\*  \*  \*

In 1978 both Guihua's Xiao Ying and my elder son Lujiang ended their primary-school education. Moreover, at the countywide examination both succeeded in scoring enough points to enter a middle school. At the last stage of the selection process, both were ordered to have a general checkup at our county's hospital. It happened that Guihua was the very doctor authorized to sign their forms. When she found my son to be in excellent health, she was extremely happy. So overjoyed, in fact, that she insisted on inviting me to eat a meal at a big restaurant.

"They say 'like father like son.' Your Lujiang is going to follow in your footsteps. I wonder if they have a saying 'Like mother, like daughter'?" Guihua smiled. "Actually, I don't want Xiao Ying to become a doctor. I want her to share your English, to go abroad one day."

"Well, that's funny, I want my son to become a doctor! To study English is dangerous. He might get into trouble—like me."

"All right, all right, Shuyi, I am afraid we've joked enough. China today is not as it used to be. I'm sure in the near future you will stand in front of a blackboard and say 'Good morning' and 'How do you do.' Your turn to enjoy sunshine has come at last."

"I hope so, but I still have a few worries. Your Xiao Ying's middle-school problem is like a little pony which has been tied safely to a big tree. My boy's middle-school problem is still questionable. We see only its shadow, and we can't catch a shadow. Anyway, it's very kind of you to invite me here today. Had it not been for the big change in our society, how could I have the honor to enjoy a delicious meal at a table here in public with you?"

Again, I waited and waited. On the sixth day one of Lujiang's classmates was instructed to report to the First Middle School. My boy's points in the examination were higher than that boy's, but he got nothing. No more joy at home. Both my father-in-law and my wife had words with me. They shared the same viewpoint: that Lujiang's failure to enter a middle school was due to my bad name and past history. I was so depressed that I burned Guihua's newspapers and other magazines. And my father-in-law gave orders for all of Lujiang's used textbooks to be burned. He said, "The world today is not ours. To use a pen is not our business."

"All right," my wife agreed, and threw Lujiang's books into the fire. "Don't worry! You'll still have your rice bowl. Work in the fields. Don't go to a school."

"I'm going to her now!" My boy looked at me and then said to his mother, "Give me some apples. I am going to ask her. ..."

"What are you going to do now?" I asked.

"To see the doctor."

"Your face is too thick!"[3] I scolded him loudly. "No more 'the doctor' from now on. You are old enough to keep a clean face for me."

"No, Baba, not a doctor to heal a person. I was thinking of becoming an animal doctor."

On further inquiry, he said Guihua's daughter had told him that a friend of theirs was going to organize a short-term training course for animal doctors. With the chief organizer's help, he might have a chance to join their training program. My wife offered her opinion: "That's a good idea, I must say, but this country is changing with each passing day. A good animal doctor has to use a pen. When you were just a baby, once you showed us you would become a farmer. So don't build your hope on animal doctoring. The best profession for you is to face the earth and dig the ground."

"Studying to be an animal doctor is easier than entering a middle school. When I master the skill we can raise many pigs and sell them and earn more money. At least it's better than being an ordinary peasant."

"No," my father-in-law finally said. "Everybody has to listen to me. I am your grandpa; I have the power to decide your career. Come on, just follow me. Let's go right away."

With these words, they dashed off. In another flash my father-in-law turned back and added in an angry voice, "I'll let them see my grandson can still manage to maintain a living without a schooling in town!"

After a little while my wife said, "I'm going to see them. I know he is taking Lujiang to visit an old carpenter. Money is kept in the same old box. You go and buy a new saw and other tools of the best quality and some presents for the old master carpenter."

My wife also went out. I began to think how best to make my boy into a good carpenter. As I was preparing lunch, somebody knocked at our gate. It was Guihua and Xiao Ying.

"Oh, my doctor, welcome home, welcome home! What wind brings you here?"

"If there is no business, what's the use of visiting a temple? Where's Lujiang? We came to report some good news for him. He has been selected at last."

While I went on making lunch, she told me the final details of my boy's examination: "Xiao Ying learned that your son's name had been crossed off their list, not because of health or some other reasons, but mainly because of his father's past history. You were punished in Kunming, they said, so a new decision was made to let another peasant's son enter the school first. Well, that was wrong. Some of them still don't understand the present policy in selecting a student. As soon as Xiao Ying's father and I heard this, we rushed to their office right away and explained each practical problem of yours for them to consider and make a second study of your son's admission. We even argued with them, and after talking for a long, long time, they wrote another note, allowing him to enter. Xiao Ying is going to report to the First Middle School in Jinghuazheng, and Lujiang is to report to your commune's middle school."

"Thank you very, very much indeed! Now one shadow has turned into a concrete object. We can touch it. Just tell me what you would like to eat for supper. We must have something special today."

Late in the afternoon, everybody returned home. We did everything to make ourselves as happy as could be. When we finally saw them off at the end of our village, Guihua said, "Go back to the reservoir and work as usual. You needn't bother anymore about Lujiang's school problem. I will take care of that."

\*     \*     \*

Back at the reservoir, in order to let people eat more fish, the reservoir headquarters made a new plan. The technician Xiao Zhang and I were sent to a village near Xiaguan to visit a fish farm. Our main job was to learn about some advanced experiences in fish breeding and to buy several pails of baby fish. While we were in Xiaguan, we were amazed at the dozens of changes in the town. All along the pavements, people were selling their goods quite openly. How different from my last trip here to sell chairs! I didn't see any policemen or market-control officials stopping and accusing anyone. Selling and buying had become free.

In a tea shop, or in the lobby of a hotel, or beside a bed in a hotel dormitory room, many, many people chatted about their personal affairs. It was easy to hear a conversation like this:

"What business has brought you to Xiaguan?"

"Oh, very important. This time I am afraid of nothing. I am going to struggle with the staff at my former work unit until they have completely settled my past political problems."

"You look crazily happy!"

"Of course I'm happy! Formerly my colleagues treated me like a counter-revolutionary. Now Comrade Hua Guofeng is in support of me. His brilliant policy has forced them to apologize. They will have to repay me all my past salary. And pay the hotel bill as well! They are too busy to clear up everything within a short time. I will have to keep on waiting and waiting at this hotel. Ha, ha!"

During that short stay in Xiaguan I also paid a visit to an old school friend of mine. We hadn't seen each other for more than twelve years. We were both in exceedingly high spirits, and our conversations covered nearly everything about the past. He was also a victim in 1958, but because he lived in a larger town the recent changes in our country had affected him immediately. Sometime before we met, the nation had offered him a permanent job in Xiaguan as a librarian.

He said, "The world doesn't belong to Chairman Mao's wife anymore. My mishandled problem has been cleared up. ... What about *your* second-life problem?"

"Well, this year, my present job at a big dam seems not so heavy. At least it's lighter than carrying stones from sunrise to sunset, a little better than being a peasant who is always working in the field. Everyone treats me in a friendly way. But, I still think a job using a piece of chalk to teach ABC is more suitable."

"Certainly you can realize that! I know all about your past history. We all wanted to serve the people, but unfortunately, for a time, some of our top leaders drank too much wine and, consequently, put hundreds of thousands of good people in the wrong places. Lao Mao was great. He saved our country. However, he was not a perfect leader. Over several years he also made many, many mistakes. What a pity to let so many intellectuals suffer and suffer."

"Yes, our paths were zigzag ones," I replied. "We are over forty, nearly half-a-hundred men; it seems too late to do anything now."

"No, no, no! In a way I agree with your viewpoint. Our days of full fresh energy ended in the long past. But didn't you say you have two boys at home? Because of the coming generation you must wash yourself clean. We will die soon, but our children will have to live on for many years. If the children's parents are considered bad people, they can succeed at nothing in our society."

That evening I was so excited that I couldn't sleep a wink. Yes, everything in China was going to turn. Warm sunshine would return to the earth soon. When that sunshine reappeared, I would have a share.

Xiao Zhang and I returned to Jianchuan. I had hoped to find some news waiting for me, but still there was nothing. The letters I had sent to Kunming seemed to be having no effect. As we say, "If the kettle doesn't whistle, move it around a little." I made up my mind to write another letter, this time giving a detailed denial of my "confession" at that study class.

After I pushed my letter into the green box I felt as though a bird, shut up in a cage for many, many years, had flown out into the wide sky. I felt incomparably happy. My strength and energy increased each passing day. I began, for the first time in years, to sing songs.

## NOTES

1. *Yan'an spirit:* This was the spirit of self-reliance, self-denial, hard struggle, courage, and diligence developed during the Long March (October 1934 to October 1935) and then, after that, in the Shaanxi-Gansu-Ningxia Border Region established at Yan'an. *Dazhai spirit:* Dazhai was a "model brigade" located in Xiyang County, Shanxi Province, that also emphasized self-reliance. The slogan "In agriculture learn from Dazhai" was used extensively from 1964 until the end of the Cultural Revolution.

2. *Gang of Four:* Madam Mao, Zhang Chunqiao, Wang Hongwen, and Yao Wenyuan made up this "gang." They were arrested shortly after Mao's death in 1976 and charged with every excess of the Cultural Revolution from criticizing worthy schoolteachers to organizing their own armed forces.

3. By this Mr. He means "You are shameless!"

# 15

# I LAY DOWN MY HOE

One afternoon in 1979, sometime before the Spring Festival holidays, I scattered some vegetable leaves into the reservoir for the fish to eat and returned to my old host's house. As I entered the gate, I suddenly saw a little boy, dressed from top to toe in new clothes, playing in the courtyard. He threw down his stick and, stretching out both his hands for me to carry him up, ran toward me.

I picked him up and kissed him, "Oh, Xiao Di,[1] my little son, you are here! It's great! How did you manage to climb up so long a distance?"

"Mama carried me on her back. Sometimes I ran myself," he replied proudly.

"Mama? Where is she?"

"Over there." As he said this his little finger pointed at my room.

I immediately thought something unlucky had happened at home. I put Xiao Di down and rushed into the room. Cuilian was making my bed.

"Hello. What's happened at home?"

"Very great!" was the answer. After giving me a gaze, she asked unhurriedly, "Can you guess?"

"Well, 'very great' can be said when a house has fallen down or a big pig has died."

"No, no, no, it's something good, not bad."

"Lujiang won a prize at school?"

"Yes, he did win something, but that isn't it."

"What in the world has happened? Out with it, please!"

Her eyes looked wet. Slowly she searched her breast and took out two letters. In a trembling voice she said, "The sun is rising."

The first letter was from Kunming, sent by my former organization. The main points ran something like this:

> *Your letter has been received. Like many other intellectuals, you were put in a wrong position. We regret this. We were touched by what you have been doing over the past years. We understand your present circumstances. This is just a simple note*

*to tell you that we are now informing your local government to consider your problem. We believe they will soon make some suitable arrangements for you. When we are not so busy we shall send them another formal detailed report.*

The second letter was from our county's government office:

*In accordance with the note we recently received from Kunming, we have been to the Educational Affairs Bureau two or three times. Now a new decision has been made to make you a teacher. Please come to the office for an interview.*

By the time I had finished reading the second one, tears were streaming down. Yes, these two, especially the one from Kunming, were just what my county's Educational Affairs Bureau had been waiting for. They were written by the authorities concerned. There were two round red official seals at the bottom of each page. What my wife had said was true. The sun had appeared above my home. I read them again for a second time and then for a third, fourth. ... I couldn't dry my tears because each time I read, more kept on running down like a stream.

Finally my wife said, "I came up here for two reasons: One is to tell you the great news, to meet you here. The other is I wanted to thank your host, the old grandpa, in person. When we enjoy a cup of water, we must not forget who dug the well. But he wasn't anywhere to be seen when we arrived. I brought some home-produced meat and vegetables with me, and I have prepared a special dinner. It is almost ready now. You go back to the headquarters office to invite the Party secretary, and don't forget to bring Xiao Zhang. Invite them all to come here and have a farewell dinner."

As she was saying this, my old host appeared at the gate.

"You are home, Great Uncle," I said.

"Father," my wife called out. Taking hold of his hand, she added, "I'm Lao He's wife, your daughter. Today I come here to thank you."

She got down on her knees, but the old man immediately helped her up. "No, no, that was nothing. It's not worthwhile mentioning it. I was pleased to hear your leg has recovered."

And he was even more pleased to hear that I was going to accept a teaching job.

"I always thought you were a good man. Now everything has turned out as well as I hoped at the very beginning. I've enjoyed your company. The door is open for you every day. I shall miss you."

"Just the same here, Great Uncle. Your care is deeper than the sea. We shall carve your kindness on our hearts. I'll always remember the days I spent here at your house."

I decided to be off that very day. After dinner, the old man, Xiao Ming, Secretary Gao, and Xiao Zhang, together with many other villagers, all came to see us off. We were reluctant to part. As we turned back outside the village, everybody waved. How could I forget the bitter past? Simultaneously my wife and I remembered that sad goodbye we had exchanged outside our home village almost two years before. We stood face to face, smiling knowingly.

The hills looked lovely. Everything looked beautiful. We heard the sound of the valley brooks. Some of the roadside willows had just woken up. Many nameless wild flowers along the slopes were beginning to come back to life. Formerly, the beauty of every spring belonged only to nature. Birds, trees, and flowers were the masters of spring. Today, spring had come back to the people. It belonged to me, to my wife, and to everybody else who was living on this land.

*       *       *

The next day, first of all, I went to report the big news to Guihua. Then I went to the Educational Affairs Bureau. Having carefully placed my two letters on the desk there, I sat down quietly. I was expecting something like: "Now everything goes well with the present policy. Just wait for a moment. I'll write you another note to become a teacher." But the man who was interviewing me just scratched his head again and again. Finally he said, "I now know which commune you belong to. I also know the name of your home village. But I've received no written information on these two letters. Sorry, this is also an important policy. I cannot give you anything before I have a written form from your production team and another one from your commune office."

I left the building and went back to see our team head—Mr. Zhao.

"Aha, why?" Mr. Zhao laughed cunningly. "Homesick? You missed your wife?"

"Yes, Mr. Team Head Zhao, I very much missed my wife. I missed her so much that I am purposely coming to tell you this: From today on, I am *not* going to work at the reservoir."

"Oh, you prefer to be a manager of an underground factory? It's too funny! You are still dreaming of becoming a big capitalist. Let me repeat this to you: The Gang of Four has fallen down now. Our brilliant new leader Chairman Hua is continuing Chairman Mao's great cause, leading us on a New March. This means eliminating capitalism and walking on a great socialist road. Now you are coming back to restart your former underground factory. I am afraid you want your head to roll off onto the ground!"

I replied, "I want to tell you just the same thing. All because the Gang of Four has fallen down, that's just why He Liyi is not going to work at the reservoir."

"How's that?"

"Because someone won't allow me to work there."

"Your wife?" Mr. Zhao knocked heavily on his desk. "What an audacious person you are!"

"Not my wife. Here you are." I placed the letters on his desk. "See for yourself. Like a group of our nation's sanitary workers, these two letters have come to clean up the polluted air in our village."

"It's false, false!"

At first he looked carelessly, quickly, but those two round red seals winked at him. Then he looked at me for a long, long time.

I said, "The relationship between you and me ends here today." As he was rereading the letters carefully, I added, "What I want you to do is this: Get a piece of paper. Very simply, write: 'The bearer of this letter is He Liyi of Shangbaodian Village, Production Team One, Diannan Commune.' Then you sign and stamp it with your official seal. That's all."

Under the pressure of those two letters, he wrote the note for me voicelessly. Handing it to me, he said, "All right, but I wonder, I wonder. ...."

"No wonder at all, Mr. Zhao. Tomorrow I will become a 'manager' again. This time it isn't an 'underground' factory but an 'open' one. It is a 'factory' that your children will have to come to; otherwise they won't bring you a rice bowl."

With Mr. Zhao's note, I went back to see the man at the Educational Affairs Bureau. No more problems of any sort. They gave me another note to teach in a small junior middle school as a temporary substitute teacher. The pay was 30 *yuan* a month. Since we were still waiting for the "formal detailed report" from Kunming, I was not yet qualified to become a permanent teacher. Nevertheless, all my friends and all my relatives were overjoyed to hear that I had become a chalk-eater at last.

The first time I entered a classroom was on the 13th or 14th of January, 1979. I was very poor at the time. I wore a shabby jacket. All the other teachers wore wristwatches. I took a big clock with me. Many people, not only students but also some teachers, came to watch and listen outside the windows. Some laughed at me. However, there weren't any problems with my English. Before long, everybody treated me with respect.

In China at that time there was a big political difference between a permanent teacher and a substitute one. Although I was called a teacher, my permanent residence booklet was still in my home village. I lived and taught at a nation's school, even received a salary there, but my name was not in the nation's book. I was still not one of Mr. China's people; I was still considered to be an ordinary peasant living in my home village.

For this reason, I was not qualified to be issued with Mr. China's grain coupons at the end of each month. I was supposed to eat what I produced in my own field. I couldn't even use the school canteen because it demanded grain coupons at each meal. For several months I had to run back and ask my wife to give me rice, vegetables, cooking oil. When a class was over, I made a fire on a portable stove and cooked meals for myself.

Substitute teachers had to face all sorts of other discrimination as well. We were not entitled to enjoy the nation's free medical care. If we went to see a doctor, we had to hand over our money at the clinic's window. There were some restrictions, too, in borrowing a book from the school library. And if we went to get hot water from the school's boiler, we had to wait until other permanent teachers had filled their thermos bottles first.

As soon as I had been offered the substitute job, many friends from Kunming and other bigger towns had written advising me not to accept it. One of them wrote: "A substitute teacher is a false one. When they have enough teachers, it is you who gets the sack. This job is like a piece of cloth wrapped around something too hot to touch with our fingers. As soon as the hot object is put down, they throw that cloth away." Yes, in my heart I knew this was perfectly true. However, all in all, I thought the job was okay. In the past I seemed to have "no face" whenever I met or talked to Guihua. But such difficulties disappeared after I became a substitute teacher. I seemed to have regained some of my self-esteem.

Most important of all, I became master of my monthly payment. Before, my pockets were always empty. Whenever I wanted to buy something, I had to look at my wife's face first. Now I went out and bought a new jacket, a hat, a pair of shoes, and even underwear. Of course, none of these were good-quality things, but they were new. Walking down a street, I could buy something for my sons to eat or play with. I took my younger son to my school, and he stayed with me for a few days. Anyway, whenever I recalled my bitter past, I enjoyed being a substitute teacher.

Way back in 1955, in Kunming, Guihua and I had exchanged a good fountain pen and an embroidered pillowcase as goodbye gifts. Then it happened that I got the pen and she the pillowcase. Our two families loved each other, and now that the Gang of Four had fallen we could freely enjoy ourselves whenever we gathered together.

Three days after International Labor Day there comes our Youth Day, May 4th. In China we combine these two days together and celebrate on the same day. That day in 1979, our county's First Middle School organized dozens of special activities: entertainment programs, scientific reports, a small-scale sports meet, "tell me a story" meetings, wall-newspaper exhibitions. Talented students from all the middle schools in our county, the prize-winners' parents, leading officials of various organizations, and school delegations at all levels were kindly invited to take part. It was quite a big thing.

Right after breakfast, I was told to go and join in the activities. The main reason was that Lujiang was going to receive a prize for his outstanding performance in an English competition. My son told me that Xiao Ying was also a prize winner. This made me think of the fountain pen I had been keeping for fourteen years. In order to encourage the girl, I thought it would be a very good thing to return it to the original owner's daughter.

As I entered the school compound, I first saw two old men—my father-in-law and Guihua's father, Uncle Li—talking under a willow tree. My two sons were playing on the lawn. Xiao Ying was showing and explaining a row of wall-newspapers to my wife. The principal received me warmly and led me to his office. At first I refused his invitation to give a talk on learning English, but he persuaded: "Today is a special red-letter day for our school. All these guests didn't come primarily to enjoy themselves but to learn something from us. You are not young, everybody knows that; but your English foundation is the strongest of all the teachers in our county. So you must go and give a brief lecture."

In the school's best classroom I was warmly greeted by more than thirty teachers of all subjects. After a brief introduction, in which I told them a bit about my personal history, I sat down and discussed learning and teaching English in our area. I hadn't prepared a thing beforehand. I talked about this for a while and then suddenly ran on to talk about another problem, but the emphasis was centered on how best to teach our national minority people's children. Time and again they demanded more, and only after two hours was I able to escape.

I decided to go and look for my father-in-law and my little son, but as I came to the main building I saw Xiao Ying showing her prizes to my wife beside a flower bed. They were talking excitedly and examining a large English-Chinese dictionary. In a flash, my two sons and the two old men also appeared. I admired Xiao Ying's prizes and showed my left thumb, which means "you are very good" in China. With my right hand I gave her a little box, adding, "I've brought you one more."

She opened the box and exclaimed, "Oh, Teacher He, you are being too polite now. I have four or five pens already."

"Yes, but this one is special. We've had this pen since before you were born, more than twenty years now. There is a moving story about it. Ask your mother to tell you the story behind this pen."

At that moment Guihua arrived, still wearing a white hospital cap on her head. "Wait a minute; before I tell you the story of that pen, let me give *you* something," and with these words Guihua produced a bundle wrapped in a piece of red cloth. "It's something as old as that pen. Xiao Ying, I want you to present it to Teacher He."

What was it? I accepted it, glancing at everybody. I opened the bundle and found a silk pillowcase, the very one Guihua had embroidered for me in Kunming.

"Let me see." My father-in-law gazed at it.

"Let me see first." My wife snatched the pillowcase and seemed to fall into a state of meditation.

"It seems so familiar. I've seen it before. I thought I'd lost it somewhere," my father-in-law said.

"You lost it in the hospital at midnight when Lujiang had whooping cough. I accidently found it early the next morning. I embroidered it for Teacher He in Kunming," Guihua slowly said. "Oh, more than ten years ago now. That year I went to your house many times. It was I who injected the boy, but I didn't mention the pillowcase. Now, let it go back to its owner."

My wife looked at me and then approached Guihua. Grasping her hands tightly, she said, "My dear sister Doctor, we really owe you a great deal. It's a simple pillowcase, but it has a long story. Come on, Lujiang. I want you to bow to the doctor." My son looked very shy as my wife pushed him forward. "You know she helped you to enter a middle school last autumn. But now we also know that when you nearly died at the age of three, Xiao Ying's mother saved your life. Do you understand?"

"Yes," my son said. "And she gave you a leg in the hospital."

"I'm so happy you understand that. She has done more than I have. So, hereafter. ...."

"... Xiao Ying's mother is also my mother. I will always feel I have two mothers."

Guihua hugged my son. Then, turning to her daughter, she took off her white hospital cap and said, "For you, I want you to understand this: Before Liberation I was an ordinary village girl in the countryside, like your Aunt He. Now you see, this is a doctor's cap. You might ask how this happened? Well, too long to tell you the whole story. In the first place, our country, our Party, must be kept in mind. But your Teacher He also helped me a great deal in becoming a doctor. He taught me many, many things. Therefore, you must take Teacher He as your father."

In another big building, gongs and drums suddenly sounded. "I'll take my two grandfathers to see some more programs in that hall," my son said, and led them off. Xiao Ying took the two mothers away in the direction of the playground.

Just then a bike hurried in. The rider was the office director of our county's Educational Affairs Bureau. He got down and shook hands with me. "Teacher He, I've got something very good to report to you."

"What news?" I asked hurriedly.

In a flash I was surrounded by a throng of people.

"We received it yesterday afternoon, from Kunming. An official note from the authorities at your former organization. They say that what was done to you in 1958 was wrong. Now everything has been corrected in accordance with our new policies. They further say that a *permanent* teaching post is to be arranged for you. They hope you will contribute more good service toward the realization of our four modernizations."

"Congratulations, Teacher He!" I heard from all sides. Guihua and her husband were the first to shake hands with me. The two grandfathers rushed back from the hall. Our children jumped for joy. We were all on top of the world. Late in the afternoon, our two families had a big supper at Guihua's house to celebrate.

*     *     *

I knew well that I was not a "red expert" of China. I had almost forgotten the basic tenses of the English language, not to mention the complicated forms of the remaining tenses. But I was determined to devote myself wholeheartedly to the teaching and learning of English, to march forward and recapture my lost territory. I was too old to achieve more for my country, this I knew; but I still thought I could do a little. As early as the forties, my main goal had been to copy the example of my Shanghai teacher Miss Xue—to pave the way for hundreds of children to learn English and then offer more service to our country. Now, after years and years of bitter struggle, this road was open to me.

**NOTES**

1. Xiao Di is Luzhong's nickname. It means "Little Brother."

# PART THREE

# 16

## AND I TAKE UP MY CHALK

**S**hortly after our Labor Day celebrations, the head of the county Educational Affairs Bureau handed me a formal appointment directive. It stated that I was to be a permanent teacher of English at the Second Middle School of our county. Without hesitation, I accepted this directive and said goodbye to all my friends. The Second Middle School is situated about seventy *li* away from my village in a district called Madeng. I began preparations to leave.

As a matter of fact, I didn't report to the school at once. After gaining control over my personal income during my three months of substitute teaching, I had gradually saved a small sum of money into my pockets. So, before I went to take up my new post, I bought a ticket and rushed to Kunming.

To my wife I said, "The main purpose in hurrying to Kunming is to buy some weapons—as many English textbooks and reference books as I can afford. My future job at the Second Middle School fills me with all sorts of worries. A substitute teacher can sometimes do things in a careless way, but now that I have been appointed by the government to be a formal teacher of the country, oh dear, the situation is quite different. I really have nothing. People at the Second Middle School will laugh at me and look down on me if as an English teacher I have no English books about me. With nothing in hand, I might face many problems in the classroom."

It was a glorious June day when I arrived in Kunming. The first thing I did was to go to my former organization, the Yunnan Provincial Committee for Border Area National Minority Peoples' Affairs. From the head official down to the man who swept the floor—all were strangers to me. Fortunately I managed to locate a Mr. Hou, one of the three most important officials at the time when I was working in the organization. He had retired but lived nearby. He received me warmly and was kind enough to take me immediately to see the new officials concerned. On that very day these officials gave me 90 *yuan*. They even arranged a bed for me in their guest house. Besides this, all my meals were to be free.

The officials discussed arranging a suitable job for me, and spoke by telephone with government officials in my home county. Unfortunately, the negotiations between them came to nothing. This is what they told me: "Sorry, but it was your own fault. You didn't do things in the proper order. Why didn't you come to see us earlier, *before* we sent that order asking your home county's government to arrange a job for you? You know, carrying out a nation's policy isn't like playing a game among children. Once a formal decision has been made, no one is able to change it."

The "formal decision" was my appointment to the Second Middle School. If this permanent job hadn't already been assigned to me, I might well have been able to arrange a job back in my old organization in Kunming. Now I could do nothing but accept some money to help pay the necessary traveling expenses and leave my former organization's guest house.

Borrowing a good-looking jacket from an old friend of mine, I paid a visit to my Kunming Teachers' College, now Yunnan Normal University. I was extremely happy to find and meet up with Mrs. Chen, now serving as the headmistress of the college's kindergarten. She told me of the death of my old teacher Mr. Chen during the Cultural Revolution. He had been cruelly treated and suffered a very sad death. He was yet another victim of that campaign, like hundreds of other old intellectuals of China.

At the college itself, the staff members in the foreign languages department were all complete strangers to me. However, I managed to get an interview with their dean. He was so moved by my personal story and the details of my study of English that he immediately arranged a written and oral test to try my actual skill. As I was taking my leave, he pointed to a typewriter in the corner and added, "By the way, I was wondering if you could type?"

"Yes, but that was twenty years ago."

"Our department needs a typist at the moment. Hopefully you will become our typist. Come and show me how you place your ten fingers."

Really, I hadn't touched a typewriter for over twenty years, but I hadn't forgotten the right position for my fingers. Within a few seconds I showed him the twenty-six letters. He said, "This year, as the number of students is growing, more and more English teachers are needed. Your oral English is okay; it sounds natural. Secondly, you know how to type. The Party branch secretary will easily agree if your written papers have been done well. Good luck!"

The dean was out when I came to call on him the following morning. A young man in the office gave me an incomplete reply. He said, "I was late this morning, but I heard the dean say, 'This man looks like a potted flower in winter. Its roots are still living, and if we take good care of it and keep on watering it for two or three years it will certainly turn out well and bear a beautiful flower.' Congratulations, Mr. He!"

On the third day the dean told me in person, "You got only 42 percent for your written papers. This outcome was not so good, but it was not the worst mark compared to those of some other people we tested last month. Don't worry about it. You know everything takes time. I'm afraid you'll have to wait for a few days longer. Another important meeting will be organized tomorrow or sometime later this week. You must be patient."

Two days after that, the dean's reply was just the same: Wait for another two days. On the seventh day I went to see him at his home. His son told me that his father had left for Beijing to attend a meeting that morning. Sadly I took my leave. Just then the dean's wife returned and led me back inside. Seated at their table, she began speaking: "My husband would like you to come and work in his department. After a series of discussions the college authorities made a decision to transfer your work from your homeland to Kunming. But unfortunately such an exceptional decision doesn't go along with some of the regulations issued by the highest authorities of our country. The college officials ran here and phoned there, but your county officials didn't agree. They don't want to let you go. We are very sorry, but really nothing can be done at the moment."

Handing me a small package containing books and some other printed materials, she continued: "He spoke highly of you, but none of us can add something new to the nation's policy. He also told us you might face some trouble back in your homeland if you stayed on in Kunming too long. In conclusion, he said that the best way for you is to return and teach at the school where your county wants you to teach. Last night he collected together some used books and teaching materials. They are yours. Take them home and try to make good use of them."

The hand of our Jianchuan officials had seized me very tightly. In a way it seemed that a policeman's bracelet had clamped shut around my wrist. In an effort to change their minds, a friend of mine took me, on the eve of my departure, to see an important man from our Jianchuan County. He was a very famous scholar in the field of cultural affairs in Kunming. It was said that many of my county's important officials were his good friends. The old scholar listened to my past story with interest. Finally he wrote a letter for me to take home and hand to the leading county officials. He assured me, "With this personal letter they will agree to let you teach in Kunming."

\*          \*          \*

I returned home on the 27th of June. Right away I rushed to town and produced that special letter for the county officials to consider. Several days later, at our county Educational Affairs Bureau, the middle-aged office director said, "All the organizations are under the leadership of the same country; but you must know, business is business. Each organization has its own affairs. First, your former organization ordered us to arrange a job for you in our Jianchuan. So we did offer you a job. Be an English teacher. It's a new type of school. It's a good school. Have you got any other problems?"

Before I could reply, another young man in the office put in angrily, "Do you know, outside the gate there are many, many people who are waiting to find a teaching post. You'll be sorry later. If you refuse to use our piece of chalk, one day you will find yourself shouldering a long-handled hoe in the field! Which is heavier? You just consider and compare the weight of those two tools."

"No, young man," the office director stopped him. "I must point out something to you. What you said just now wasn't the policy of our country. You were simply threatening. Yes, many people are asking us to let them teach, but do you know how many of them can teach ABC? We are not supposed to force people. We should make him take our advice with his heart. Show him some convincing facts, lead him to accept our arrangements with reason. We all know he was wronged in the past. Now the country wants us to correct the past wrongdoings. We were asked to give him a job. He knows ABC and our county needs ABC teachers very much at the present stage." He stood up and showed the young man the door. "You leave now. This isn't your business." He thought for a moment and then, turning to the other middle-aged office workers, added, "You too, all of you, leave the office!"

Everybody went out except the office director and me. Offering me a cup of tea, he began his chat with a brief introduction about his own past and present. He was actually a Han Chinese, but he had learned to speak our Bai dialect fluently. He had graduated from the Institute of Southwest National Minority Peoples in Sichuan Province. In response to Chairman Mao's call, he had volunteered to work in a poor and backward area. So he was sent to our Jianchuan County. Before long, he became a local Bai. He went on to relate many of the problems facing our county. Finally he said, "Originally, our Jianchuan was among the most backward counties of the whole province. The so-called Cultural Revolution made us go from bad to worse! We are lagging behind all the other counties. Education is a must, a foundation for speeding up cultural development and the economy. At the moment, the shortage of qualified schoolteachers is our biggest problem, particularly in the field of foreign languages. Our First Middle School is known as the best school of our county. To tell you the truth, none of their English teachers has graduated from a four-year college course in the department of foreign languages. One of them did study a four-year course, but not English. He studied Russian. You probably know what their actual level is.

"As for our Second Middle School, last term they found a half-qualified teacher of English. Actually, he has received only several weeks of hurried training. Most of the students over there are the children of mountain-corner national minority people. In a way, they are what we call backward people, but all of them have a strong desire to learn more. At the moment about 360 pupils, 20 percent of them girls, are divided into six classes. They have only one teacher of English. One teacher can manage to teach only three classes. The other classes are looking forward to learning English from someone. Just think of the past when you and I were young, what we and our parents felt when we had no teacher to tell us how to work out our lessons—what a pity to leave them undone!

"Mr. He, for the sake of hundreds of students and hundreds of their parents, could you give up the idea of going to Kunming? I do hope you'll consider my opinions and stay in Jianchuan County. Just offer what you have to our own Jianchuan children. People of all circles in our county will be grateful to you. Everybody will remember you."

I was silent for a long time. The office director stood up and ended the chat. "All right, Mr. He. The young man is a newcomer. What he said a moment ago was wrong. You are older. You forgive him. As for my opinions, no hurry to answer me right now. Go home and reconsider the whole situation, but I hope you will change your mind and go to teach at our Second Middle School in Madeng."

After hearing his opinions, I began to hesitate. There was something to the office director's point of view. I stopped thinking of going to Kunming. Returning home that afternoon, I told my wife what I had been considering. She got excited and said, "Right, perfectly right. I put both my hands up high to show I am for your decision. Stay in Jianchuan. This is our homeland. This is our birthplace. This is also the birthplace of our ancestors. Thousands and thousands of our children are waiting for us to feed them. Our own two boys are among them. Go to Madeng. Take Lujiang with you. I will be responsible for everything in the house. All in all, you just use your ABC to make our home county look more and more beautiful. Let the sad things become smoke floating above the chimney. Let the northwest wind blow them away."

My village wife's words sounded like those of a woman from a college. I was deeply touched. It made me give up all my previous thoughts completely. The next day I went to tell the office director my final decision. On my way home I bought two tickets for Madeng District.

\*　　　\*　　　\*

My elder son and I left home for the Second Middle School on July 4, 1979. My wife saw us off at the commune bus stop. It was Lujiang's very first time to enjoy a bus ride. He looked out of the window and shouted, "Goodbye, my home village! Bye-bye, Mama, bye-bye for some time."

"Yes, yes, only goodbye for a short time. Don't worry about the pigs or the chickens at home. Hereafter, our everything will be all right."

"Perfectly correct. But Mama, you look unhappy. We are going to have a new life. You must smile and celebrate."

"I know that already, but the other day I was told the weather there is extremely cold. Shall I hurry back to bring your grandpa's sheepskin coat? I'm afraid that father and son, two people, sharing one old sheepskin coat is not enough."

"My grandpa's tattered sheepskin coat can only keep our bodies warm. You must know we have received another 'special coat' which is more precious than everything else in the world."

The mother could make neither head nor tail of this.

"The long-awaited time has come to our family. After a storm we have fine weather; sunshine comes out and the land begins to warm up. That sunshine warms not only our bodies but our minds as well. Formerly my father went to our commune's middle school when people had all gone to bed. Can you remember? But, after all, our country didn't forget him. Today, he is going to be a permanent teacher! Bye-bye. Take care of everything and don't worry about us."

The distance between Jinghuazheng and Madeng is about 140 *li*. Not very far, but the trouble is that all the way the bus has to stagger slowly along a narrow and zigzagging upward mountain road, go through a large number of thick woods, and pass quite close to some about-to-fall-down rocks. In the dry season, the whole distance usually takes four hours to cover. During the rainy or snowy seasons, the passengers have to spend almost a whole day on the bus.

Formerly, before the nation's liberation, people on the Jianchuan plain gave Madeng a special name: "The innermost corner of the county." Their meaning was that Madeng was a most mysterious and hidden corner, filled with nothing but mountains, rocks, and lots of dangerous wild animals. When I was a little boy, if I or one of my sisters repeatedly did something wrong, my father would scold us: "Be careful. If you are not going to turn over a new leaf, tomorrow I shall tie you up and take you to Madeng and leave you there to be their slave." Then my mother would add, "Yes, let him wear a tree leaf for trousers, sleep beside a fire, and eat potatoes all the year round!" Madeng was known as a "four noes corner": No four sunny days following one after another; no four feet of smooth, flat terrain; no person able to read or write can be found within four neighboring villages; no four coins can be found belonging to one person. Nobody could confirm if the "four noes" were true or false, because nobody in or around my home village had ever been there before!

At about one-thirty the bus driver called out loudly, "Ladies and gentlemen, all passengers for Madeng be ready to get down!" Looking out of the window, I noticed a group of boys and girls waiting beside the road. As soon as my son and I stepped down, they formed a noisy circle around us. Their principal and two other teachers shook us warmly by the hand. We followed them upward. After we'd passed through a market square and into a field not far from the foot of a hill, some buildings came into view. Another quarter of an hour's walk brought us to the school. Hundreds of boys and girls rushed out to meet us. As we walked, the principal waved and shouted excitedly, "Come and welcome Teacher He, our school's new teacher of ABC."

Hundreds of students said "Hello" to me. Many nodded with the sweetest smile on their faces. As we arrived in the main school courtyard, someone behind us called out, "How do you do?" Turning back I returned the caller another "How do you do?" I stopped and asked them to repeat after me, "We are fine, thank you."

Some ran away at once. The principal immediately waved them back. "Why, don't be so silly! This is just the way to learn a foreign language. Come on, everybody. I will learn from Teacher He, too. Don't be afraid. Let's do it together, okay? Teacher He, will you please repeat it again and we will repeat it after you."

"One, two, three, 'How do you do?'"

Some stood at a distance, but many got closer and repeated after me twice.

I was sleepless that evening. The principal's friendly welcome had left a good and deep impression. How the mountain area children struggled to carry my luggage! How the other teachers greeted me! Their lovely smiles made me extremely happy and proud. That afternoon, after getting down from the bus, I was rather fatigued from the bumpy ride, but the moment I saw the students' eager-to-learn eyes all my weariness disappeared. I thought, "If I had gone to teach in Kunming nobody would have given me as warm a welcome as the one I have had at the Second Middle School today."

The next day my son told me, "Within only twenty-four hours, you haven't even entered a classroom, and they have already given you a nickname."

"How do you know?"

"Well, I overheard them talking when I went to the toilet this morning."[1]

"What did you hear?"

"They said your name was 'Old how do you do.' For me, they say 'Little how do you do.'"

"Well, that's all right. It sounds good. At least this new nickname is better than the one our villagers gave me. Do you remember what they used to call me?"

"Was it 'Mrs. He's tail?'"

"No, they did call me that for some time, but many people also called me 'Mr. Slow-Coach.' You must know, having one's name changed is not easy."

*       *       *

Madeng, with a population of 50,000, is one of the seven districts that make up our Jianchuan County. Five of these, including Madeng, are classed as higher, colder, and poorer "mountain districts"; the remaining two, Dongning and Diannan, my home district, are classed as more prosperous "half-mountain, half-plain districts." People living on the plains grow rice, the best kind of staple. In the mountain-corner districts the staples are coarser: potatoes, corn, barley, or buckwheat.

Jianchuan County, on the whole, is a county of Bai people. But other national minority peoples live in many corners of the county as well. In my home village, all the local people are Bai. But in Madeng, about 80 percent of the population are Bai, and the remaining 20 percent are Yi, Lisu, or Moslem. Each group has its own customs, traditions, and costumes. The Yi and Lisu each have their own language as well. The Moslems of Jianchuan speak our local Bai language. Once a week, on market day in Madeng Town, all gather and mingle together in a colorful throng to buy and sell.

This market square, the very one I walked through on my first day in Madeng, is the political and economic center of the district. Local organizations such as the commune government offices, the Culture Station,[2] a branch of the People's Bank, a small post office, the hospital, the department store, and the elementary school all cluster around it. Our school is not far away, and I enjoy walking over the hills to look around and shop.

Madeng is 2,800 meters above sea level, so my wife was correct—it *is* colder than my home village on the Jianchuan plain. Plenty of water can be found in the valleys, but, at present, long stretches of dry land remain on the mountain slopes. Most peasants farming these slopes rely on Heaven for their water supply. The dry seasons, winter and early spring, are especially troublesome. In our school, we often have to take turns carrying water to the kitchen during these seasons. In 1985, Mr. China gave us money and we made an "iron dragon"—a water pipe. But we still suffer from water shortages.

In the field of education, a junior middle school made its first appearance in the early sixties, but it had no qualified teacher of English. In 1977, this became the Second Middle School. It was a one-class school in its first year, but in 1978 it became a complete middle school with several classes and a senior department as well. Broadly speaking, the level of knowledge of our local Madeng schoolchildren is lower than that in the schools of all the other advanced districts. The high mountains that surround Madeng have kept the children from the outside world. Yet Madeng students show an eager-to-study spirit and work hard; and so, starting in 1980, a few of the local children have been selected to receive further education at higher-level colleges in big cities.

I was their first qualified teacher of English. The villagers called me "Local King of English." With the Gang of Four just fallen, the contents of our textbooks were in a constant state of change. Nevertheless, they didn't seem as difficult as the ones we had used forty years previously, and I found no unsolvable difficulties in understanding our textbook English.

My main problem was that each term, when I was instructed to teach the beginners' classes, I found it a troublesome job to make all of the students understand my explanations. The cause was that three different languages were spoken at our school: Bai, Lisu, and Yi. In addition, it is a rule in China that Mandarin must be spoken in the classroom. So, altogether we had four different languages. Some of the new students, selected from faraway mountain and valley corners of the district, had never heard Mandarin before. And I had to use this Mandarin to teach English!

Often this happened in my classroom: First, I had to explain the thing in Mandarin. A few couldn't understand. The second step was to translate, to put the Mandarin explanation into the students' various local languages. Well, the next problem was that I myself belong to the Bai nationality. As for the other languages, I knew only a little. Therefore, I often had to look for another student to be my assistant and interpret. In order to tackle this problem more thoroughly, I was forced to learn some of the local languages.

Another of my problems, an important one, was that this was the very first time in the history of Madeng that English was being taught and learned. In a village, when a father wanted to have a look at his son's English exercise book, he didn't say, "Let me see how many points your teacher gave you for your English." Instead, he said something like, "Let me see how you drew your chicken-duck feet."

When a mother heard her daughter reading English, she would say, "Oh, I don't think the blue-eyed people talk like that!"

"Why, Mother, our teacher taught us this passage. On the other side of our earth, people really speak like this."

"Well, as I listen, it sounds like some strange birds singing in the forest. The way you write looks like a little chick walking in the sand."

Once, at a student's home, as I was talking to a father about his daughter's homework, a part of our conversation ran like this: "Today, with Deng Xiaoping's policy, it's easy to lead a happy life even if we do not study English. We were born here, grew up here. In the future, we shall die here, too. We haven't the least intention of letting our children go to a foreign country. What's the use of troubling our mouths to learn to speak their language?"

"Tell me, since the founding of our People's Republic in 1949, how many times did Chairman Mao go to a foreign country?" I asked.

"Well, I was twenty-two in 1949. So far as I can recall, Chairman Mao went to the Soviet Union only once in 1950. Perhaps that was all."

"That's right. Now tell me this: Since 1978, when there appeared many wise leaders like Hu Yaobang, Li Xiannian, and Zhao Ziyang, do these new leaders learn from Chairman Mao and stay at home year after year?"

"No, they travel to foreign countries all the time."

"Do you think this is because our leaders are poor, so they want to look for good things to eat in other countries?"

"No, today we common people have more than enough to eat and drink. Our officials have still more and more."

"Do you know why they always want to go abroad?"

"Well, they say they go abroad to buy foreign goods and see how other people do things."

"Right. To study English doesn't mean we want to enjoy a pleasure trip from country to country. It's all because the knowledge we obtain from our own textbooks cannot satisfy our needs. If we want to lead a happier life, we have to learn more about the advanced experiences of other countries. But the trouble is they do not write of their achievements in Chinese. Therefore, our children have to learn foreign languages."

I talked to this one and then to that one. By and by, more villagers came to understand the importance of learning a foreign language.

*     *     *

Three months passed by quickly. While teaching in a classroom I was extremely happy, because all my students looked at me with smiling faces. They enjoyed learning ABC. They had an English teacher and also a textbook, so they were overjoyed. I found them amiable, honest, and, apart from a few naughty ones, enthusiastic. As soon as I came down to my bedroom I had to hurry with dozens of chores, such as sweeping, making a fire to cook, chopping the vegetables, washing the rice and all our clothes. My elder son Lujiang was old enough to carry a pail of water and wash vegetables, but as a student he had a timetable that was full every day of the week. I was responsible for nearly all the meals. Each day, after finishing supper, correcting all my students' exercise books, and helping Lujiang with his English homework, it seemed that I had nothing special to do. For sports activities the school had only one or two basketballs, and at that stage Madeng had no television reception.

I would have liked to gather together all my spare time and polish my rusty English. But without more materials I could really do nothing to learn something new to pass on to my students. In China we have a saying: "A wife cannot make a good meal if she has no rice." All I had were the 1,600 words found in our six junior middle school textbooks. I had no chance to speak English, nowhere to sit down and listen to English for a little while. I had no radio of my own. No English books or magazines could be borrowed from the school's library or from any other source. And no English printed materials were to be found in the local market square's little bookshop, even though I was quite willing to pay for them. I had brought some books with me from Kunming, but not enough even to fill one shelf from end to end.

So I could do nothing special for my students. Only four hours of English lessons per class each week, with at least fifty-six, sometimes sixty, heads in each class. There was no extra time for oral practice. Sometimes I felt my job was a meaningful, enjoyable one, but at other times I thought it was like making a bad bargain in the street. I have lots of customers. I sell my goods like hotcakes. But can I sell exactly the same things year after year? Do I have a large storehouse? A textbook, a blackboard, a piece of chalk, and finally my own mouth. That was all.

When Saturday came, both father and son felt rather lonely. Most of the other teachers had gone to spend the weekend with their families. I liked to read near my charcoal fire quietly for a long, long time. My son had a dislike of fires. He used to go over his lessons in bed, with a blanket covering his legs. The bed and the fire were our only friends to keep father and son company.

Sometimes he would ask, "Baba, charcoal isn't cheap. Why not pull a cover over your legs like me?"

I would say, "Our lamp by the bed is too poor. Sooner or later you will have eye problems."

"All right, all right. Let's go to sleep then," he would say.

"Yes, yes, the best way is to go to sleep earlier. It's cheaper, and it will make our bodies strong."

Quite a few Saturdays were spent like this in the beginning. But even before my first term ended, things began to change for the better. New friendly contacts began. When I took an after-supper walk in the nearby villages, the students' parents often insisted that I drop in and have a cup of tea with them. Wherever I went I was very interested in learning how people lived. I often asked questions like, "What did your father do?" "How many pigs are there in your family?" "What is your daughter going to do when she grows up?" The father of one of my students, after getting to know me better, was kind enough to lend me his own shortwave transistor radio.

How marvelous! With a little radio sitting on the desk I could hear not only what was happening in the nation's capital but also a thousand interesting things from every corner of the world. All sorts of radio frequencies added new "programs" to my life. With the coming of Voice of America and London Calling, presented by the British Broadcasting Corporation, my thoughts often jumped from country to country. To tell the truth, I couldn't follow much of the programs, but I thought I understood a little of everything. I just loved to hear what was spoken on the air, just loved to train my ears as often as possible. After that peasant lent me his radio, coldness and loneliness disappeared from my bedroom.

In 1958 one of the "reasons" I was sent away to reform my thoughts was "He listened to foreign countries' reactionary broadcasts." If I restarted listening to these broadcasts, would they punish me again? This was the biggest question I had to consider seriously. If someone was going to send me away to reform myself, the other four members of my family would be involved. If I returned the radio to the owner, where could I learn something new? These two thoughts fought battle after battle, troubling me for days and nights. By the end of 1979, the war had ended. My final decision was: I am willing to risk everything to save my knowledge of English.

With this firm determination, I placed a piece of paper in front of me and wrote down some words to the BBC's Chinese Section. I wrote in Chinese. I showed it to my son. Who would have thought it possible—the boy tore it into pieces!

"They live in England. They speak English. You are a teacher—what's more, a teacher of English. This is a good chance to practice your English. Why not?"

A few days later I tried again. This time I wrote the letter in English, beginning: "Dear Chinese Section's Ladies and Gentlemen, Your radio broadcast station is indeed a very big one. It is so big and so good that I can hear your voices at our school. I am a student. ...."

My son read it. Turning to a letter in his textbook, he said, "Look, here is a letter written by a boy named Mike to his friend in Australia. He didn't write 'Ladies and Gentlemen.' The second thing is you must tell them you are a teacher, not a student."

Several days later I wrote another letter. It began: "Dear Respectable Chinese Section's Respectable Comrades." This time, my son had something to say about the word "comrade": "What are you? You are a mountain-corner teacher of English in China. They are big radio officials in London, a very big capital city. You are too ordinary. It will make them angry if you use the word 'comrade.'"

Several days passed. I wrote and tore, wrote and tore. It took me almost a month to settle the wording of that first letter. I remember that the one I finally posted began with "Dear friends." I wrote a similar letter to VOA.

About thirty years ago, in 1948, when I was a middle-school student in Kunming, I wrote a letter to a film star in Hollywood. My teacher corrected the letter. It created a lot of excitement when I received a photo from that American film star. Her name was Linda Darnell. At that time America and China were good friends. This time, although things had changed, I was still in a state of half-belief and half-doubt. I thought my letters to the BBC and VOA would be like two stones falling down into a big sea—nowhere to be seen again.

I was wrong! First, in less than six weeks, came two books from VOA. Then I received several large yellowish paper bags containing two or three sets of teaching materials from the BBC. I was wild with joy to get these valuable books. Now I could seriously begin my you-die-or-let-me-die struggle with the English language.

I wrote letters back to thank every one involved at both the BBC and VOA. In response to these letters, I received a reply written by a secretary named Sara Lim, a member of the BBC's Chinese Section. For a time, I thought this secretary was a gentleman, so each time I wrote I addressed the receiver as "Dear Mr. Lim." This Sara Lim wrote back again and again; we exchanged letters nearly twice a month. She sent me more printed materials, including a big English-English dictionary such as native English speakers use. As time went by, the sender began to give me more and more information and even described some personal affairs. It turned out that the mysterious secretary was a lady! And she was particularly interested to learn that I was not a young teacher but already had a teenage son.

In our Bai area we have a saying: "At home we rely on our parents for everything. Going out away from home we have nothing to rely on but friends." After all, one's own effort is always a limited one. Just as Sara was introducing me to a huge family of international pen-friends, Guihua moved away. Shortly after I became a formal teacher in Madeng her father, Uncle Li, sadly died. Everything changed. Her husband had become homesick. Sometime in 1980 he took Guihua and Xiao Ying back to his own homeland, a small distant county in the northern part of Gansu Province. I never thought our short meeting before I reported to my Second Middle School was to be our last goodbye.

## NOTES

1. Many people in China do not have private toilets. Work units and local health departments provide public toilets for their residents.

2. Culture Stations are set up by local authorities to promote literacy and culture. Anyone may drop in to read magazines, borrow books, talk, sing, play chess or cards, and, on special occasions, watch plays.

# 17

# A NINTH DISH OF EGGS

**M**ore and more big changes were taking place in my village. Each time we received a letter from home we heard good news. My wife's letter said:

> It seems that all the market-control officials have died quietly. Nobody comes to stop me from selling things in the street. I never hear of anyone going into a house to search, or threatening by saying, "You'll be arrested if you are making an underground factory!" There are no more political or class-struggle meetings. All the old important officials at the Team Committee have been replaced by a band of young men. It will give you a big laugh, father and son, to hear that Mr. Zhao our former team head is now an ordinary peasant. We villagers elected the new committee at a team meeting, and the members have been approved by the higher-level authorities. They seem very fair in solving our village problems.
>
> The village public property has been reasonably divided among the commune members. It was the same with the land. Each household received an equal share of dry land and watery land.[1] Those who had the interest and skill put in bids for the pear orchard, the apple orchard, the rice mill, and so on. They promise to give a certain amount to the government each year, and the remainder is theirs to keep. Mr. Ma's son used to be considered the poorest fellow in our village. Do you recall how he used to ask people to give him one cigarette from house to house? Now, he has become very rich and married a beautiful wife. All because he was contracted to take charge of our village pond. Nowadays he is paying his former "debts" by offering cigarettes to all he meets. I don't smoke, but the other day at the edge of our village he ran after me and forced me to accept some cigarettes. He said once long ago you gave him a cigarette. When you come home for a visit he will certainly bring us a lot of fish.
>
> People go to work according to their own convenience. Our loudspeaker never hurries people, but everybody goes around more quickly. Most of the households have fulfilled the country's public-grain requirements ahead of schedule and, in addition, have harvested more than enough to eat. Rice—big, pure white, as white as snow—we now have not occasionally or when a festival comes but at each meal, every day of the month.

*My hens lay plenty of eggs each week, and the pigs are growing surprisingly big and fat. The old man is also all right. Luzhong is getting anxious to start his schooling. In addition, we received 200 yuan from your former organization in Kunming. This money is meant to help us with our difficult problems at home. I have ordered some new tiles. If possible we will complete our new house by the end of the year. Everything seems okay. We always hope and pray that God will protect you, father and son. May you teach and study well.*

In my reply, I wrote:

*The rope which tied my thoughts for many years is beginning to fall down. I am becoming brave. I am only an ordinary teacher, but I feel as if I am also one of the masters of the school. If someone asks me something, I no longer tell half and keep half. I tell the asker exactly and plainly.*

One afternoon in August 1980, my wife and young son unexpectedly arrived at our school. The moment I led them into my room, Luzhong opened up a cardboard box. Holding it politely with his two hands, he gave me a new shortwave radio.

"This is my mother's fattest pig. It's yours now," he said smiling.

"Pig?"

My wife said, "They say foreign people often speak in shortwave radios. So I sold our family's fattest pig and bought this for you to celebrate your appointment as a formal teacher."

"You are so thoughtful! Indeed, very, very kind." I was touched by my wife's gift, but I added, "Someone here lent us one some time ago. Everything went by smoothly, even if we didn't own a radio. The situation is different at home, though. How can you do farmwork if you run short of meat in the house? Selling a pig is a big thing."

"Don't worry about home. Hereafter, regarding your foreign language, the English ABC, I'm afraid I can do nothing for you because I am only a village woman. But many things remain to be done at our house. Please believe I'll shoulder that responsibility. You just put your energy into your teaching work at school. You are still a poor teacher compared to other teachers of the country. Be patient. After completing the new house, if my family economy goes well, I shall buy you a Shanghai-made watch."

"There is no hurry to let my wrist look beautiful. I won't be late even if I have no watch."

She said jokingly, "Now, you tell me this: Was I wrong or silly in choosing a good husband? At the beginning, when you first came to our house, people said you were a criminal, you were a bad egg who tried everything to oppose Chairman Mao and socialism. They all advised me not to marry you. But I pushed away the fearful gossip. I thought you must have been wronged by some top officials. Some day, God in Heaven would open his eyes and reveal all the facts for people to see the truth. Now, I think the whole village has come to understand everything."

*      *      *

After the autumn harvest of 1980, happy laughter filled the villages. That year there was only my wife and an aged, almost seventy-year-old man at home, but the rice they took in from our watery land was three times more than in previous years, when that land was under the control of our village production team. My wife and father-in-law were unable to do many jobs, but since much grain had been harvested they started to raise a big mother pig. Within five months the number of pigs had grown to fifteen or twenty. My wife sold a little piglet and bought several hens. The number of chicks also grew rapidly. My wife said she was tired out every day; nevertheless, like me, she now enjoyed her life.

The year 1981 was a great one for our family. First, after overcoming numerous difficulties, my wife finally managed to wake up those sleeping logs and complete our new house. Regarding the building of a house, we Bai people have a common saying: "There is a house inside a house." The first stage of building is to erect the main poles straight into the ground and cover the roof with tiles. As we can at least keep out wind and rain, this is already called a house. But we cannot sleep in it comfortably, because time and money are needed to add a staircase, walls, and windows. These things are called "another smaller house." We thought it was a big success in our family's history to complete both these houses.

The second big event in 1981 was that Lujiang was selected to enter the senior department of our school. In Jianchuan County, more senior departments were added to our middle schools after the country's Liberation, but they can still take only a limited number of students. Each year, more than half of all junior middle school graduates cannot continue their studies in a senior department. They have to return home to be earthrepairers. That year, there were altogether seven junior middle school graduates from our home village—but only my son's scores on his examination papers qualified him to enter a senior department.

The third big event was that I opened a door to West Germany. One evening, my new radio took me traveling to that country. Without delay I wrote a letter to the Voice of Germany's English Department. Three months after posting my letter I received a registered reply congratulating me on winning "the prize for the most outstanding letter to be received by the Asian English Department this week." The prize was a transistor radio; I felt like "a blind cat who had met a dead rat." However, I waited and waited for this radio. I lost count of how many letters I wrote in connection with it. I was about to sit down and write a letter to the West German ambassador in Beijing when the radio suddenly reached our school. I—no, the whole school, and people of all circles in our commune—was over the moon the day I received it. In celebration I handed out cupfuls of wine, good-quality cigarettes, and two little bags of candy. Heaven knows how many stations my new radio can receive. Perhaps it is the Number One radio in the whole province.

The fourth important event in 1981 wasn't any sort of success at all. It was another heavy load on my shoulders: My wife sent my younger son to join me at my school. She wrote in a letter:

> *I am very sorry, but you are his father. You know I am only an ordinary village woman. I only know how to feed a pig and how to plant rice and wheat. As for how to make our children gain more knowledge, I can do nothing at all. I think I have fulfilled what a mother was supposed to do for the children. You'll have to accept him and make him go to study at a nearby elementary school.*

From 1981 on, my five-member family was divided into two branches. My wife was responsible for our home and the old man. At school, I was to teach four classes and look after my two sons. It wasn't easy to make sure that everything went by smoothly. One more person meant one more bed, one more bowl, one more pair of chopsticks. On weekends it was I who did three people's washing. On Sundays it was I who mended the holes in our clothes. People in our school often said, "From Monday to Saturday morning Mr. He is a schoolteacher. But from Saturday afternoon to Sunday evening he is the mother of the house."[2]

*     *     *

My home village wasn't far away, and several regular buses came and went every day. But once I became a formal teacher of the country I made up my mind to stay at school most of the time. The local people were very surprised when they learned that we didn't go home even for the Spring Festival. They gave me a new nickname, "The Temple Watchman." But for vacations I had a special plan for my two sons and myself. At first, both of them rejected my idea. But I talked to them again and again. I made several comparisons between our bitter past and the happy present. Then I pointed to a bright future for them to see. In the end both listened to me.

Every day, early in the morning, they had to memorize some important passages from their textbooks. After this they could read anything they liked at the commune's Culture Station. They had to spend one-third of the day going over their school lessons. Late in the afternoon, we three would go to the back of our dormitory to weed and enlarge our private vegetable garden. We dug a little bit every day, and gradually that wasted corner became a beautiful vegetable garden. After supper, the three of us would take a walk around the nearby villages. We returned with three bamboo baskets filled with animal droppings, which we scattered over our garden. Our vegetables grew tall and lovely. Later I sold them to the student dining hall and bought a pair of new shoes for each of the boys.

During the winter vacation of 1982, we made another plan to earn some extra money. The school needed mud bricks. I signed an agreement with our principal. We three carried earth and water, mixed them up together, and formed bricks. The weather was cold. A mud brick can't be produced if you run away from mixing the mud with your feet. Sometimes my sons' feet and fingers were blistered from the mud and cold. I encouraged them: "At home we have to do heavy jobs every day. This job is cold and heavy, but we needn't do it all the year round. Very soon it will be over." After half a month we succeeded in producing 3,000 mud bricks. We received 30 *yuan* for them. With that sum of extra income the two boys bought lots of exercise books and two good-quality pens; they even paid their school fees. We bought more candles, because although a power station had been completed two years before we came to Madeng, the school authorities shut off that public electricity as soon as a vacation began. We also bought some additional sugar and eggs. The boys were very happy when they ate something we had bought as a result of their own hard work.

As for myself, I used the vacations to enrich myself. During term time I could hardly keep up with my teaching, let alone improve my English level. This was the true reason why I kept on staying at school, vacation after vacation. If I had idled away this valuable time with festivities, I'd have had no hope of recapturing my lost English territory. Therefore, I abandoned all other trivial pursuits and began a serious last-minute struggle against the English language. In order to accomplish this task I began translating some interesting folktales from Chinese into English during my spring vacation of 1980. I sent the first few completed stories to a friend of mine in Kunming, asking him to show them to a famous English teacher in the city. I failed. This is what that famous teacher wrote:

> *A mountain-corner middle-school teacher wishes to translate something? You are dreaming! Can a frog at the bottom of a deep well eat the flesh of a swan up in the sky?*

This blow didn't hurt me at all. On the contrary, it gave me more strength to try again and again. Each week, whenever I had a moment of spare time, I translated a little. Soon I had completed the folktales of several national minority people. My special friend Sara kindly agreed to let me send all the stories for her to read and see. In 1982 I was overjoyed to receive some big extra news from London. Collins Publishers had decided to publish my folktales. Like the day I was accepted as a college student and the day I received that formal document from my former organization, this was another great, great day in my life.

Soon after Collins made the decision to publish my stories, a famous editor, Susan Dickinson, asked me to write a brief autobiography. One day in the summer of 1982, as I was wondering how to begin this autobiography, I wrote a letter to the British Embassy in Beijing asking for information about England. Before long, I received a reply from a secretary at the embassy. He also sent a good dictionary and a monthly magazine called *In Britain*. I wrote a letter to the magazine's address in London. Several weeks later both the editor and her secretary wrote back to me. In March 1983 my letter was published in their magazine.

After this, more and more international letters flew to my mountain-corner school. Really, that magazine was the leading engineer behind my Second International Bridge. During the second half of 1983, I was often wanted on the telephone. It was the young man from the local post office hurrying me to run down and pick up my international mail. The senders were all English speakers. I read each letter carefully and repeatedly. I even studied the notes and "instructions" printed on the envelopes and packages. We exchanged photos, stamps, drawings, tapes, magazines, newspapers, books. Earlier I had complained because I had no ammunition with which to fire at English. Now, up and down along my bed, I had dozens of boxes full to the top.

During my second year a few students began calling at my room to ask how to subscribe to English magazines. Later, after seeing the bundles of replies I had received from my foreign friends, many more wanted to find foreign penfriends. I corrected their letters and introduced them to some British middle-school students. Each time they got a reply, they were over the moon. Once I overheard a little girl say, "If I can't speak English I'll look like my mother who cannot speak Mandarin, so she can do nothing but prepare meals for us. My father learned how to speak Mandarin, so he is able to make a living in other counties."

Once, while visiting home, I delivered a detailed report for my wife to hear. I told her about all the materials I had received from my international friends abroad. She thought for a while and then said, "I think, very, very possibly it's because for a time you were a sort of little local king in the underground world. Your foreign friends somehow were forced by another bigger king to be your slaves. However, you were not a cruel despot but a kind-hearted king. After several years of underground training, all of you were set free. Some were born in Australia. Some were born in America or in England. While you were living in that underground world you had too many shortcomings, so you were assigned to be reborn in a poor country—our China. Later, the others found you were in trouble in a mountain corner of Yunnan. You had done some good deeds for them before; therefore, today they are coming to return something to you."

*           *           *

On July 1st, 1983, I unexpectedly received a letter from my publisher saying that a new typewriter was on its way to Yunnan for me. The publisher had
succeeded in asking a lady, Claire Chik, to bring it to China. She had been invited to teach English at the Kunming Institute of Technology. Shortly after
this I received a letter from Claire herself, saying that her husband had gone
on ahead of her and her daughter for a brief visit to Kunming, and had left the
typewriter with a friend there. The friend was waiting for me to pick it up.

Just at this time, by a curious coincidence, I was selected by my county authorities to attend a big and important meeting of schoolteachers from our
whole province in Kunming. They would pay my traveling expenses. I arrived
in Kunming on July 17th and the meeting began the following morning.
About 700 teachers of all subjects from 130 counties were taking part. The
teachers of English, about 60 in all, were organized into one big group. We
began with a report delivered by a top official from the Yunnan Department
of English Studies.

At first, all my group members looked down on me. I came from a distant,
unknown, mountain-corner school. I wore poor, handmade shoes. Under my
arm I carried no handsome briefcase with a zipper. And no watch at all, not
even the cheapest, could be found on my wrist. My fellow teachers, however,
wore beautiful suits of the best quality, and some even carried big tape-re-
corders under their arms. During the breaks I felt too ashamed to talk to anyone. Once, as I passed by a group of them, I tried to have a look at what they
were doing, but they held their heads higher and returned me a sad and ugly
look.

On the second or third evening, I took up Claire's letter and went out to
find the address where my typewriter was waiting. It took me three hours to
find that address. But when I finally succeeded—there was my portable typewriter. I just couldn't find the proper words to express my love for this machine. I returned quietly, but in less than ten minutes my room was full of
teachers. It looked like I had organized a "press conference." In the fifties it
was easy to see secondhand typewriters in some Kunming shops, but later
everything changed. As teachers of English, most of us had at least heard
about a writing machine, but hardly any had ever seen a typewriter before.
"Just come and enjoy for a moment's pleasure! Foreign people's writing machine! The very first time in my life... ," they shouted at the tops of their
voices. "That mountain fellow got a writing machine from Britain!"

By the next morning the news had spread in all directions. A poor mountain-corner teacher had suddenly turned into a language expert! In the dining
hall or during breaks, crowds of strangers came up to greet me. Those tape-
recorder carriers lowered their heads and warmly invited me to borrow at any
time. They no longer gave me an ugly look but, instead, a sweet smile.

*          *          *

I returned to my Second Middle School on July 31st. Madeng had changed since my first arrival three years before. At that time there was only one restaurant, one hotel, and one department store. Each was crowded and slow every day of the week. Our Mr. China was the owner of all these businesses. In the market, fresh vegetables were scarce. One could get a few only on market day. Lots of people had to rely on dried vegetables. Nobody could be found to repair a watch, a radio, or a shoe. For entertainment we had to rely on an open-air film show once a week.

Now, private-owned businesses had overtaken state-owned ones. There were five private restaurants, and nearly each one had at least two or three guest rooms for travelers to sleep in. Small shops and stalls selling all sorts of things had sprung up in every corner of the market square, and people could buy things conveniently and quickly. As I walked through the square, I counted the number of watch-repairers and shoemakers. There were twenty-one in all.

Just a few short years ago the local people seldom traveled from place to place. But shortly after the Gang of Four were swept away, several regular buses were full every day. The narrow highway has since opened the local people's eyes and linked them to the outside world. Hundreds of trucks, mostly loaded with coal and logs, are kept busy from early in the morning until late at night. Traveling vegetable-sellers hitch rides on these trucks and come to sell good things produced by people from other distant counties, so we can buy a variety of fresh vegetables any season of the year.

In 1982 the county government gave Madeng District a big sum of money to build a television station. About ten TV sets were bought collectively, and after this we could enjoy a TV program on the TV set at school or in some other organization.

In the fields, wearing a pair of straw shoes has become a thing of the past. Nearly all the young villagers now wear a pair of rubber boots when weeding their plants. And whenever it begins to rain, instead of large straw hats umbrellas can be seen everywhere. When I first arrived at our school, the students often wore shabby clothes. Only a few teachers wore wristwatches. All students came to school by Number 11 bus.[3] Gradually, many of the students have begun to wear stylish clothes, especially the girls. Some even wear high-heeled shoes. A third of our *students* now wear wristwatches, and many come to school on bikes.

*          *          *

From time to time I returned home for a day or so. On these occasions, a problem appeared as soon as I got to my gate. This was the question of my elder son's marriage. Lujiang himself never talked a word about "looking for a girlfriend" or even hinted at anything like this. And I thought it was too early to consider this problem. Everything came from his mother. Each time I met up with my wife, she pestered me to answer some questions relating to my elder son's marriage problem.

In our home village, nearly 80 percent of the young boys and girls of Lujiang's age had already had their marital futures settled. This marriage business is compared to a farmer's job. The farmer has to plough and plant in time. If you do it late, you lose all hope of getting in a good harvest. For a typical village woman like my wife, full of feudal ideas, this concern wasn't anything strange. All she wanted for her old age was to cradle a grandchild in her arms and wander around to spend the time. This was considered most honorable. The earlier the better.

According to our nation's marriage law, no parents are allowed to meddle in their children's marriage affairs. The newspapers say that nobody is allowed to offer a big sum of money as a dowry. Well, the policies say this and most people do that. Lots of marriage engagements, in my home county at least, are handled exactly like people making bargains in a street. I was not a millionaire. I hated people who bought wives for their sons, and therefore I refused to hurry anyone in my house to search out a girl for Lujiang. However, the village people hurried my wife. I was the breadwinner of the family, so my wife came to hurry me. She said, "You know someone has found a good one for us. She has been to elementary school for four years and can write a letter. You must tell Lujiang to come back and see her. I can arrange a good chance for them to meet and talk."

Another time she told me a different story: "They couldn't wait for us. She has flown away; too late to pick that flower now. But I have another one for you to consider. She has never been to school, but her other qualities are very good. A year older than our son. And they tell me she works like a little tiger but eats like a bird. What's more, the price is reasonable."

Again I turned a deaf ear to her marriage propaganda. I said, "My mighty Mrs. He, I am sorry to tell you, but my wallet is always empty. I do have several boxes, but unfortunately they are boxes of chalk and books under my bed. Mr. China's regular salary is too little to buy a wife for our son. We'll have to wait and see how things develop or change in the future."

Then I added jokingly, "Just do things in a cheaper way. Do you remember how much I paid for you before we married a long time ago? Why not arrange something like we did in the past?"

"Oh, I have no pleasure to joke with you! In our case, it was you, the man, who came into my house, so it was all free. Today, we want the girl to come into our house. We must pay for that."

"Well, anyway, they marry each other. It makes no difference whether the marriage is in the boy's house or in the girl's house."

"No, no, no! How we suffered to bring him up! If you make our son marry into the girl's house, that means when the tree is about to bear fruit you let other people pull the tree away and pick the fruit."

"The girl will be our son's wife. I am not marrying another third wife. Don't trouble me. You ask Lujiang. As a father, I can only offer some personal opinions for him to consider. I just hope he is able to marry someone who can use a pen to earn a living, not a girl who carries a hoe and goes to work in the field."

"Well, it sounds nice. Sometimes I also hope that, too; but I think if he marries a girl who works in an office building or teaches at a school we might become poor when we are too old to get around. Just think, who is going to bring you a cup of water, not to mention a bowl of rice with some good vegetables on top, if they are away at work all day?"

"Sorry, I haven't got the patience to quarrel with you about this. You'd better go to a state-owned farm and reform your thoughts."

Many times our conversations ended in a bad mood.

Actually, in regard to my elder son's wife problem I had firmly made up my mind: Under all circumstances I am determined to let him get a wife completely by his own efforts. I used to tell my son this: "There are many good girls in the world, like there are always plenty of fish in the sea. If your knowledge-box is a heavy one, lots and lots of girls will struggle to help you carry it. So, do nothing but simply think of a good way to arm yourself with knowledge first."

But behind my back my wife said to Lujiang, "When the authorities ask you to fill in your application form, you must tell them that you wish to work in our home county Jianchuan. Being an elementary school teacher in our village will give our ancestors a lot of honor. Ask the officials concerned to make you a little teacher. Don't be too ambitious. An elementary school teacher has got an iron rice bowl. Don't worry. As soon as you get an iron rice bowl I can easily find a beautiful wife for you. If you prefer to choose the girl yourself, all you have to do is tell me her name and address. I can ask for help from many people. If you listen to your father and study at a big school, they will force you to work in a distant area; then we shall miss each other."[4]

Each time he heard something from his mother, Lujiang immediately came to report. Then at once I gave him some good "medicine." Gradually Lujiang came to favor my words. In agriculture my wife knew more than I did, but in arranging other matters my two boys believed I could do things better. Both father and son united together.

\*         \*         \*

In February 1984, for the first time in four years, my sons and I went home for the Spring Festival. Both my father-in-law and my wife were extremely happy. On the last day of the old year, before noontime, everybody got busy giving the house a big cleaning. After this, in order to celebrate our five-member-get-together New Year's Eve in a big way, my wife prepared eight special dishes. My father-in-law said, "The last few years we had only four or five dishes. This year is grander."

Following our Bai tradition, before we sat down to eat, we placed these eight good dishes onto a table which was set in the middle of our central room, something equivalent to a sitting room. Having placed everything neatly, we lit incense and arranged it around the food. The whole family knelt down in a row in front of the table and knocked our foreheads to the ground three times, to thank our ancestors. Then we lit some candles and set off many strings of firecrackers to ensure that all the evil spirits were driven out of the house for the coming year.

As the noise and smoke faded away we began to worship the Kitchen God, the Gate God, and then the Pigsty and Cowshed Gods. I emerged from our kitchen holding a large tray on which a ready-to-eat pig's head and tail, other delicious dishes, and little cups of tea and wine were all placed in good order. I lifted the tray high above my forehead and went around the house. All the other members followed me from the kitchen to the gate, and then we turned to the animal pens. Each time I arrived at a door I lifted my large tray higher three times. My followers' job was to scatter a few drops of tea and wine in front of each door and then to kneel down on the ground and bow three times. These activities were meant to ask the various gods to protect the house, people, and all the domestic animals.

In addition, we decorated our flowerpots with a red square of paper on which the word "spring" was written. Just outside our gate my father-in-law's grandfather had planted a persimmon tree. Every year when the Spring Festival came around we made a red-paper ring and placed it around the trunk. Outside our duck and chicken coops my son pasted another piece of red paper, on which he wrote: "Let the chicks grow up safely in all the four seasons, and let every hen lay thousands of big eggs." The doors of our house, both inside and out, were beautifully decorated with all sorts of pictures. It is a tradition to paste a pair of antithetical couplets on either side of each door. These red-paper couplets can be bought ready printed from a shop, but the messages they bear nowadays are political slogans such as "Celebrate our Motherland's Achievements!" or "Enjoy Today's Prosperous Life!" For our doors that year we decided to write something meaningful ourselves. Lujiang and I wrote the following:

**On the door to my father-in-law's room:**
- **(left)** Enjoying Eighty Years of Age
  and Living in Happiness and Peace.

- **(right)** Two Grandsons Preparing Hard
  to Go Around the Four Seas.

**On the door to our kitchen:**
(left)     I Work in the Mountain Valley
to Promote International Mutual Understanding.

(right)    She Maintains a Good Home
to Make Every One of Us Happy.

At our New Year's Eve dinner, just as my little boy put out his chopsticks to touch the fish, I made an ugly face and said, "Don't touch that. Let your mother eat it herself. It's too salty."

My father-in-law loved his grandson very much, so he said, "Oh, you must not stop him. Let him eat as much as he likes to."

My wife said, "No, you try it first before you say things. I know your habits. I put only a little salt in. It's really very delicious."

"No, no, no! All your dishes are good-for-nothing."

On hearing this, my wife was no longer all smiles. She said slowly, "Well, is the quantity not enough? You are unwell these days. You eat only a little, but honestly I've prepared more. After all, none of you are tremendous eaters. You just eat a little bit first to see if my dishes are really too salty. I can make another dish for you if. ..."

My father-in-law took a sip of wine and said solemnly, "Be careful, don't you know what the date is today? Others will laugh at us if we quarrel at the table this evening. Never think the peak of that mountain over there must be higher than the one you are now standing on. For me, this grand New Year's Eve supper is quite big; everything is more than enough. Last year's was poorer."

All of a sudden I changed my face and smiled, "All right, eat, eat, eat! Everybody help themselves to whatever they like to. I was joking. But before we begin I would like to share one more special dish, a ninth dish—from London. I myself prepared it a long time ago. Two huge eggs!"

I rushed to my desk and returned with a small sheet of paper, sent to me by Collins Publishers of London. I placed it on the table and pointed at "£500" with my chopsticks. Turning to Luzhong I said, "Your grandfather is too old to read. Your mother, though younger, is a village woman. You have studied at school for three years. I want you to read this loudly for every one of us to hear how it sounds to the ears."

"Well." My little guy looked at it for a moment and then continued, "One zero, two zeros, and then before these two zeros, there is ... but what is that before the number five?"

"That's money, money, English money!" I shouted. "We cannot eat these two special huge eggs on the paper, but they are magic eggs produced in England. Later, when they get to our house, we will ask your mother to let our biggest hen hatch them. Within a short time, two big chicks will be hatched out. When they grow bigger they will give us more and more special eggs."

That evening we laughed and laughed. Later that year, when the advance from Collins arrived, like lightning the mother hired a group of villagers and began repairing our broken house. Our old house had been built when my father-in-law was four years old. After it stopped raining outside, a "small rain" had continued in our house for a long time afterward. We had to place all sorts of buckets and pots around our upstairs rooms. We were very happy now to be able to solve this troublesome house problem.

## NOTES

1. In the early 1980s, collective farming was replaced by the Production Responsibility System. Communal land and properties were distributed among commune families and groups of families in partnership, in return for a specified annual payment to the government.

2. The weekend begins on Saturday afternoon or evening in China.

3. *Number 11 bus:* This means "on foot"; number 11 is formed by the two legs.

4. Elementary school teachers, especially in rural areas of China, are not required to be college graduates.

# 18

# OUR FIRECRACKERS
# ANNOUNCE BIG NEWS

**O**ur Dali Autonomous Region formally opened its doors to foreign guests in 1984; before this date it had been a "closed region." A big hotel, the Er Hai Hotel in Xiaguan, equipped with modern facilities, was ready for use. Unfortunately, only a very few of the hotel staff could speak any English. In Xiaguan there were plenty of English teachers in each middle school, but it was said that although these teachers were good at school-textbook English, when conversing with English-speaking tourists they didn't know how to begin.

By chance, an old friend of mine named Mr. Wu learned that the Er Hai Hotel was in urgent need of a person who could speak understandable English. The hotel was under the leadership of the Foreign Affairs Office of the Dali People's Government. The secretary of this government happened to be a good friend of Mr. Wu. At the Foreign Affairs Office Mr. Wu gave them a few details of my past and present, and the government secretary immediately agreed to write a letter of recommendation for me. Then Mr. Wu wrote, urging me to meet him in Xiaguan. Everything was done in a hurry. At my school, I was officially allowed to leave for Xiaguan to see a doctor. I had indeed been troubled for several years with severe stomach problems, which I now used as a pretext to get away.

Once I got to Xiaguan's Er Hai Hotel, however, the officials there would not let me leave. Within a week, both sides—my school and the hotel—had begun to criticize each other bitterly. The reason was that I belonged to Jianchuan County, and unless the Jianchuan officials formally released me I had to continue teaching English at the Second Middle School. What was more, I had been permitted to go to Xiaguan to see a doctor, not to work in a hotel. It caused some trouble. The final result of their negotiations was that the Dali Foreign Affairs Office "borrowed" me to work for them for only a short period of time.

With the lady manager taking the lead, a drive to fire at English began at once. The hotel staff were enthusiastic. Every day, a two-hour English class in the morning and another two hours in the afternoon were organized. I translated the menu and various wall signs into intelligible English. Not all the tourists brought interpreters with them, so time and again I was recommended as a guide to accompany groups of foreign friends around the Bai villages for a day or two. And if people at the Foreign Affairs Office came across problems in receiving international guests, a car was ordered for me to hurry there and help them out. "Life is like a dream!" I said to myself as I recalled my past miserable experiences selling little wooden chairs in the streets of Xiaguan.

One day early in May, I fell ill with a recurrence of my old complaint. Since coming to Xiaguan I had been to the hospital many times to see about being admitted as a patient. But each time I went, the staff at the window somehow found an excuse to refuse my admission. They treated me coldly, telling me the beds were all full. The problem was that I came from a distant mountain corner and had no personal connections in the hospital. It happened that a baby girl at our hotel also fell ill. While I was interpreting for her parents, I naturally had a golden opportunity to get to know some of the doctors in the hospital. They were all very grateful to me for helping them treat their very first foreign patient. When I mentioned my health and hospital problems to one of their best pediatricians, a Dr. Yao, she replied, "Why, no problem at all! Believe me, I can make them find out all your health problems. Just come and stay, the sooner the better."

Why the sudden change in attitude? All because I could speak a little English. Many important doctors and nurses also had a strong desire to improve their English. With a view to learning something from me, I was warmly hurried to stay in their hospital as soon as possible. They gave me a bed in the Third Department, used only for Dali's top officials and other important people. In that department everything was excellent—professional doctors, well-trained nurses, the best medicine, special treatment. If you wished to, you could enjoy a TV program, play badminton or chess, or read magazines in their reading room. To show my gratitude, I volunteered to teach them "hospital English" in the mornings.

The doctors finally decided that their knives would have to dance into my belly and arrest an enemy—an ulcer. The date for the operation was set for May 23rd, 1984. On the day of the operation my wife came to the hospital. It was her very first visit to a big town. To tell the truth, I was rather nervous: I didn't know if she would return home smiling—or weeping over a coffin. The doctors' knives danced in and out, up and down, for five hours. Everything was carried out successfully.

Two days after the doctors removed my stitches I was transferred back to my original bed in the Third Department. I restarted English classes on that very day. My school authorities paid the main part of the hospital fees, but when my wife hurried to Xiaguan to look after me she had left an aged man at home. He was too old to do the fieldwork, yet it had to be done in time. We were forced to pay "double wages" to some villagers to plant our rice fields. As soon as I was well enough to cook for myself, my wife hurried home to her rice plants. On the last day of June, I was well enough to wave goodbye to all my students at the hotel and the hospital and return to Madeng.

*     *     *

After the fall of the Gang of Four, our country used a new method to select good students for universities. We call it the "dragon dance" method. The person who holds up the dragon's big and heavy head has to be strong and swift in performing the dragon dance. The person who plays the dragon's tail might be a weak person but is still warmly welcomed to participate in the dance. So it is with selecting college students. Since 1978 annual university entrance examinations have been held on the same three days throughout our country. These examinations have become more and more competitive with each passing year. The better the university, the higher the score it demands. Those who score above 450 points are chosen to attend a top college in Beijing or Shanghai. Since the academic level of our province is lower than that of other advanced provinces, only a few are selected for Shanghai or Beijing each year. In order to improve this situation, the country allows a candidate from one of our backward national minority areas to enter a college at, say, the 300-point level with only 270 points. However, not all the minorities are entitled to these 30 free points. Those who live on mountain tops or deep down in valleys are entitled to them. Those who live on the more prosperous plains are not. As my home village is classified as a half-mountain, half-plain village, our children are not entitled to the 30 points. Nevertheless, many national minority children from poorly developed areas can enter a two- or four-year course with the help of those free points.

Lujiang graduated from our middle school in mid-1984. Ever since I had become a formal teacher, in addition to teaching English to the minority people's children, my main job had been to turn this country bumpkin of mine into a university student. Well, conditions in our newly established Second Middle School were poor. Some of the teachers, including myself, were not as good as those in bigger towns and cities. Sometimes we simply had no qualified teachers of geography, history, math. ... But regardless of whether it's an advanced school or a poor school, the same university entrance examination papers are used nationwide. So, year after year and term after term, father and son stayed at school and gave up all the long vacations. I used to cheer him up by saying, "If our radio gets sick, we can repair it. If that flower outside the window dies, we can plant another one next year when spring comes. However, Time flies like a hunter's arrow and what we lose we can never get back. You must grasp each passing minute now."

Our nationwide examination that year was scheduled to take place from July 7th to 9th, 1984. Until the end of June I had been away in Xiaguan, and during my absence my two boys had suffered a great deal. The young one had had to return to my home and attend our village elementary school. Lujiang had stayed on, somehow managing to tackle all the difficulties by himself. But two or three weeks before the examination, a cold-ghost began bothering him day and night. When I returned to Madeng I found him feverish and weak. I feared my soldier was too ill to join the battle.

That year, not only the teachers of our own school but all the teachers of the whole county had gossiped a great deal about my son's university chances. They even bet on it. Today I still remember some of their remarks: "Four months before your son's graduation you ran away to teach hotel English in Xiaguan, but here you lost your son's chair at the university." And "Remember the saying: 'The most embarrassing thing for a shoe-mender is to wear broken shoes.'"

We saw many doctors, but when we awoke at sunrise on July 6th we found that Lujiang's illness had worsened. He had no appetite. He felt dizzy and seemed very, very tired. He was so sad that he began to sob. We sobbed together. At ten that morning, after a long period of comfort and persuasion, we took a bus down to Jinghuazheng. Fortunately, as we alighted we bumped into a doctor friend who had worked for some time near our Second Middle School. Lujiang was swiftly admitted into our county hospital. That night he was given an intravenous drip.

The next day Lujiang was still feverish but nonetheless insisted on entering the battlefield—a huge classroom building with more than 500 students from all the districts firing at the question paper. The first two days he couldn't think clearly and failed to answer many questions. On the third day, the day of his last examination, the fever was gone. He felt better. That last day was his most important examination—English.

That year, the dragon dance went by rather slowly. Day after day and week after week we waited. We wrote many, many letters to Kunming to ask our friends there to get the news. We rang the examination headquarters several times. Our hearts could never feel warm unless we heard reliable news. Gradually all the secret policies for that year became known. For engineering, physics, and other scientific subjects a student had to earn 335 points. But a student of foreign languages had to get above 370 points in order to be admitted to a four-year university course. What was more, such a student had to pass another test. We call it a face examination, an oral test.

At last my son got some news. He had scored 390 points. With this total he was told to take the face examination in Dali the next day. We practiced oral English throughout the night. When the time came, he was interviewed by three professors in separate rooms for twenty minutes. He came out in all smiles and said, "Everything turned out just as we planned. Those three were surprised at my English—so eager that they forced me to describe my English teacher. And when I told them a little, they said, 'No wonder.'"

We returned home, happy because the face examination had been successful. But as we waited, day after day and night after night, we again became anxious and nervous. At about two o'clock on August 31st, a village boy ran into our house and shouted excitedly, "Lujiang, someone in the commune office asked me to tell you this: Hurry to them right now! They want you to get a special message from Kunming."

An hour later Lujiang returned home holding up high in his left hand a formal note:

### Admission Notice of Yunnan Normal University

*Following the ratification of Yunnan Normal University together with the Headquarters of the University Examination Board, He Lujiang of Jianchuan Second Middle School has been accepted. He is warmly welcomed to major in the English language for four years at the university's Foreign Languages Department. All the new students are required to be prepared with a complete set of quilts, a mosquito net, a personal residence note from the local government, books, and school fees, and to report to the university between the 10th and 12th of September.*

What a relief! What a joy! Well, in the eyes of Western people, becoming a university student is considered too ordinary a thing. But in China, especially in a distant district full of minority people, it is quite a big thing. In our Jianchuan, 504 students had taken part in the university entrance examination. Only 39 were formally selected. And of those 39 only 19 had scored enough points to enter a four-year course. The other 20 could enter only a two-year program. In spite of being ill, and in spite of not qualifying for the 30 free points, my son came in thirteenth in our Jianchuan. Moreover, he was the first pupil from our Second Middle School to enter a real university. A few had qualified to enter two-year programs in the past, but Lujiang was the very first to be accepted onto a four-year course. One of my colleagues said, "Your Lujiang has broken our school record."

Placing this most important and priceless formal note on the table carefully, we gathered round and held a small-scale family party in our kitchen. First we read the note aloud together. Then we played our two radios at the same time. To add some more music, we clapped our hands and hit a bowl and cup with chopsticks. After a while my wife ran to the market to buy some fish and firecrackers. Late that afternoon, just at the time when the villagers were about to have their supper, we lit our firecrackers and declared the big news in the village square. This news moved as fast as the American space shuttle.

Now people far and wide knew, and they shouted out, "This year the very first big-school student has appeared in Shangbaodian Village!"

*         *         *

My wife seemed to be showing her teeth all the time. I asked, "Is anything wrong with your mouth?"

"No, no, no!" she answered. "You made me become the mother of a big-school student. I am too excited all the time. If I was in a sad mood you could never see my teeth."

"All right," I said. "You sit down, please. Let's suppose, or let me pretend, that I am not a schoolteacher but a newspaper reporter coming from a big city. Now Mrs. He, would you tell us something about what you felt after you heard the news, or just tell us why it makes you show your ugly teeth all the time?"

She replied, "Generation after generation, to the best of my knowledge, nobody was able to read or write in our family. I learned to write my own name and recognize a few words while working in our iron factory, but actually my ability is a limited one. On the other hand, after Lujiang and Luzhong followed you to Madeng they learned more and more every day. As I thought of my miserable past and looked at our two boys, I felt extremely happy. I wanted to do something for you. I thought and thought, and finally I sold the biggest pig and bought you a shortwave radio. I wanted you to improve your foreign language and then teach our own two boys well, so when they grew bigger they wouldn't be oppressed by others. You cared not much about our house for many years, but instead you taught the two boys well. Finally, this year, the old man and I can enjoy your fruit. Just think, our Lujiang is the very first big-school student not only in our He family history but also in the whole village, the very first true student who is now opening the university's gate for the whole village to see, to learn from, and to copy as an example. Those are the reasons why I am so happy. Sometimes I feel very sorry and sad, too. ...."

"I know that," I put in. "You feel sorry and sad because you know my monthly income is limited and I can never give you several thousand *yuan* to engage two wives for our boys. Isn't that it?"

"Oh, no! Not now," she said in a sad manner. "For several years I controlled everything in the house and treated you as my servant, not my 'big man.' I hated you when I heard you talk about English and made you vow solemnly never to mention it. Now the world has turned upside-down. It is through your knowledge of English that we can maintain our family. I was absolutely wrong. Away from your help, how could I have made Lujiang into a big-school student? Our neighbors have made a lot of money, but they have nothing special to celebrate. We are poorer at this present stage, but Lujiang is going off to study in Kunming. We have a huge success to sing and dance about."

"Well, just say things right to the point, directly." I knew what she was thinking, so I urged her a bit.

"All right." She paused a little and glanced at me secretly. "I was thinking of something to celebrate the occasion."

"You mean you want to hold a party and invite people to have a big meal in our yard?"

"Yes, just think of this: The very first university student in our He family. ..."

"No! A foolish thought. I don't think it's a good idea. We are not what they call 'new-type millionaires.' Our London eggs are almost all gone, you know that well. You must get a scale and weigh your purse before you plan to do something. Lujiang's acceptance as a big-school student doesn't mean that you and I have grown a 'bearing-money tree.' Anyway, here I must repeat one of our country's political slogans: 'What we have achieved is only the first step on our Long March.' According to all the living information I have received, in the future we will still have to pay a lot of money each month to complete his four-year course of study. The living standard in Kunming is much higher than it is in this village. Besides, if he is to obtain more knowledge, I am sure he has to buy a lot of books. We can't do things as we have done in the past. The Second Middle School is a mountain-corner school in a national minority people's area, while our Kunming is becoming an international city. Remember, 'If the rat is a big one, so is the hole.' As his parents we have the responsibility to make sure he has all he needs for big-city life. We must first of all try our best to make him look like his classmates in all repects. That is why I pushed away all the old things and bought everything new—a good fountain pen, a pillowcase, sheets, blanket, quilt. Are you still planning to make some shoes for him? Handmade shoes look poor and ugly. As a university student in a big city he must wear machine-made shoes. For myself, teaching in that poor school, there is still no need to use a watch. But for Lujiang's tomorrow, I must buy one for him before he leaves home. Without money you can do nothing. I hope you will give up that idea."

"Never mind," my wife replied. "Our family's reputation in recent years has not been so bad. Speaking from the point of view of education, we are Number One, culturally the richest in this village. As soon as you nod your head, I have the magic power to borrow several thousand *yuan* and show you the money before the sun appears in the east tomorrow morning."

"No, no, no! A hundred noes, a thousand noes! Not you, but I have to return the money. You'd better stop that. If you persist I think we will have to discuss it at our Family Congress, which we must hold tomorrow or the day after tomorrow."

\*     \*     \*

Luzhong was eleven in 1984, just at the start of his grade four.[1] After show-ing him all the good and new things bought for his older brother, I asked him, "What do you think after seeing your brother's exhibition?"

"You are a heartless father! At school I didn't steal. At home I didn't say dirty words. I am all right at everything, but you use a different policy toward me. Just have a look at my school bag and my clothes. ... This month I am a fourth-grade pupil. What on earth have you bought me?"

"Oh, I never would have imagined someone as little as you could say such things! But all right, all right. Later I shall make it up to you. For now, all I want to say is this: Your elder brother has become a big-school student; what about you?"

"Me?" he seemed surprised. "Here is my answer: The 15th of a month fol-lows the 1st of the month."

"Well, everybody knows that."

"You understand only half of what I mean. Everything takes time. I am the 15th of the month. My brother is the 1st. I will certainly, perfectly certainly, follow his example one of these days. Just wait and see."

"You have given us a meaningful answer," my wife said. "Our family is like a country. At the beginning we put the stress on heavy industry; that's old brother Lujiang. Later, when the time comes, we will put the stress on devel-oping light industry; that's you, young brother Luzhong. With up-to-date heavy and light industry, our family will become a stronger and happier fam-ily."

Just then, in came the oldest man of the family. The little one showed my father-in-law a seat. "Grandpa, now you sit down. It's your turn to say some-thing about my brother's success."

"Well," the old man began slowly, "they say the present generation is al-ways cleverer than the previous generation. I am a living example. Actually I am now nothing but a useless, stupid old man. I cannot give you a report like a county-head does at a big county meeting. My so-called report can be summed up in four points: First, knowledge is above all. The more you learn, the less you do not know. So, while you are in Kunming's big school, work harder than ever before. Second, always be very careful of the 'face-problem.' You must protect not only your own face but the face of the He family, the face of our village, and the face of our country. No matter what you do, no matter where you go, be kind and polite to everyone and help others and say good words. Third, never forget our miserable past. Even if you become a rich man or a top official, you must never change your heart and look down on your parents and ancestors. The God in Heaven will punish you if you do that; then certainly you will suffer in the other world. Finally, Mr. China spends a lot of money on bringing up big-school students. When you graduate, you must do something good for our people to pay back our country with your knowledge. ... Well, I think that is all."

The next day, while we were chatting in the village square, an aged woman said to my wife, "Congratulations! Will you please, without any reservations, tell us your secret of giving birth to a big-school student? You just look at our village. From south to north and from the top downward, many women have given birth to several children, two times or sometimes even three times more than you, but now most of their children can only enter the biggest school on earth, Field University. We ate the same food and dug the same ground and shared the same good things given by our country, but in the end you achieved much more than we did. There must be some secrets. Don't be too selfish."

"Yes, of course. Actually, I have nothing special to share. My secret is very simple: I pray, pray, and again pray, at each meal three times at the table, and many more times when I go to bed."

"Yes, yes, but tell us exactly how many loads of incense and how many times you lit candles and then knelt down to ask our General God of Ancestors to make your son become a big-school student?"

In a joking manner she replied, "Well, at the moment, being ordinary peasants, we are too poor to buy what my son describes as an electrical calculating machine to figure out the amount in a flash. But people in foreign countries also believe in God. The name of their God is Jesus. The same one as ours, I think. Foreigners are very good at operating many strange electrical machines. England's radio and Voice of America and radio stations of many other countries mentioned Lujiang's father's name high up in Heaven. That means not only I myself and all our relatives but both sides asked God to help my son. Up in Heaven it is the same as on the earth where we now are living. The gods of the foreigners are all modern-equipped ones, very powerful. They also helped my son and protected him in all his battles. Since everybody kept their fingers crossed, he won the final victory."

"Mother, be careful," Lujiang suddenly put in. "You must not talk superstitious things here in public—it's dangerous."

"Oh, it doesn't matter!" the woman said. "We are all old village women. I don't think they will come to arrest us. Like your mother, I also have two sons. But they have always refused to learn. Mr. Big-School Student, what is your secret? What was the main force which made you work hard at school?"

"I can tell you lots of things, but as I compare them one by one, I think the main force came from my mother. My mother's story touched my heart. Look, over there." Lujiang pointed to the east of our house. "My success today cannot be separated from that vegetable garden. That big vegetable garden is the Lius', but originally it belonged to us. The original owner was my grandfather's grandfather. It was handed down to my grandpa. My mother once told me this story, saying it took place about forty-five years ago, before Liberation. At that time, we were so poor that we were forced to sell a piece of land. Well, as you know, the buyer and the seller had to sign an agreement in black and white. If the seller didn't give the buyer a written agreement, the buyer would not hand over the money. Today, more and more people go to school and receive an education. But forty-five years ago, in our village, it happened that Liu Lijiu's grandfather was the only so-called country-scholar around. No other person was good enough to hold a pen and then write an agreement.

"My grandma and my mother got down on their knees in front of his bed and pleaded with him for almost the whole night. My mother was holding a hen. They thought a big hen might please old Mr. Liu. Suddenly, without any warning at all, someone in his house kicked my mother over. The hen jumped up. A second later it was nowhere to be found. Old Mr. Liu said to my grandma, 'If you offer me a fat pig or twenty hens, I might consider. Or, no pig and hens, but you must give me another, smaller piece of land.' He meant that vegetable garden over there. On the following day my grandma had to agree. Understand now? No way out. My grandpa couldn't write, and my mother was just a little girl. Under such circumstances we had to offer two pieces of land: a piece for the buyer, and the other smaller one for old Mr. Liu who wrote out the agreement for us. My mother's true story was an unforgettable lesson for me to remember. After hearing it I made a solemn vow. My young brother and I have to study harder and harder at school; otherwise someone will come to cheat us again, as often happened in the long past."

In my own home county, despite the fact that the government advises us not to use money when settling a marriage, the "price" for marrying a girl is shooting up with each passing year. In 1984 the girl's side first asked for 600 *yuan* wrapped up in red paper and placed on a tray. They also asked for lots of best-quality cloth. Lastly, they wanted you to organize a big eat-and-drink party. The boy's parents had to spend at least 1,200 *yuan* to complete all three steps. And this was only to make the engagement! After a year or two, when the wedding took place, the boy's side had to make another payment of 500 *yuan* in the presence of all the wedding guests. His parents also had to spend about 500 *yuan* on the wedding party. After the engagement, if the girl changed her heart and wanted to marry another new boyfriend, she would return that 600 *yuan* and the rolls of cloth. As for the other several hundred already spent on organizing the party, the girl didn't care. If the boy changed his heart and loved another girl, he couldn't get anything back at all from the original girl. So, that engagement was a dangerous thing. If something went wrong, it was like throwing a needle into the Pacific Ocean—that big sum of money could never be found back.

Each month my regular salary was about 65 *yuan*. I had to let my two boys eat, drink, and study. I had to give another part to maintain the house. How could I have enough left over to buy an expensive wife? I refused to talk to my wife about this problem and sometimes scolded her, but she kept on troubling me about my son's marriage problem. Now everything changed. The mother put up her hands and waved a white flag. Going to study a four-year course meant getting an unbreakable rice bowl. What was more, the bowl given by the university would be a gold-covered one, a hundred times better than the iron bowl given by a low-level school education. With an iron rice bowl in hand, Lujiang would have to pay a considerable sum of money to get a wife. However, if he had a best-quality gold-covered rice bowl, there would be no need at all to run here and there after a wife. Many beautiful girls would run after him and open their mouths first.

Although people now say the price of a wife will go up to 10,000 *yuan* in later years, there is no need for me to worry about it. I believe my son is going to find a wife of his own choice and arrange a modern marriage.

**NOTES**

1. In China, children start elementary school at age seven.

# 19

## MRS. HE
## GOES TO KUNMING

**O**n the evening of September 4th, 1984, we held a Family Congress. It was a secret but very special congress in our village. The chairman was Mr. He, recently promoted to family chairman after becoming a permanent teacher of the country. The other old man in the house had lost all his power several years before. Like a humble representative coming from a little-corner developing country, the old man's membership existed only in name. We even refused him permission to listen to our speeches. He was forced to make friends with his bed and tea and tobacco.

That night a candle was our only light as we still found electricity too expensive to use. The congress took place in the kitchen. Here we could often see the cat chase a rat, a cock fly over the table, or some hungry pigs bumping about. We had no comfortable chairs either; but our meeting lasted for five hours, until long after midnight, and nobody felt sleepy. He Luzhong was our only listener. After young Mr. He Lujiang delivered an opening speech, we began to discuss various problems. Sometimes we sang a little and the meeting was conducted in a friendly way. But at other times we got angry and shouted at one another. In the end we all agreed to issue the following statement:

1.  To satisfy Mrs. He's lifelong wish, a special small-scale eat-and-drink party will be organized to celebrate the record-breaking first-university-winner He Lujiang's admission to Yunnan Normal University.
2.  All the He families in the whole village will kindly be invited to come. Mr. He's elder brother's family, together with his four sisters and their families, and all his great-aunts with their children, will be warmly welcomed to celebrate this special occasion. In addition, two elementary school teachers who taught Lujiang for some time, the new team head, the village's one childless old couple,[1] and the

248

oldest man and the oldest woman in the village will be invited to come and spend the afternoon.

3. Another old Mrs. He, now almost seventy-five years of age, is the most important guest. This aged Mrs. He is a famous old-fashioned midwife of the village. Twenty years ago, when Mrs. He was giving birth to Lujiang, she was the first woman who ran to our house to give first-aid help. It was this aged Mrs. He who first picked up the newborn baby from the ground. For this very reason, Lujiang must invite this famous midwife to sit in the most honorable seat. What's more, He Lujiang must offer more wine and more cigarettes to her, and kneel down on the ground to thank her for her special care.

4. The host, of course, will be Mr. He, the breadwinner of the house. At the party he is also the chief director. All the attendants have to obey his orders unconditionally. The father can go everywhere in the house, but his main job is to welcome and say hello to all the guests the moment they enter the gate. He is the first person to shake hands with the comers. In the kitchen, Mrs. He is naturally the chef. She must prepare each dish well. Lujiang is responsible for handing out cigarettes, once every fifteen to thirty minutes. The young ladies usually do not smoke, but Lujiang has the duty to insist that each accept and take a cigarette home. He Luzhong's job is to offer a cup of "happy tea" to everybody. He must hold the tea-tray carefully. If he breaks a cup he will be punished by having to stand in the corner alone for ten minutes. The old man's job is to boil water at the fireside.

5. About 100 people, including two- and three-year-old children, are expected to come to the party. But there might be some unexpected guests. So Mrs. He must prepare for 120 people. Everybody in the house has to bear this in mind: If, suddenly, a stranger or villager who is not on our namelist drops in, all family members must welcome the comer with open arms and offer food, drink, and cigarettes.

6. This sort of party is a new event in the village's history. Therefore Mrs. He is going to do some little break-the-record things: (a) Eight small children can form a table and enjoy exactly the same dishes as eight big eaters sharing a table. (b) As a rule, the hostess makes some false dishes. She prepares something cheap at the bottom of the bowl and then covers it up with a tiny fish at the top. Then she calls it a "dish of fish." This time Mrs. He is going to serve a bowl completely filled with fish, from top to bottom. (c) Mrs. He is going to supply many bottles of wine and let the wine-lovers drink as much as they can. All the ladies have to drink a little.

As for the children, ask them to lick a little drop with their chopsticks.

7.   When all the guests are being asked to sit down at the table, He Lujiang must straightaway bow his head politely and say, "Thank you very much for coming to honor us. Do please have a drink of happy wine." He must do this from table to table. When the guests are about to leave the house, Mr. and Mrs. He and the two boys have to stand in a line at the gate and thank all of them with one more cigarette and a warm handshake.

8.   Mr. He is going to accompany Lujiang away to Kunming. As the long-handed-down tradition goes, before the father and son leave for Kunming they will have to prepare six to eight dishes, a bowl of rice, tea, wine, and other things. These they will take to their graveyard to "report and say goodbye" to their ancestors. As for burning incense in two different temples to ask for protection along the way, two well-known aged women will be asked to do that job.

9.   On the morning of their departure, father and son will carry nothing in their hands or on their backs. They will just walk. The mother is going to carry everything in a bamboo basket and accompany them to the bus station. Before they set out, Lujiang must kneel down in front of his grandpa and then do the same in front of his mother, to thank them for everything in the past twenty years. As soon as they leave the house, little He Luzhong is going to light some firecrackers and wave to all the people hurrying by with their early-morning pails of water on their shoulder poles.

10.   When father and son arrive in Kunming they will not have enough money to order a taxi or a porter. They will have to carry everything themselves and go to the university by Number 11 bus. In order to economize further, this time they are not going to purchase a ticket to walk in a park or go to see a film. Buy nothing, eat cheap food, and Mr. He will sleep in an ordinary hotel. However, in order to let young Mr. He study well, they will select a cheap wristwatch for the son's use.

11.   Mr. He is going to take Lujiang to meet several important professors in the university circle. He is also going to take Lujiang to meet and visit with several old friends in Kunming. Everywhere the goal is the same: They wish that their friends and acquaintances will offer a little help in overcoming the difficulties of the city.

12.   Strictly observe Bai people's national customs. Politely treat people of all circles in the same way. Not only respect the aged people but also pay great attention to the young ones.

13. All these decisions will be written down in a book and kept by the mother. Everybody has to pay attention to the decisions of the Family Congress just as if they were from a government document.

Everything at our party went well. Then, on September 8th, Lujiang and I left home for Kunming. Many, many people in our village rushed out to wave goodbye. We heard, "Come and see our village's first real big-school student going to Kunming now!" Our new team head and his wife also ran out to see us off.

The team head said to Lujiang, "You have opened the university's gate for our village's younger generation. We all hope you study well at the university. Work hard every day. You must learn more than your father did. You must set a good example for our children's children. We will always be pleased to hear good and successful news from you. Above all, we hope you will bring honor and credit to our whole village."

All the way from our gate to the bus station the mother did nothing but urge Lujiang again and again to be modest and prudent. She became a most garrulous woman and chattered interminably. It reminded me of the day I left my home county for Kunming in the early forties. Who would have thought that was to be my last goodbye to my own mother? That morning, when I heard my wife's this and that, I fell into a deep meditation. A mother's love is great, I thought. I hoped that my son would bravely temper himself in our present-day China's lively life. I also hoped nothing wrong would happen in my country, so that Lujiang and millions of other young people could contribute their best to our modernization. Let Lujiang's generation make up what their parent's generation had lost. Let all the youngsters bring credit to my people and country.

*        *        *

Not long after Lujiang's departure, Luzhong wrote a letter to his elder brother in Kunming:

**Dear Elder Brother,**

*Hello, how are you? Our midterm exams have come and gone. Altogether we had nine subjects. I have been home for two days to see mother. I miss her, and so father kindly agreed to let me go home.*

*Mother is all right, in good condition. She has finished harvesting our crops. It is said that Mother's autumn harvest turned out to be Number One in the whole village. No need to worry about going hungry. Next year's wheat and broad-bean seeds were scattered the day before I returned. Mother has sold one of our two fat pigs. She got about 200 yuan for it. Mother says she is going to ask a butcher to kill the other one three weeks before the Spring Festival comes. Besides, another old hen has hatched twelve chicks. Mother says you are to take good care of your health and study your lessons well.*

*The last thing to report is some big news: I got a prize. It was Number One, the highest prize. My total marks in our midterm exam were the highest in my class. The principal gave me 5 yuan at a big meeting. The second got 3 yuan, and the third got 2 yuan. Shame, shame, a hundred shames on Mr. Zhang and Mr. Nie. It was these two who handed out the money to us winners, but they couldn't give a cent to their own children. I must gather my efforts. We won the victory, a big victory indeed. I'll guard my seat and defeat all those who come to attack!*

*Your brother,*
**Luzhong**

At his university in Kunming, Lujiang just makes me smile. You know, in my eyes this boy is a mountain-corner "tortoise." All his classmates are well-trained city "hares." The present-day struggle among university students is not a simple matter. During his first term the tortoise found it hard to catch up with the hares. Later, many scores have proved that he is going to win the tortoise-hare race.

*       *       *

Early in 1986, my father-in-law fell ill. He couldn't breathe normally and his legs, arms, and breast swelled up. We wanted him to stay in a hospital, so we sold all the bigger pigs. But he refused to be treated by modern medical science. My wife watched him during the day and at night either I or Lujiang watched. When we returned to our schools, two men came to sleep beside the old man's bed. We had to provide them with tea, cigarettes, something good to eat, and a little pocket money. In February I painted my father-in-law's coffin. Then all other necessary preparations were made for assigning our old man to watch the mountain.

In September, Luzhong and I received the sad news at our Second Middle School. The next day we hurried home to organize the funeral ceremony. In order to keep up with our changing society, I couldn't prepare the simple ceremony that we were used to before 1979. Compared with some of our county's 10,000-*yuan*-a-year households, we were still poor. However, Mr. China had given me an unbreakable rice bowl. Under these new circumstances, how could I bury my father-in-law quietly, without a big and noisy funeral ceremony? Just as the old man was about to pass away, in came another payment for my folk tales. My wife said, "You know, when my mother died, we really had nothing at all in the house. No tea, no wine, no firewood, no rice even— nor a bowl of meat or fish. But our neighbor, Liu Jingyuan's grandfather, lent us 20 *jin* of rice. By offering that rice, we were able to ask ten men to carry my mother's coffin out. Her tomb was nothing but a pile of earth and several rough stones. Now with our book-master's special help, my father's funeral can go by smoothly."

Many of our village's aged men and women came to our house and held a meeting. Everything was carried out exactly in accordance with their opinions. We employed a band of Buddhist leaders, a group of classical music players, and many important old-fashioned scholars. We gave out piles of white-cloth headbands to a large number of mourners, and also provided plenty of meat, fish, tea, and cigarettes. The whole village came out to watch. The male mourners knelt down on the left side, the women on the right. After weeping on the ground for fifteen minutes, we started for the graveyard. It is a tradition for the women to knock the coffin with their bodies, creating problems for the eight men who carry it. The male mourners followed the coffin to its destination; the women returned home after half a mile in twos and threes, crying all the way. The funeral director secretly assigned several women to watch my wife, who might otherwise have run after the coffin and created trouble.

As it was I who had followed my wife to her house, my position was that of the dead person's son. I had to follow the coffin bent over, with my back facing the sky and using a very short bamboo walking stick. Whenever the coffin passed over a bridge, I had to lie down on the road and let the coffin go above my body. They say this custom helps the dead cross a bridge safely to Heaven.

We spent several hundred *yuan* to build the tomb. Twenty-five strong men worked for five hours to complete it before sunset. Those men were carefully chosen and most kindly treated. We invited them to drink and eat many best-quality things for several days. A stone tablet was bought in Dali County, and four stone-experts were hired to prepare everything. They constructed the tomb in our He clan cemetery, directly in front of the tombs of the oldest ancestors of our clan, near a tall pine tree known as a "mountain god tree." As soon as the tomb was completed, eight bowls of good vegetables, tea, wine, buns, and incense were placed in front.

Before the funeral, I ran here and there and luckily managed to employ someone to use his camera and take color photos. Too bad the man was an ordinary worker, so he failed to take meaningful pictures. Nevertheless, this was the first time anyone had done this in our village's history. All of the villagers came around to our house to see our color funeral photos. The relatives were pleased.

At first I had planned to use 600 *yuan*, but as we discovered when we summed up everything at the end of the funeral, we had spent about 1,100 *yuan*. This funeral service was recognized as the biggest one ever in recent years. The reaction from people of all walks of life was very good. My wife was the happiest.

\*      \*      \*

During the Spring Festival of 1987, Lujiang returned home and we held a four-member Family Congress. The goal of this congress was to carefully plan a trip to Kunming. All the participants showed a firm resolution to realize this dream regardless of the circumstances. Also decided was that the mother should most kindly be invited as a special guest. This point was first put forward by the youngest son: "Dad and I were kept at school. Brother Lujiang was at the university in Kunming. You know that throughout 1986 Mama was the only person to look after Grandpa who was lying in his bed for several months. That wasn't an easy task. It took a lot of trouble to please a dying man. We must give Mother a reward for that. In my opinion, no one is allowed to make her offer any of her homemade things. For her the trip must be absolutely free of charge."

"A good son you are," praised the chairman, Mr. He. "You have submitted a reasonable proposal. Now, please listen to the chairman's second decision. Our family's next winner in our coming trip will be He Luzhong. At the present stage he is only a schoolchild and the youngest one of our family. So it's reasonable to let him enjoy a free seat. None of you is allowed to make him offer the scholarship money he has saved three times. He earned that all by himself through working hard at his lessons. It's up to him how to spend his 15 *yuan.*

"As for Lujiang, you have been in Kunming for several years now. You know which is which and where is where. You are kindly invited to be a guide in the city. You are to be responsible for our everything there. Never, never forget our miserable past, particularly how your mother suffered to bring you up. Now the right time has come for you to return something good to your mother."

"All right, all right," Lujiang said impatiently. "In the forest, the stupidest monkey knows how to climb up a tree. I know too well how to return my mother's care." Then he added, "What about you, may I ask?"

"Well." I paused for a little while and then replied, "For our unprecedented trip next year, I shall act something like an official of a country. But all the way from our home village down to the provincial capital, your mother will look like a queen. This four-member family's queen is very special. She has no power to rule other people, but when we begin to travel she will do nothing but eat, drink, look, see, and play. I'll automatically force my honorable position down and do everything for her like a maid-in-waiting at a palace. Also, I shall prepare myself to be a treasurer of our little country. From now on, I must make lots of regulations on economic policies. I must begin to save each cent. By the time we are ready to leave, all my pockets will be filled with money."

Everybody agreed with one voice: Overcome all the difficulties and be fully prepared for a trip to Kunming in the spring of 1988.

*         *         *

Right after I finished going over the winter examination papers, Luzhong and I hurried home. Who could have predicted that the day before our departure the mother would turn down our decision. Her face turned pale when I told her the sum of money, about 1,000 *yuan*, we would have to spend on the trip. Pointing at our yard she said, "You measure the length of this line, from the point I am standing at to that corner. We must buy half a truck of good-quality stone to fix it."

Then she took me to have a detailed look at our kitchen. She said, "The chimney doesn't work properly. Too smoky, very easy to catch health problems. Not a thing looks bright and clean."

Finally I followed her to see the room she meant to prepare for Lujiang's future wife. She said, "Do you think Lujiang's future wife would be pleased with this ugly room? The ceiling, the four walls, and the floor. ... We need several hundred to make a nicer room for his big-school-student wife."

She listed many other family problems for me, but in my heart I thought of everything in a different way. Sometimes I answered, "Yes, yes"; sometimes I praised her, "Oh, really you are a good mother, very thoughtful." But in the end I went to town and bought the bus tickets. That evening we quarreled. She told me that one of her fattest hens had died mysteriously early that morning. She said, "Your honoring me with a trip to Kunming is good. Many people envy me, but on the other hand, things in our house are important, too. I'm afraid we'll have to reconsider everything. If we give up the trip and you let me have that 1,000 *yuan*, I'll show you five bigger pigs or at least forty big hens. Please consider my opinion."

Once again I told her, "You are indeed a model housewife and a good economist, too. But I want you to know, taking a walk in a Kunming main street or having just a three-minute ride in an elevator will make you feel as happy as going up to Heaven to visit Paradise. Tell me, can you do that here? It's not easy. You'll be sorry if you miss this chance. Furthermore, everything in the market is shooting up each passing day. Last year, for 12 *fen* they gave you a large bowl of noodles. This year, two times 12 *fen* can buy only a smaller bowl of noodles. Next year, probably you will have to pay 36 or even 40 *fen* for a small bowl. The other problem is that Lujiang has prepared a room for you and another bed for Luzhong and me. We are going to have our meals in their dining hall. The price at the university is many times cheaper than out in a street restaurant. Lujiang is going to leave his school after he graduates in July. If you ignore this, who else will be kind enough to prepare free beds and cheap meals for you? Don't forget, if you go next year, you will have to double your money many times."

"How about you, father and son, go to Kunming alone. In order to save some money, I would like to wait for you in Xiaguan. I prefer to travel by turning the pages of those colorful foreign magazines. That saves a lot of money and is very safe as well. What I am longing for is an overall physical checkup in a higher-level hospital. So, you and Luzhong go yourselves."

I turned a deaf ear to my wife's words. I knew that my younger son was on the side of his father. Therefore, very late on the eve of our departure, I divided my 1,000 *yuan* into four shares. Finding a needle and some thread, I sewed 300 *yuan* inside Luzhong's shirt and 400 into one of my wife's dresses. Then I sewed 200 *yuan* into my underwear, leaving the remainder in separate pockets.

Early the next morning, before dawn, I woke the others up. Leaving some instructions for our neighbor Liu Jingyuan, we three left home for the bus stop. I had to fool my wife, saying we would not go to Kunming. We would just go to see some wise doctors at Dali People's Hospital. She was half-hearted about it. On seeing the way we left, many villagers wondered a lot. Everybody had learned that Mrs. He was going to see her older son in Kunming, but why did she look unhappy? The younger son pulled at his mother's hand again and again. Sometimes I shouted at her, "Go faster or you will be late for the bus! The driver isn't your son. He won't wait for you."

On our way to the bus stop a woman from the next village watched and watched and then asked, "Why, what evil has she done?"

I jokingly answered, "Well, a thief-wife she is. She stole my money yesterday. I am going to the police station to give her a lesson."

At about noon, we arrived in Xiaguan, the little capital town. The mother wasn't very pleased, but anyway we had brought her this far. Her Mandarin is poor and most of the people in that town speak Han people's Mandarin. So it became very easy to control her. In fact, as soon as we got off the bus, she dared not refuse my orders. The very first thing I did was to buy another three tickets for Kunming. We stayed in a hotel close to the bus station. That afternoon, I took my wife and son to see a film. In the evening, we called on some of my doctor-friends. We gave them our home-produced presents and told them we would come back to see them after our return from Kunming.

That year our province had bought several large go-faster-than-all-the-other-models buses from Poland. The four wheels started moving at seven A.M. sharp. In a county called Nanhua we took a forty-minute break for lunch. At four-thirty in the afternoon, Luzhong was so excited that he refused to sit still in his seat, as if the seat were made of sharp thorns. Our beautiful City of Spring had appeared in the distance. What happened to the mother? All the way she didn't talk, nor did she drink or eat. The smell of the four-wheel-walking-machine, to use her words, was too terrible. She had a serious attack of travel sickness and complained of a "seasick ghost." Someone in the Polish bus gave her several tablets, but to no avail. She kept on vomiting repeatedly. At four forty-five, the bus safely reached our destination. I looked around again and again, but Lujiang wasn't there. The mother was so sick and so tired that she simply couldn't walk an inch further. She couldn't even stand up. I called a taxi.

"Hello, Young Master. Look at this woman. She is too sick to walk. You just say how much to Yunnan Normal University."

"The distance isn't too far, but the road is a sea of cars. Give me 6 *yuan* and I'll take you there right away."

Both Luzhong and I were frightened to hear the sum he asked for. Luzhong said, "Can't you judge from our clothes? He is only a mountain-corner schoolteacher, not the principal or a rich factory manager."

"Oh, you are from a distant county? All right, I will make it 5 *yuan.*"

My wife couldn't catch the Kunming driver's local accent, but the man showed his five fingers. She tried hard to stand up and said in our Bai local dialect, "Let's go on foot. Lujiang has become a bad son now. He should be waiting for us here before our arrival."

"Teacher, you are a newcomer so you don't know the distance. It's a long way to drive. ..."

"Please go away, Master. You go and deceive another rich gentleman. I was here before you were born. Within ten minutes I can walk to my son's university. We will go by Number 11 bus."

Just then I heard a familiar voice crying for help: "Father be quick! Kidnappers are dragging me!"

I turned my head and saw that the so-called kidnapper was He Lujiang. He nodded and smiled and, removing his fingers from in front of Luzhong's eyes, hugged his young brother. A little smile appeared on the mother's face. Lujiang took a picture of us then and there. Slowly we three followed Lujiang to his eight-people dormitory room on the third floor of a big building. It was nearly empty, as Lujiang's fellow students had gone home for their winter vacation. That first day in Kunming, Lujiang prepared a good meal for supper, but the mother was too tired to eat anything. Luzhong and I slept in the same bed in Lujiang's room. The mother slept in the girl-student's dormitory, a seven-story building.

The next morning, February 1st, we didn't get up until nine o'clock. The university had a very big dining hall and we could order nearly everything. Though cheaper than in the street, the dining hall was expensive compared to our village standard, so we gave up eating there. Lujiang borrowed an electric cooker from the wife of one of his teachers. We had brought with us forty home-produced eggs and several pieces of dry meat. And there was a vegetable market not so far from the university. Every morning Luzhong and his mother went to buy fresh vegetables. With these things, we made one of their classrooms our kitchen. What we had was simple and ordinary, but it seemed more interesting to have our meals in the classroom than to eat in a noisy restaurant.

At the table that very morning, the following decisions were made: We would visit the Kunming Zoo, February 1st; several Buddhist temples, February 2nd; the Seaside Park next to Lake Dianchi, February 3rd; the Bamboo Temple, February 4th; the Golden Temple and Kunming International Airport, February 5th; the main streets, the tallest buildings, and the biggest department store, February 6th. Late in the afternoons and in the evenings, we planned to visit our old friends and schoolteachers, see colleges and institutes, go to theaters, or watch TV programs. On the seventh day we would wave goodbye to Lujiang.

*         *         *

Lots and lots of villagers admire city people's lifestyle. They always think a big city must be an extremely good place to live and work. In recent years many have struggled very hard to get into a city. However, somehow, a distant village woman like my Mrs. He seemed quite uninterested. Every day we three tried every means to make her happy, but she refused nearly all our arrangements. Every time we asked her to follow, she returned us a reluctant attitude. We all wanted her to grasp this opportunity and enjoy as much as she could. But as soon as she heard we would go to a place or buy something, her very first question was, "How much will that cost?" No matter where, her comments made us feel sad. I really couldn't count the number of times she said, "Not for me! I am over fifty—too old. It's too expensive. It won't make me grow fat. I don't mind if all the people in Kunming say I am an ugly-looking mother."

One evening Lujiang and I exchanged our thoughts for a long, long time. In speaking of our mother's reactions, we had the same feelings and also shared the same point of view. For this typical countryside woman, the turn from a distant village to a million-people city was too large. How could we succeed in forcing her to get used to everything in the city? We had done all we could to make her enjoy herself over these several days, but she just would not accept our invitation. We simply didn't know what the best remedy was to cure her problems. Finally, our policy was: Don't be too strict and too serious with her. Let things go by in a natural way.

One afternoon, we took her to see a very big department store. We meant to let her choose a favorite dress of modern style. She said no perhaps a hundred times. Lujiang said, "Mother, this week we are not in the village. We are in our provincial capital. You must copy how Kunming people dress."

This is what she said: "It sounds nice, but not for me. You talk such things to your future wife. You seem to enjoy seeing the way Kunming ladies wear their dresses. Ladies ought to look like ladies. Crazy! They must protect, no, they must not let other people see the skin of their chests. I hate to see those girls who show their chests. I like only our Bai people's national costume.''

Once the younger son said, "You know all the city people wear high-heeled shoes. This evening I will steal and throw away your handmade shoes. I don't think father will scold me. A pair of high-heeled shoes will certainly make you grow taller.''

In response to this, the mother said, "Am I the shortest woman in Kunming? I am a peasant. I am not an international-level basketball player. No use to look taller.''

At the university we were twice invited to watch TV programs. We also persuaded the mother to see two American films. One film was the story of several street jazz dancers. The other was entitled *Flight 704.* The screen wasn't a square one; it looked like a half-round one. Later we learned that this was called an arc screen, the first one in our province. The price for one ticket was six times higher than for other ordinary theaters. After the film was over, we asked how she liked that special arc film and she said, "Oh, I enjoyed seeing their beautiful snow-capped mountain peaks. It seemed as if I had traveled to America. But I would not have followed you to that theater if I had known the price before we got in. Really too expensive. With the money you spent on that round-screen film I could buy lots of things in our home village. Money here and money there. Anyway, Kunming is not for the village people. It belongs to the rich. Let me go home earlier. ...''

One day, in the middle part of a hill on our way to a temple, a middle-aged tourist from Pakistan kindly agreed to take a picture for our family. He was surprised because three of us could speak a little English. After we finished taking the photo, the Pakistani tourist went in one direction and we went in another. Our plan was to see the temple, but the mother feared to climb higher, so we made her wait near a big rock. When we came down from the top, the mother was all smiles.

"Strange! You begin to smile today," Luzhong said. "I wonder what made you happier.''

She answered, "I recognized him as soon as he waved to me and even came near to greet me. He was the foreigner who took the picture for us a moment ago. He said something in English but I didn't understand, so I just nodded and said 'yes, yes' many times. He said more and more. Well, I knew to say 'no' wasn't polite or nice. Therefore I said 'thank you' two or three times. Finally he shook my right hand and said 'goodbye.' By that I knew he was going away. I said 'okay' to him two times. He looked very pleased and returned me many more 'bye-byes.'''

One evening we meant to have a bird's-eye view from the top floor of Kunming's tallest building, the seventeen-story Kunming Workers' Palace. Once again the mother insisted on waiting for us on the third floor. On our way back to the university, I asked, "Did you have a good time?''

"No," she said. "While waiting on the third floor I saw lots of young peo-ple dancing under colored lights. As soon as music began, each man held a lady around her waist and then each couple turned round and round. Some pairs looked somewhat crazy. Oh dear, just terrible. Shame on those thick-faced young people. As I watched them from the windows, my face grew red-der and redder."

Turning to Lujiang, she added, "I don't think you big-school students do shameful things like that?"

"Sometimes we have dancing parties too, but it's not easy to learn to dance beautifully. I just watch them."

"Good. You may dance, I think, but at home, in your own room, with your wife. You must not dance with another lady in public."

One late afternoon, as we were about to have our supper, the mother sud-denly said, "Oh dear, maybe I lost my scarf. Maybe it's still under my pillow. Anyway I must go back to my room and look for it. Please wait for me."

With these words, the mother rushed to the girl-students' dormitory. She should have returned within five minutes, but after ten Lujiang and I went to look for her. Holding the key in her hand, she was slowly walking from door to door, trying to find something on the floor. Lujiang was angry, "What's the matter with you? Here is your room, Number 49. Didn't I tell you to re-member the room number by heart? You will be caught as a thief if you touch this door and then that door."

"I am sorry. I ignore the room numbers because it seems you big-school students are using another type of number. Your numbers don't look like the ones I saw in our home county. All the doors look the same. My own way is to mark my room with something special. This morning I picked up a broken brick and another short stick, shorter than a chopstick. When I left I put them here; but when I returned just now, my brick and stick were nowhere to be found."

One night, at about one o'clock, one of the university's night-watchers came to knock at our door. The man asked, "Is the middle-aged woman in Number 49 your mother?"

"Yes she is. What's the matter?" Lujiang asked anxiously.

"We welcome your parents, but please follow me to see her room."

Lujiang was frightened. He said, "Really she is my mother, an ordinary vil-lage farmer. What wrong can a village woman do?"

Luzhong and I woke up and followed them. As we went downstairs, the man said, "I saw the light was on. I knocked and asked why she didn't turn the light off. Very funny, your mother said there was a 'ghost fire' in her bed. It was too hot to sleep. So she just sat beside a desk, leaving the light on."

As we entered the mother's room, Lujiang said, "I am awfully sorry. My in-tention was to surprise my mother. I should have told her before I made a 'ghost fire' in her bed. You see, my mother was so poor when she was young that my grandmother and her shared a straw-made mattress even on winter days. So this time when she came to see me at the university, I wanted my mother to return with something special. I thought about it for several months and finally I decided to use a part of my scholarship to buy her an electric blanket. I wanted her to enjoy a warmer bed. This morning I secretly spread the new blanket under this cotton sheet. Since I wanted to give her a surprise, I didn't tell her a word. It was my fault."

Well, I am a middle-school teacher, but to tell the truth, this was my first time to see an electric blanket. Lujiang's present to his mother surprised all of us. It was so great that nearly half of our village's housewives later came to see Mrs. He's special present from her university-student son. It was the very first electric blanket in our home village's history.

From the beginning to the end of our trip, Luzhong was the happiest boy. Through purchasing goods at the vegetable market and in the streets, his Mandarin improved a great deal. Within only a week, he learned the Kunming people's special accent. I took him to see two of my former teachers. He saw with his own eyes how educated people arrange everything in their houses. Every day, he liked to watch university people. He was particularly overjoyed to be the short-time owner of a bicycle which Lujiang had borrowed for him. Wearing his older brother's sports vest designed for university students, he played many times with that bicycle. Each time he rode it, he asked, "Do I really look like a young university sportsman?"

His mother replied, "Yes, yes. The day before yesterday, your father said he would buy me a beautiful dress as a remembrance for our trip. I am getting on and on. A beautiful dress makes no sense for a village woman. Use that money to buy a pile of books for your own use."

The next day, we arranged a trip to several bookstores and returned with about thirty new books. On our way back, the younger son took the mother to a watch shop and bought a golden-like strap for her. The young son said, "You know I saved my scholarship at school. You gave up wearing a nice dress. In return I give you nothing but a golden-like strap to decorate your iron rooster.[2] Our neighbors will wonder at your iron rooster when they see that golden strap."

*       *       *

Altogether we spent about 1,200 *yuan* on our trip. (As my salary had increased, I received a little over 100 *yuan* each month from Mr. China.) The total sounded quite a big sum, a whole year's income, but it included everything—taking lots of photos, bus tickets, hotel fees, meals in the street restaurants, presents for our neighbors, all the presents we gave each other, Lujiang's school fees, and hospital fees for my wife in Xiaguan. The elder son Lujiang had gone to a lot of trouble preparing our accommodations and making other arrangements for us. So, on the day before we left, we gave him 350 *yuan*. (This sum, too, was included in the 1,200.)

The mother said, "You must understand that your time to study more isn't long now. Your graduation is a big event in our family. We have so many problems at home, but nevertheless your father and I can overcome all the difficulties. You use half of this sum to buy a Western-style suit as a graduation present. The other half is for emergencies. Money is not easy to earn. Remember, spend each cent with reason."

Unbuttoning her apron, the mother tore open the cloth and counted the money.

"Thank you, Mother," Lujiang said. "Father and you may take me on trust that I will be a good son. Just wait and you shall see how I have been using my money and also what I am going to do with this money."

With these words, Lujiang rushed out. We didn't know what he was going to do. We waited and waited. Two hours later, he returned with a square hard-paper box.

"This is for you and my young brother to use at school," Lujiang said to me. "Well, everything must be equal and fair. I bought a special electric blanket out of my scholarship for mother. As you will be leaving for home tomorrow, too, I want you to have something like my mother's blanket."

"Oh, I know what he has bought!" Luzhong cried with excitement. "Look, Mother, you can't read the words, but as soon as you see the picture on the box you'll know what it is."

"It's an electric rice-cooker, and I also bought a smaller electric pan." Lujiang placed them on the desk and showed us how to use them.

"Well, it's kind of you, but for our family I'm afraid it's still early to enjoy these modern facilities. You know the weight of our family's wallet," I said.

"Yes, we must count our limited money before we buy something. You wanted to make your father happy, but what about your Western-style suit?" the mother asked.

"Here it is," and Lujiang produced a new suit from another bag. "I had already bought one some time ago with my own money."

"All right," said the mother. Then she asked again, "What about all sorts of fees you will have to pay before your graduation?"

"Don't worry about that. I know how to make both ends meet and arrange my things well. I am old enough to solve all the difficulties. But can I forget those troublesome years at the Second Middle School? Every day, from spring to summer and then from autumn to winter, as soon as you put down your chalk box, you had to make a fire first. The damp firewood, the smoke. ... We two brothers were too young to help. As a result, it was you who had to do lots of chores. I understand that at present our family is still poor; but compared with the bitter past, we are doing much, much better. I reconsidered everything and finally decided to buy an electric pan and rice-cooker for you to use at school. With this modern equipment you will be able to keep your room clean; and, above all, it saves time. I hope you and Luzhong will like them."

"Yes, yes," the mother began to smile. "You are perfectly right, very thoughtful. But you two boys must not laugh at me. I am afraid your father is too old to enjoy electricity. They say electricity helps us a lot in building our country, but they also warn people, saying electricity is an invisible enemy. It will kill you in half a minute if you do not handle it properly. Before you take it home, you must give him a lesson on learning the instructions."

"Oh Mother, there's no need for you to worry about that," the young son said. "It's easy. I am only a middle-school student, but even I can work it."

*     *     *

On the seventh day, we waved goodbye to Lujiang and safely returned to Xiaguan. This time, on the way back, Mrs. He didn't mention anything about the "seasick ghost." We talked to each other and sometimes ate.

We three stayed in Xiaguan for four days. This time our main business was to see some doctors. We stayed in a hotel, and for our daily meals we ate in an ordinary restaurant. Sometimes the three of us shared one single plate of vegetables and three smaller bowls of soup. My wife said, "Nobody is closely following behind. Who knows we three shared only one plate here in Xiaguan? Remember this: When we get to our home village many people will come and ask many, many things. If someone asks about the food, you just tell them we tried all the best-quality things in Kunming. Tell them your father took us several times to eat in the most expensive restaurants. Tell them we saw many foreign films. But you must not tell them we cooked our meals in your brother's classroom. Tell them we have bought lots of electricity. Tell them we had a wonderful time seeing the elephants, tigers, lions, and bear-cat.[3] Tell them we saw the whole city at the top of a seventeen-story building. But you must not say I was waiting on the third floor while you climbed up to the top."

Right after the doctors gave us the mother's health report, we returned to our home village. That afternoon, the moment we passed through our gate, Liu Jingyuan told us that all our hens, chicks, and the cock had died. Then, suddenly, our yard became a noisy market square. We had a very good time showing our rice-cooker and the blanket. Formerly, the death of one small chick would make my wife cry, but this time she smiled and said, "That's nothing. Never mind. I returned home with something a million times more precious than some chicks or hens."

Then she showed all the villagers in our courtyard the health document from Dali People's Hospital. "Look, I am sorry I can't read, but Mr. He or Luzhong can tell you that on each piece of paper their high-level doctors confirmed that I have no serious health problems. All my previous worries have gone away. Isn't that very precious? With good health I will be able to raise more hens and pigs and then become rich. As long as I enjoy good health, my hens and pigs might return me more money than the amount Mr. He receives from his school. This time he took us to see the provincial capital. In another year, I might take him to see our nation's capital."

## NOTES

1. As Mr. He explains, "In nearly all the villages, more or less, childless people exist. In my village, we also have such a couple. The wife is blind. Before 1979 the man was responsible for looking after the team cows and buffalo. Every day he drove out the cattle and spent his time along the hills. His wife can't see, but she can cook and feed their pig. On Sundays or special occasions, the boys and girls of our village school go up into the hills and collect firewood for their use. As for rice and other daily necessities, the Team Committee gives them some out of our public grains. And every year when winter comes, our Mr. China gives them a sum of money."

2. *Iron rooster:* watch.

3. *Bear-cat:* panda.

# 20

## POSTSCRIPT

**S**hortly after the mother, the young son, and I returned from our trip to Kunming, another new school term began on March 1st, 1988. A week after that, two document-like letters reached my hands on the same day. At the local people's post office, as I opened the large envelopes I could hardly believe my eyes. I scratched my head violently. Then I jumped up and hit the wall with my fists. The postwoman watched and seemed frightened. A girl student from our school was also there at that moment. Her eyes growing bigger, she asked, "What's the matter, Teacher He? Has someone at home passed away?"

The postwoman said to the girl, "Go and send for a doctor straight away."

"There's no need to trouble a doctor," I said. "It's a red event, not a white one.[1] I have received an extra-huge news from London."

One letter was from the director of the BBC's Summer School. I had begun applying to that school as early as 1983. Every spring, as soon as I heard news about the school on my radio I asked them to send me an application form. I tried my luck each time but failed five times in succession. Contrary to my expectations, this sixth reply said that I had won a place and also a scholarship to cover all accommodations. The second letter was from the chairman of the Sino-British Fellowship Trust promising to cover the traveling expenses from Yunnan to London.

The next day I wrote to my son: "You must be quiet for some time. It's too early to celebrate. More and more people will laugh at me if one day my huge news changes like a cloud on a windy day. I have to get two wings—a passport from Mr. China. I am not an eight-o'clock sun early in the morning but a six-o'clock sun late in the afternoon. Our officials may think it a waste to send me abroad when I am about to retire and take a long rest."

But the news spread in all directions. For a time my name became a household word throughout the county. Every time I was wanted on the telephone, nearly the whole school crowded around to watch and listen attentively. If I said "Okay, thank you," they began to smile and clap for joy. As soon as the news reached their ears, my relatives rushed to my house.

When I took my documents to our county town, the officials said, "It's quite a new problem. So many people go to Beijing or Shanghai, but we've never heard of anyone asking to go to England before. We will have to ask the officials at the provincial level first. For now we need the BBC's acceptance letter; real money, a check, or at least a written guarantee from England; and a written document from your school telling us you are a good teacher. In addition, you will have to show a formal health report and nine photos. ..."

My going-abroad problem became so big a thing that the officials organized meetings to discuss the matter again and again. I had to bow my head lower to 90 degrees and say "thank you" and "please" a thousand times. It took two months for the leaders of our county government and important officials in our Public Security Bureau to agree to sign their names. Our Educational Affairs Bureau office director (the same one who had persuaded me to stay in Jianchuan in 1979) said, "Teacher He, we really want to thank you and praise you. I know what you have been doing in Madeng these past nine years. You made our Second Middle School your home. You were diligent and planted an English seed at the bottom of the hearts of our national minority people's children. Really you deserve recognition as an honorable people's teacher. As for your two wings, don't worry. Our county's Educational Affairs Bureau is in full support of your going abroad to get further studies and then contributing more services to our Jianchuan County."

But this county-level yes didn't mean "Here is your passport." It meant only "We agree to forward your application to Kunming. Whether you are qualified to receive a passport or not is the Kunming top officials' business." Week after week I waited in my room. In the middle of June a young police officer (a former student of mine) handed me an envelope and said, "Your going abroad is unprecedented in Bai people's past history and perhaps never to be repeated again." Inside the envelope I found a yellowish passport, a true passport, No. 739915, given to me by the People's Republic of China. I sewed a secret pocket inside my underwear and placed it there safely.

My wife gave me piles of advice on how to behave myself in a foreign country. Finally she said, "I think people in England can offer you several glasses of milk like we give cheap cold water to others at home. They can easily eat chicken or meat three times a day, but I'm afraid their machine-made food and chemical-fertilized vegetables are not as good as the books say. They won't make you grow fatter or taller within a few weeks."

On July 5th, I waved goodbye to my wife and young son. From that moment forward, many, many first-time things happened to me on my Long March to London. I traveled to our glorious capital city of Beijing by train—the first time in my life I ever left our Yunnan Province. And then, after a never-before-experienced ride in a giant passenger plane, I arrived in London. My first surprise was that people there parked their cars upstairs. Meeting my mysterious pen-friends face to face, as well as the broadcasters in the BBC's

English by Radio department, was great and interesting. I didn't want to make trouble for my London friends, so every time I stayed for the night I asked them to report my arrival at the policeman's station. They laughed and said "not necessary." Each one of them invited me to dinner and to many pubs, performances, parks, and historic sites. At our BBC Summer School I won second place in a speaking competition and a bottle of whiskey for being voted "most outstanding personality." I had a wonderful stay in London.

At the beginning of September, I safely returned to our nation's capital. The next day I went to find a special shop called Returned People's Department Store. Nobody is allowed to buy or even look at the goods here unless they show a passport. Their prices are the cheapest in the city, but only U.S. dollars are accepted. After I counted the money I had left in my pocket, I decided to buy a TV set.

In Beijing there were thousands of "returned people." The Returned People's Department Store opened at eight-thirty, but a line began to form before six. I got up at four-thirty; it took me two hours to walk to the building as there was no bus at that hour. I thought I would be among the earliest arrivers, but hundreds of people were already waiting by the time I finally got there. As soon as the window was opened, people began to push and even quarrel. The office hours were over just as I was about to reach the window. On the following day, when my turn finally came to show my passport, the man inside the window said, "Sorry, your yellow-covered passport doesn't work in this store. Can you see, in that gentleman's hand is a blue-covered one.[2] That's the passport we want to check here. Your yellowish passport belongs to the Department Store for Overseas People. Most of their customers have returned from Taiwan or Hong Kong. ..."

I was so disappointed. Bearing the new address, I started to explore the capital. It took me almost another whole day to find the store. Things there were more expensive than in the first store, but still cheaper than in an ordinary shop along a Beijing street. Unfortunately, suitable TV sets were not available that day. I would have to come back to Beijing in December if I wanted to buy in that shop. I decided to change my remaining foreign money into *yuan* and to buy a good Japanese color television in Kunming. Beijing made my head ache.

From Kunming to Dali I took an evening bus. For safe transportation of my new TV, I bought an additional ticket in advance. But when the time came for me to put my television into the bus, the driver strongly refused. The bus was about to start. The situation suddenly became a big problem. Just then a traveling fruit-seller spoke to me in a whisper: "Aside from offering some extra money, you can never stop the driver-master's shouting."

I gave her 20 *yuan* at once. Then I stood aside and watched. She went over to the driver and handed my 20 *yuan* to him, saying, "This is for you to buy

some cigarettes and tea. Please accept. Look, the TV's owner is over there.
..."

The fruit-seller helped me move my TV up into the bus. The driver saw us,
but this time he had become a "blind driver." From Dali to my home county
I had to buy another seat for the TV once again.

My two sons were extremely happy. The young son said, "Great! Ours is
the third color TV in the whole village. Now there's no need to knock on
other people's doors and say a hundred 'Let me in please.'"

But who would have thought that as soon as my wife learned the big paper
box contained a color electric-showing-machine her face would turn white.
The growing number of people in our yard were waiting for my wife to say
something, but she just stood there silently.

"I can never bear the coming trouble," she spoke in the end. "You three repeatedly praise your TV, but in just a few days all of you will go back to
schools, leaving that machine for me to offend people. I want to be quiet. If
you turn on the TV and then say, 'You go away!' people will hate you. If you
open your gate, you have to offer cigarettes and tea, and then sweep the floor
when they leave. Each drop of water has to be carried home, and we do not
have so much money to buy extra firewood. In time we'll have to paint the
walls and employ a carpenter to repair our benches. Sell your TV quickly or
don't come to my table for supper."

Some burst out laughing, but others said, "Yes, quite true. I am for the
mother. A TV is not a joy; it is a troublemaker. It's too early for us to enjoy a
TV program."

When my wife's supper was ready we sat around the table. I had so much to
tell, but I dared not speak a word. We knew the mother had become a bomb.
After supper, we kindly invited all the people to watch until the TV programs
came to an end for the night. Only poor Mrs. He stayed on in the kitchen. She
wanted to go to bed but couldn't pass through the crowd. This lasted four
evenings.

My wife kept insisting that we sell the television, but Lujiang said, "I must
have a TV when I marry one day."

His young brother immediately put in, "I also have half of this TV. You'd
better stop dreaming of enjoying a TV with your future wife."

My wife said, "All I want is a peaceful life. I don't want anyone to scold me
behind my back. I want to keep a good relationship with all the people in the
village."

On the fifth day, we three left home for school, telling people we would
take the TV with us. Then at school we told people, "Sorry, too troublesome
to ask the driver's permission, so we left it at home."

To this day, we let the television sleep quietly under a bed. We can't find a
good solution for this troublesome TV problem.

\*        \*        \*

Middle-school teachers usually retire around sixty in our country. In my own case, I could easily manage to keep on grasping my job for several years longer, because my home county constantly lacks English teachers. But each year the number of jobless people outside the Educational Affairs Bureau is not small. Many of my countrymen would say "What a selfish Mr. He!" if I showed no inclination to return home. So I thought it better to ask for an earlier retirement in 1988. It took a year for the authorities to discuss and approve my demand.

When the printed decree was sent to me in February of 1989, I complained about it. The government's policy stated that I could begin to rest on the second day after I received the document, but I was reluctant to leave my students and Madeng, that out-of-the-way mountain corner, and its local straight-talking people. I asked the county authorities to let me stay longer. With their approval, I kept on teaching for another term. Finally, arrangements were made for me to leave school for home in July.

In our Bai area, since the number of people accepted officially and formally to be written in Mr. China's book is small, to retire is greater than a wedding or a son or daughter's acceptance to university. People usually celebrate a retirement in a big way. But I took no pleasure in organizing a big eat-and-drink party. At our family congresses the young son always stood firmly on my side. But with regard to my retirement, he moved his seat closer to his mother. The elder son strongly opposed my opinions. The mother maintained that if our money was not enough to show people a break-the-record party, then at least several not-so-bad tables with two bottles of wine and eight bowls of good vegetables must be prepared to entertain those who accompanied me home.

She said, "You had a return full of disgrace and shame in 1962. Having taken off the rightist cap at a state-owned mine, you were allowed by the government to return to your birthplace. If you compare 1962's return to 1989's retirement, you will see the difference is quite clear. This second time, your return from a school is openly recognized as glorious and delightful. Before 1979, many people looked down on you. Now, thank God a million times, it's time for you to feel proud and elated."

This family issue was forced to a vote. I failed, three to one.

The 6th of July was our big day. On the afternoon of the 5th, the local Madeng government's educational and cultural units organized a special party in my honor. What touched me was the local people's hospitality and kindness. From distant corners they came to say goodbye to me. Many brought homemade articles such as handwoven bamboo baskets, hand-knitted woolen tablecloths, and a white yak's tail to dust the bed. On the eve of my departure, my old brother and Lujiang came to meet me. The next morning the school authorities prepared a car and a truck to take me and my belongings home. They pasted big-character posters, saying "Warmly Welcome and Salute Mr. He's Honorable Retirement," onto the vehicles. They also pinned a big red-cloth-made flower onto my jacket and fired a pile of fire-crackers. Many important people from our school and local leaders of all the organizations concerned saw me off in person. The school gave me two long benches as a goodbye gift.

Our party was a great success. That evening my wife said, "I am most grate-ful and contented, all because you returned home with a good reputation. While standing on the roadside waiting to meet your car and truck, I was on top of the world. When you introduced me to those important officials who had accompanied you all the way from the school to our house, I counted al-together thirteen—including your principal, Party branch secretary, back-bone teachers,[3] representatives from your Students' Association, and some Madeng officials. Leading officials from the Educational Affairs Bureau at two levels—the government of Jianchuan County and Diannan District—also came to honor us. You saw with your own eyes, all these plus many respect-able aged people of our village and a large crowd of smiling friends and rela-tives gathered in our house. They sat down around our tables, gave speeches praising you and thanking you, and ate the food I prepared. That was the greatest honor in the world. In our Shangbaodian Village we have several 10,000-*yuan*-a-year families, but do they have the power to invite all these people to eat, as we did in our house?"

*        *        *

After 1979 my elder brother and his only son worked very, very hard. In 1983 they paid some money to one of the poor peasant families who had moved in after the Land Reform Movement and bought back one-third of our old house. In 1987 they paid another big sum and bought back the other two-thirds. However, the remaining two families kept on staying there. In 1990 my brother added more money and they finally moved out. Altogether they paid almost 4,000 *yuan*. Then, early in 1991, they spent still more money and had all the broken things repaired. Each time I go to visit I sit first under the pomegranate tree and have a cup of water from our old well.

## NOTES

1. A *white event* is a funeral; a *red event* is a happy occasion such as a wedding, the building of a new house, or the acceptance of a family member into college.

2. Yellow passports are issued to people who "self-finance" their trips abroad; blue ones go to those who are sponsored by the government.

3. *Backbone teachers:* These are teachers who have substantial experience and take on a heavier workload than other teachers.

# ABOUT THE BOOK

He Liyi belongs to one of China's minorities, the Bai, and he lives in a remote area of northwestern Yunnan Province. In 1979 his wife sold her fattest pig to buy him a shortwave radio. He spent every spare moment listening to the BBC and VOA in order to improve the English he had learned at college between 1950 and 1953. For "further practice," he decided to write down his life story in English. Humorous and unfiltered by translation, his autobiography is direct and personal, full of richly descriptive images and phrases from his native Bai language.

At the time of He Liyi's graduation, English was being vilified as the language of the imperialists, so the job he was assigned had nothing to do with his education. In 1958 he was labeled a rightist and sent to a "reeducation-through-labor farm." Spirited away by truck on the eve of his marriage, Mr. He spent years in the labor camp, where he schemed to garner favor from the authorities, who nevertheless shamed him publicly and told him that all his problems "belong to contradictions between the people and the enemy." After his release in 1962, the talented Mr. He had no choice but to return to his native village as a peasant. His stratagems for survival, which included stealing "nightsoil" from public toilets and extracting peach-pit oil from thousands of peaches, personify the peasant's universal struggle to endure during those difficult years.

He Liyi's autobiography recounts nearly all the major events of China's recent history, including the Japanese occupation, the Communist victory over the Nationalists in 1949, Mao's disastrous Great Leap Forward and Cultural Revolution, the experience of the labor camps, and changes brought about by China's dramatic re-opening to the world since Deng Xiaoping came to power in 1978. No other book so poignantly reveals the travails of the common person and village life under China's tempestuous Communist government, which He Liyi ironically refers to as "Mr. China." Yet he describes his saga of poverty and hardship with humor and a surprising lack of bitterness. And rarely has there been such an intimate, frank view of how a Chinese man thinks and feels about personal relationships, revealed in dialogue and letters to his two wives.

He Liyi's autobiography stands as perhaps the most readable and authentic account available in English of life in rural China.

He Liyi's previous book is *The Spring of Butterflies* (London and New York, 1985), a translation of Chinese folk tales.